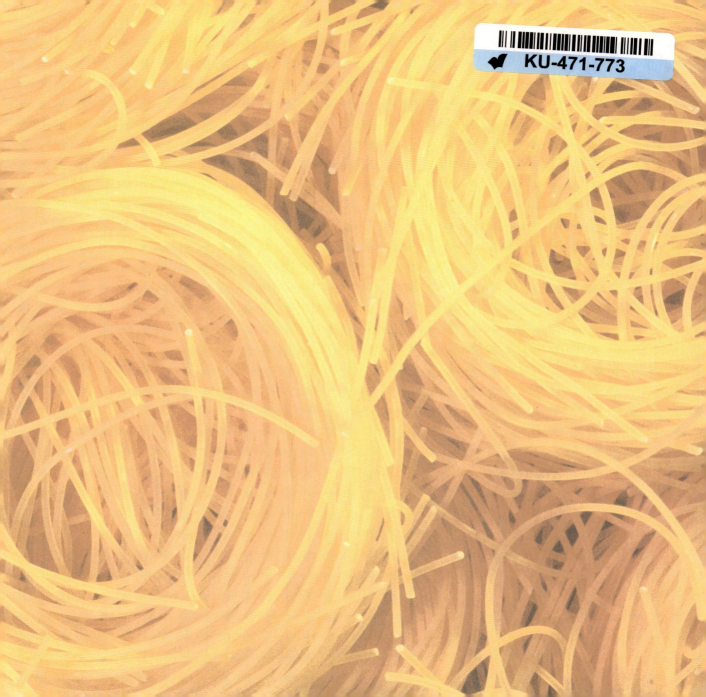

MARKS &
SPENCER

pasta sauces

simple and delicious easy-to-make recipes

Christine McFadden

Marks and Spencer p.l.c.
Baker Street, London, W1U 8EP

www.marksandspencer.com

Copyright © Exclusive Editions 2001
This edition published in 2004

ISBN: 1-84461-041-1

Printed in China

Produced by
THE BRIDGEWATER BOOK COMPANY LTD

Photographer Simon Punter
Home Economist Ricky Turner

Cover Photography Calvey Taylor-Haw
Home Economist Ruth Pollock

NOTES FOR THE READER

- This book uses both metric and imperial
  measurements. Follow the same units of
  measurement throughout; do not mix metric and
  imperial.

- All spoon measurements are level: teaspoons are
  assumed to be 5 ml, and tablespoons are assumed
  to be 15 ml.

- Unless otherwise stated, milk is assumed to be
  full fat, eggs and individual vegetables such as
  potatoes are medium, and pepper is freshly
  ground black pepper.

- Recipes using raw or very lightly cooked eggs
  should be avoided by infants, the elderly, pregnant
  women, convalescents, and anyone suffering from
  an illness.

- Optional ingredients, variations or serving
  suggestions have not been included in the
  calculations.

- The times given are an approximate guide only.
  Preparation times differ according to the techniques
  used by different people and the cooking times vary
  as a result of the type of oven used.

contents

introduction

Cooked in minutes and easy on the purse, pasta is one of the most versatile of foods, combining happily with a wide variety of sauces. Although meat-based sauces are among the best known, vegetables provide inspiration for many delicious sauces, as do fish and seafood.

Pasta comes in a large number of shapes: flat and round ribbons, tubes, quills and corkscrews, to name but a few. Each shape lends itself to a particular sauce style. For example, long, thin pasta, such as spaghetti, is best for tomato or oil-based sauces, which coat the surface and cling to it. Wide, flat ribbons, such as fettucine, go well with cream sauces. Shapes or short, hollow tubes are perfect for chunkier sauces because they trap tasty morsels in their crevices.

To cook perfect pasta, use a large pan so the pasta has enough room to move around freely. Allow 1 litre/1¾ pints of water for every 115 g/4 oz of pasta.

meat sauce with mushrooms & tomatoes
page 12

asparagus & gorgonzola sauce with cream
page 58

Bring the water to a fast boil, then add the salt and pasta together, stirring once. Cooking time depends on the type of pasta. It is ready when al dente – tender, but still firm to the bite and slightly chewy. Be careful not to overcook. It is generally better to cook the sauce before the pasta; sauces can be kept waiting, but pasta cannot – it becomes sticky!

easy

Recipes are graded as follows:
1 spoon = easy;
2 spoons = very easy;
3 spoons = extremely easy.

serves 4

Recipes generally serve four people. Simply halve the ingredients to serve two, taking care not to mix metric and imperial measurements.

15 minutes

Preparation time. Where marinating or soaking are involved, these times have been added on separately: eg, 15 minutes + 30 minutes to marinate.

40 minutes

Cooking time. Cooking times do not include the cooking of side dishes or accompaniments served with the main dishes.

prawn & garlic sauce with cream
page 78

tuna with garlic, lemon, capers & olives
page 86

Rich, hearty, meat-based sauces include the universally popular Bolognese, which needs no introduction. There are also irresistible sauces made with coarse-cut sausages or bacon and enriched with tomatoes, mushrooms or peppers. Less well-known are more delicate sauces made with chicken. These often include generous amounts of cream and freshly grated cheese for richness and flavour. All the sauces are simple to prepare and are equally suitable for relaxed entertaining or family suppers.

meat & poultry sauces

classic bolognese meat sauce

very easy   serves 4

15 minutes   1 hour
             15 minutes

ingredients

2 tbsp olive oil

1 tbsp butter

1 small onion, chopped finely

1 carrot, chopped finely

1 celery stick, chopped finely

50 g/1¾ oz mushrooms, diced

225 g/8 oz minced beef

75 g/2¾ oz unsmoked bacon or ham, diced

2 chicken livers, chopped

2 tbsp tomato purée

125 ml/4 fl oz dry white wine

salt and pepper

½ tsp freshly grated nutmeg

300 ml/10 fl oz chicken stock

125 ml/4 fl oz double cream

450 g/1 lb dried spaghetti

2 tbsp chopped fresh parsley, to garnish

freshly grated Parmesan cheese, to serve

Heat the oil and butter in a large saucepan over a medium heat. Add the onion, carrot, celery and mushrooms to the pan, then fry until soft. Add the beef and bacon to the pan and fry until the beef is evenly browned.

Stir in the chicken livers and tomato purée and cook for 2–3 minutes. Pour in the wine and season with salt, pepper and the nutmeg. Add the stock. Bring to the boil, then cover and simmer gently over a low heat for 1 hour. Stir in the cream and simmer, uncovered, until reduced.

Cook the pasta in plenty of boiling salted water until al dente. Drain and transfer to a warm serving dish.

Pour half the sauce over the pasta. Toss well to mix. Spoon the remaining sauce over the top.

Garnish with the parsley and serve with Parmesan cheese.

macaroni with sausage, pepperoncini & olives

very easy

serves 4

10–15 minutes

15 minutes

ingredients

1 tbsp olive oil

1 large onion, chopped finely

2 garlic cloves, chopped very finely

450 g/1 lb pork sausage, peeled and
chopped coarsely

3 canned pepperoncini, or other hot red
peppers, drained and sliced

400 g/14 oz canned chopped tomatoes

2 tsp dried oregano

125 ml/4 fl oz chicken stock or red wine

salt and pepper

450 g/1 lb dried macaroni

12–15 black olives, stoned and quartered

75 g/2¾ oz freshly grated cheese, such as
Cheddar or Gruyère cheese

Heat the oil in a large frying pan over a medium heat. Add the onion and fry for 5 minutes until soft. Add the garlic and fry for a few seconds until just beginning to colour. Add the sausage and fry until evenly browned.

Stir in the pepperoncini, tomatoes, oregano and stock. Season with salt and pepper. Bring to the boil, then simmer over a medium heat for 10 minutes, stirring occasionally.

Cook the macaroni in plenty of boiling salted water until al dente. Drain and transfer to a warm serving dish.

Add the olives and half the cheese to the sauce, then stir until the cheese has melted.

Pour the sauce over the pasta. Toss well to mix. Sprinkle with the remaining cheese and serve at once.

meat sauce with mushrooms & tomatoes

very easy   serves 4

10–15 minutes   40 minutes

ingredients

3 tbsp olive oil
450 g/1 lb minced beef
225 g/8 oz mushrooms, sliced thinly
4 spring onions, sliced thinly
4 garlic cloves, chopped very finely
400 g/14 oz canned chopped tomatoes
4 tbsp tomato purée

2 tsp dried oregano
salt and pepper
125 ml/4 fl oz stock or water
450 g/1 lb dried conchiglie or gnocchi

freshly grated Parmesan cheese, to serve

Heat 1 tablespoon of the oil in a large frying pan over a medium heat. Add the beef and fry until lightly browned. Remove from the pan and set aside.

Add the rest of the oil to the pan and fry the mushrooms until softened. Stir in the onions and garlic, then fry for 2 minutes.

Tip the meat back into the pan and stir in the tomatoes, tomato purée, oregano, salt, pepper and stock. Bring the mixture to the boil, then reduce the heat and simmer over a medium–low heat for 30 minutes.

Cook the pasta in plenty of boiling salted water until al dente. Drain and transfer to a warm serving dish.

Pour the sauce over the pasta and toss well to mix. Serve with freshly grated Parmesan.

sausage & beef sauce
with peppers & tomatoes

ingredients

very easy   serves 4

15–20   1 hour
minutes   15 minutes

2 tbsp olive oil

4 bacon rashers, chopped

1 onion, chopped finely

1 green pepper, deseeded and chopped
    finely

50 g/1¾ oz mushrooms, sliced thinly

4 garlic cloves, sliced thinly

225 g/8 oz minced beef

225 g/8 oz coarse pork sausage, peeled
    and chopped

800 g/1 lb 12 oz canned chopped tomatoes

1 fresh bay leaf

6 tbsp tomato purée

4 tbsp red wine or stock

salt and pepper

450 g/1 lb dried penne or rigatoni

6 fresh basil leaves, shredded, to garnish

freshly grated Parmesan cheese, to serve

Heat the oil in a large frying pan over a medium heat. Add the bacon and fry until
lightly browned. Add the onion, green pepper, mushrooms and garlic. Gently fry
for 5–7 minutes until soft.

Stir in the beef and sausage, then cook until browned. Add the tomatoes and
bay leaf. Bring to the boil, then simmer over a medium–low heat for 1 hour.
Stir in the tomato purée and wine. Season with salt and pepper. Simmer for a
few minutes more.

Cook the pasta in plenty of boiling salted water until al dente. Drain and transfer
to a warm serving dish.

Pour the sauce over the pasta and toss well to mix. Sprinkle with the basil and
serve with Parmesan.

chicken & onion cream sauce

very easy   serves 4

10 minutes   35 minutes

ingredients

1 tbsp olive oil
2 tbsp butter
1 garlic clove, chopped very finely
4 boneless, skinless chicken breasts
salt and pepper
1 onion, chopped finely
1 chicken stock cube, crumbled
125 ml/4 fl oz water
300 ml/10 fl oz double cream

175 ml/6 fl oz milk
6 spring onions, green part included,
    sliced diagonally
35 g/1¼ oz freshly grated Parmesan cheese
450 g/1 lb dried fettuccine

chopped fresh flat-leaved parsley,
    to garnish

Heat the oil and butter with the garlic in a large frying pan over a medium–low heat. Cook the garlic until just beginning to colour. Add the chicken breasts and raise the heat to medium. Fry for 4–5 minutes on each side, until the juices are no longer pink. Season with salt and pepper. Remove from the heat. Remove the chicken breasts, leaving the oil in the pan. Slice the breasts diagonally into thin strips and set aside.

Reheat the oil in the pan. Add the onion and gently fry for 5 minutes until soft. Add the crumbled stock cube and the water. Bring to the boil, then simmer over a medium–low heat for 10 minutes. Stir in the cream, milk, spring onions and Parmesan. Simmer until heated through and slightly thickened.

Cook the fettucine in boiling salted water until al dente. Drain and transfer to a warm serving dish. Layer the chicken slices over the pasta. Pour on the sauce, garnish with parsley and serve.

cannelloni with chicken, ricotta & herbs

ingredients

easy   serves 4

15–20
minutes +
30 minutes
to marinate   1 hour

MARINADE
125 ml/4 fl oz white wine vinegar
1 garlic clove, crushed
225 ml/8 fl oz olive oil

2 tbsp olive oil
4 boneless, skinless chicken breasts, diced
6 tbsp butter
500 ml/18 fl oz double cream
1 tsp salt

1 tsp freshly ground black pepper
¼ tsp freshly grated nutmeg
55 g/2 oz freshly grated Parmesan
450 g/1 lb ricotta cheese
1 egg, lightly beaten
1 tbsp chopped fresh oregano
2 tbsp chopped fresh basil
225 g/8 oz dried cannelloni
75 g/2¾ oz freshly grated mozzarella cheese

In a bowl, combine the vinegar, garlic and olive oil for the marinade. Add the chicken and marinate for 30 minutes.

Heat 2 tablespoons of olive oil in a frying pan. Drain the chicken and cook for 5–7 minutes, stirring, until no longer pink. Set aside.

Melt the butter in a saucepan over a medium–high heat. Add the cream, salt, pepper and nutmeg. Stir until thickened. Reduce the heat, add the Parmesan and stir until melted. Remove from the heat.

Heat the oven to 180°C/350°F/Gas Mark 4. In a large bowl, mix together the ricotta, egg and herbs. Stir in the chicken. Stuff the cannelloni with the chicken mixture. Pour half the sauce into a 23 x 33-cm/9 x 13-inch baking dish. Place the stuffed cannelloni on top. Pour over the remaining sauce. Sprinkle with the mozzarella and cover with aluminium foil. Bake for 45 minutes. Leave the dish to stand for 10 minutes before serving.

creamy chicken & shiitake sauce

very easy   serves 4

10 minutes   35 minutes
+ 30 minutes
soaking time

ingredients

25 g/1 oz dried shiitake mushrooms
350 ml/12 fl oz hot water
1 tbsp olive oil
6 bacon rashers, chopped
3 boneless, skinless chicken breasts, sliced
   into strips
115 g/4 oz fresh shiitake mushrooms,
   sliced
1 small onion, chopped finely

1 tsp fresh oregano or marjoram,
   chopped finely
250 ml/9 fl oz chicken stock
300 ml/10 fl oz whipping cream
salt and pepper
450 g/1 lb dried tagliatelle
55 g/2 oz freshly grated Parmesan cheese

chopped fresh flat-leaved parsley,
   to garnish

Put the dried mushrooms in a bowl with the hot water. Leave to soak for 30 minutes until softened. Remove, squeezing excess water back into the bowl. Strain the liquid in a fine-meshed sieve and reserve. Slice the soaked mushrooms, discarding the stems.

Heat the oil in a large frying pan over a medium heat. Add the bacon and chicken, then stir-fry for about 3 minutes. Add the dried and fresh mushrooms, the onion and oregano. Stir-fry for 5–7 minutes until soft. Pour in the stock and the mushroom liquid. Bring to the boil, stirring. Simmer briskly for about 10 minutes, continuing to stir, until reduced. Add the cream and simmer for 5 minutes, stirring, until beginning to thicken. Season with salt and pepper. Remove the pan from the heat and set aside.

Cook the pasta until al dente. Drain and transfer to a serving dish. Pour the sauce over the pasta. Add half the Parmesan and mix. Sprinkle with parsley and serve with the remaining Parmesan.

farfalle with chicken, broccoli & roasted red peppers

very easy   serves 4

15 minutes   15 minutes

ingredients

4 tbsp olive oil
5 tbsp butter
3 garlic cloves, chopped very finely
450 g/1 lb boneless, skinless chicken
  breasts, diced
¼ tsp dried chilli flakes
salt and pepper

450 g/1 lb small broccoli florets
300 g/10½ oz dried farfalle or fusilli
175 g/6 oz bottled roasted red peppers,
  drained and diced
250 ml/9 fl oz chicken stock

freshly grated Parmesan cheese, to serve

Bring a large pan of salted water to the boil. Meanwhile, heat the olive oil, butter and garlic in a large frying pan over a medium–low heat. Cook the garlic until just beginning to colour.

Add the diced chicken, raise the heat to medium and stir-fry for 4–5 minutes until the chicken is no longer pink. Add the chilli flakes and season with salt and pepper. Remove from the heat.

Plunge the broccoli into the boiling water and cook for 2 minutes until tender-crisp. Remove with a perforated spoon and set aside. Bring the water back to the boil. Add the pasta and cook until al dente. Drain and add to the chicken mixture in the pan. Add the broccoli and roasted peppers. Pour in the stock. Simmer briskly over a medium–high heat, stirring frequently, until most of the liquid has been absorbed.

Sprinkle with the Parmesan and serve.

chicken with basil & pine kernel pesto

very easy   serves 4

10 minutes   15 minutes

ingredients

PESTO
100 g/3½ oz shredded fresh basil
125 ml/4 fl oz extra-virgin olive oil
3 tbsp pine kernels
3 garlic cloves, crushed
salt
55 g/2 oz freshly grated Parmesan cheese

2 tbsp freshly grated pecorino cheese
2 tbsp vegetable oil
4 boneless, skinless chicken breasts
350 g/12 oz dried fettuccine
freshly ground pepper to taste

sprig of fresh basil, to garnish

To make the pesto, put the basil, olive oil, pine kernels, garlic and a generous pinch of salt in a food processor or blender. Purée the ingredients until smooth. Scrape the mixture into a bowl and stir in the cheeses.

Heat the vegetable oil in a frying pan over a medium heat. Fry the chicken breasts, turning once, for 8–10 minutes until the juices are no longer pink. Cut into small cubes.

Cook the pasta in plenty of boiling salted water until al dente. Drain and transfer to a warm serving dish. Add the chicken and pesto, then season with pepper. Toss well to mix.

Garnish with a sprig of basil and serve warm.

noodles with chicken satay sauce

very easy   serves 4

10 minutes   20 minutes

ingredients

2 tbsp vegetable oil

450 g/1 lb boneless, skinless chicken
   breasts, cubed

1 red pepper, deseeded and sliced

4 spring onions, green part included, sliced
   diagonally

225 g/8 oz dried vermicelli or spaghettini

125 g/4½ oz smooth peanut butter

1 tsp grated fresh ginger root

2 tbsp soy sauce

125 ml/4 fl oz chicken stock

Heat the oil in a large frying pan over a medium heat. Add the chicken and fry
for 5–7 minutes until no longer pink. Add the pepper and spring onions. Fry for
3 minutes until just soft. Remove from the heat.

Cook the pasta in plenty of boiling salted water until al dente. Drain and return to
the pan.

Put the peanut butter, ginger, soy sauce and chicken stock in a large saucepan.
Simmer over a medium–low heat, stirring, until bubbling. Add the cooked
vegetables, chicken and pasta to the peanut mixture. Toss gently until coated with
the sauce.

Transfer to a warm serving dish and serve immediately.

fusilli with bacon, eggs & mushrooms

very easy   serves 4

10 minutes 15 minutes

ingredients

1 tbsp olive oil
4 rashers streaky bacon or pancetta
115 g/4 oz mushrooms, sliced
225 g/8 oz fusilli or conchiglie
salt and pepper

2 eggs, beaten
115 g/4 oz Cheddar or mozzarella cheese,
  cubed

chopped fresh flat-leaved parsley,
  to garnish

Heat the oil in a frying pan over a medium heat. Add the bacon and fry until crisp. Remove with tongs, leaving the drippings in the pan. Cut into small pieces and keep warm.

Fry the mushrooms in the bacon drippings for 5–7 minutes until soft. Remove from the heat.

Cook the pasta in plenty of boiling salted water until al dente. Drain and return to the pan.

Stir the mushrooms, beaten eggs and the cheese cubes into the pasta. Season with pepper and toss until the eggs have coated the pasta and the cheese has melted.

Transfer to a warm serving dish. Sprinkle with the bacon pieces and parsley and serve at once.

rigatoni with spicy bacon & tomato sauce

ingredients

very easy   serves 4

10 minutes   45 minutes

6 tbsp olive oil
3 garlic cloves, sliced thinly
75 g/2¾ oz streaky bacon, chopped
800 g/1 lb 12 oz canned chopped tomatoes
½ tsp dried chilli flakes

salt and pepper
450 g/1 lb rigatoni
10 fresh basil leaves, shredded
2 tbsp freshly grated pecorino cheese

Heat the oil and garlic in a large frying pan over a medium–low heat. Cook until the garlic is just beginning to colour. Add the bacon and cook until browned.

Stir in the tomatoes and chilli flakes. Season with a little salt and pepper. Bring to the boil, then simmer over a medium–low heat for 30–40 minutes, until the oil separates from the tomatoes.

Cook the pasta in plenty of boiling salted water until al dente. Drain and transfer to a warm serving dish.

Pour the sauce over the pasta. Add the basil and pecorino, then toss well to mix. Serve at once.

ham, tomato & chilli sauce

very easy serves 4

10–15
minutes 1 hour

ingredients

1 tbsp olive oil
2 tbsp butter
1 onion, chopped finely
150 g/5½ oz ham, diced
2 garlic cloves, chopped very finely
1 fresh red chilli, deseeded and chopped
    finely

800 g/1 lb 12 oz canned chopped tomatoes
salt and pepper
450 g/1 lb bucatini or penne
2 tbsp chopped fresh flat-leaved parsley
6 tbsp freshly grated Parmesan cheese

Put the olive oil and 1 tablespoon of the butter in a large saucepan over a
medium–low heat. Add the onion and fry for 10 minutes until soft and golden.
Add the ham and fry for 5 minutes until lightly browned. Stir in the garlic, chilli
and tomatoes. Season with a little salt and pepper. Bring to the boil, then simmer
over a medium–low heat for 30–40 minutes until thickened.

Cook the pasta in plenty of boiling salted water until al dente. Drain and transfer
to a warm serving dish.

Pour the sauce over the pasta. Add the parsley, Parmesan and the remaining
butter. Toss well to mix. Serve immediately.

spaghetti alla carbonara

very easy   serves 4

10–15
minutes   15 minutes

ingredients

2 tbsp olive oil

1 tbsp butter

175 g/6 oz smoked streaky bacon,
sliced into thin strips

3 eggs, lightly beaten

35 g/1¼ oz freshly grated Parmesan cheese

20 g/¾ oz freshly grated pecorino cheese

1 tbsp chopped fresh flat-leaved parsley

4 tbsp single cream

pepper

450 g/1 lb dried spaghetti, chopped

Heat the oil and butter in a frying pan over a medium–high heat. Add the bacon and fry for 4–5 minutes until browned. Remove from the heat. Combine the eggs, cheeses, parsley and cream in a bowl, mixing well. Season with pepper.

Cook the pasta in plenty of boiling salted water until al dente. Drain and return to the pan.

Quickly add the egg mixture to the pasta, tossing rapidly so that the egg cooks in the heat. Transfer to a warm serving dish.

Briefly reheat the bacon over a high heat. Add to the pasta, toss again and serve at once.

With their flamboyant colours and fresh flavours, Mediterranean-style vegetables and herbs are perfect for pasta sauces. These are among the quickest and easiest sauces to prepare, ranging from the simple concoctions of chopped raw tomatoes, olive oil and basil to more complex mixtures of roasted peppers and garlic, or asparagus and Gorgonzola. Storecupboard ingredients are put to good use: jars of artichokes, peppers, sun-dried tomatoes and olives all contribute robust flavours that will please vegetarians and meat-eaters alike.

vegetable sauces

sun-dried tomato & goat's cheese sauce

very easy serves 4

10 minutes 10–15 minutes

ingredients

1 tbsp butter
2 garlic cloves, sliced thinly
225 g/8 oz goat's cheese, crumbled
300 ml/10 fl oz milk
150 ml/5 fl oz double cream
20 oil-cured sun-dried tomato halves
  (in oil), chopped roughly

salt and pepper
450 g/1 lb dried penne
35 g/1¼ oz freshly grated Parmesan cheese
10 fresh basil leaves, shredded

Heat the butter and garlic in a frying pan over a medium–low heat. Cook until the garlic is just beginning to colour. Add the cheese and milk. Stir until the cheese has melted and formed a thick sauce.

Add the cream and sun-dried tomatoes. Cook for about 5 minutes, stirring frequently, until reduced by one-third. Season with salt and pepper. Remove from the heat.

Cook the pasta in plenty of boiling salted water until al dente. Transfer to a warm serving dish.

Briefly reheat the sauce over a low heat. Pour over the pasta. Add the Parmesan and basil, then toss well to mix. Serve immediately.

sun-dried tomato sauce with herbs

very easy | serves 4 | 10–15 minutes | 20–25 minutes

ingredients

85 g/3 oz sun-dried tomatoes (not in oil)
700 ml/1¼ pints boiling water
2 tbsp olive oil
1 onion, chopped finely
2 large garlic cloves, sliced finely
2 tbsp chopped fresh flat-leaved parsley
2 tsp chopped fresh oregano
1 tsp chopped fresh rosemary
salt and pepper
350 g/12 oz dried fusilli
10 fresh basil leaves, shredded
3 tbsp freshly grated Parmesan cheese

Put the tomatoes and boiling water in a bowl and leave to stand for 5 minutes. Using a perforated spoon, remove one-third of the tomatoes from the bowl. Cut into bite-sized pieces. Put the remaining tomatoes and water into a blender and purée.

Heat the oil in a large frying pan over a medium heat. Add the onion and gently fry for 5 minutes until soft. Add the garlic and fry until just beginning to colour. Add the puréed tomato and the reserved tomato pieces to the pan. Bring to the boil, then simmer over a medium–low heat for 10 minutes. Stir in the herbs and season with salt and pepper. Simmer for 1 minute, then remove from the heat.

Cook the pasta in plenty of boiling salted water until al dente. Drain and transfer to a warm serving dish. Briefly reheat the sauce. Pour over the pasta, add the basil and toss well to mix. Sprinkle with the Parmesan and serve immediately.

tomato-chilli sauce with avocado & coriander

very easy   serves 4

15 minutes   20 minutes

ingredients

3 tbsp olive oil

4 spring onions, green part included, sliced finely

1 fresh green chilli, deseeded and chopped very finely

2 garlic cloves, chopped very finely

200 g/7 oz canned chopped tomatoes

salt and pepper

350 g/12 oz dried farfalle or conchiglie

2 small avocados, peeled and cubed

juice of ½ lime

6 tbsp chopped fresh coriander

Heat 1 tablespoon of the oil in a frying pan over a medium–low heat. Add the spring onions and chilli, then fry, stirring constantly, for 3–4 minutes until just soft. Add the garlic and fry until just beginning to colour.

Stir in the tomatoes. Bring to the boil, then simmer the sauce over a medium heat for 10 minutes, stirring, until thickened. Season with salt and pepper.

Cook the pasta in plenty of boiling salted water until al dente. Drain and transfer to a warm serving dish.

Pour the sauce over the pasta. Add the avocados, lime juice, coriander and remaining olive oil. Toss well to mix. Serve warm or at room temperature.

pepper & goat's cheese sauce

very easy   serves 4

10 minutes   30 minutes

ingredients

2 tbsp olive oil

1 tbsp butter

1 small onion, chopped finely

4 peppers, yellow and red, deseeded and
    cut into 2-cm/¾-inch squares

3 garlic cloves, sliced thinly

salt and pepper

450 g/1 lb dried rigatoni or penne

125 g/4½ oz goat's cheese, crumbled

15 fresh basil leaves, shredded

10 black olives, stoned and sliced

Heat the oil and butter in a large frying pan over a medium heat. Add the onion
and fry until soft. Raise the heat to medium–high and add the peppers and garlic.
Cook for 12–15 minutes, stirring, until the peppers are tender but not mushy.
Season with salt and pepper. Remove from the heat.

Cook the pasta in plenty of boiling salted water until al dente. Drain and transfer
to a warm serving dish. Add the goat's cheese and toss to mix.

Briefly reheat the sauce. Add the basil and olives. Pour over the pasta and toss
well to mix. Serve immediately.

tomato sauce with garlic & basil

very easy   serves 4

10 minutes   30 minutes

ingredients

5 tbsp extra-virgin olive oil

1 onion, chopped finely

800 g/1 lb 12 oz canned chopped tomatoes

4 garlic cloves, quartered

salt and pepper

450 g/1 lb dried spaghetti

large handful fresh basil leaves, shredded

freshly grated Parmesan cheese, to serve

Heat the oil in a large saucepan over a medium heat. Add the onion and fry gently for 5 minutes until soft. Add the tomatoes and garlic. Bring to the boil, then simmer over a medium–low heat for 25–30 minutes until the oil separates from the tomato. Season with salt and pepper.

Cook the pasta in plenty of boiling salted water until al dente. Drain and transfer to a warm serving dish.

Pour the sauce over the pasta. Add the basil and toss well to mix. Serve with Parmesan.

raw tomato sauce with olive oil, garlic & basil

ingredients

extremely easy

serves 4

10 minutes
+ 30 minutes
standing
time

8–10
minutes

550 g/1 lb 4 oz large, ripe tomatoes, peeled, deseeded and diced
125 ml/4 fl oz extra-virgin olive oil
4 garlic cloves, chopped very finely

large handful fresh basil leaves, shredded
3 tbsp chopped fresh oregano or marjoram
salt and pepper
450 g/1 lb dried conchiglie

Combine the tomatoes, olive oil, garlic, basil and oregano in a bowl that is large enough eventually to accommodate the cooked pasta. Season generously with salt and pepper. Cover the bowl with clingfilm and leave to stand at room temperature for at least 30 minutes.

Cook the pasta in plenty of boiling salted water until al dente. Drain thoroughly and immediately add to the tomatoes.

Toss well to mix. Serve at room temperature.

cherry tomato sauce with olives

very easy   serves 4

10 minutes   30 minutes

ingredients

4 tbsp olive oil
900 g/2 lb cherry tomatoes
2 garlic cloves, chopped very finely
1 tbsp chopped fresh oregano or marjoram
¼ tsp dried chilli flakes

20–25 black olives, stoned and sliced
pepper
350 g/12 oz dried conchiglie
rind of ½ lemon, grated
20 g/¾ oz freshly grated Parmesan cheese

Heat the oil in a large frying pan over a medium–high heat. Add the cherry tomatoes and stir until evenly coated with oil. Cover and cook for 10–12 minutes, shaking the pan and stirring once, until all the tomatoes have split.

Add the garlic, oregano, chilli flakes and olives. Season with pepper. Reduce the heat to low and simmer, uncovered, for another 7–10 minutes.

Cook the pasta in plenty of boiling salted water until al dente. Drain well and transfer to a warm serving dish.

Pour half the sauce over the pasta. Toss well to mix. Spoon the rest of the sauce over the top. Sprinkle with the grated lemon rind and Parmesan and serve at once.

roasted red pepper sauce

very easy   serves 4

10 minutes   35 minutes

ingredients

4 red peppers, halved and deseeded
5 tbsp olive oil
1 small red onion, sliced finely
2 garlic cloves, chopped very finely
2 tbsp chopped fresh flat-leaved parsley
1 tsp chopped fresh thyme
salt and pepper

350 g/12 oz dried penne or rigatoni

4 tbsp toasted fresh breadcrumbs,
  to garnish

freshly grated Parmesan cheese, to serve

Place the peppers cut side down in a roasting tin. Roast in a preheated oven at 220°C/425°F/Gas Mark 7 for 15–20 minutes until the skin begins to blacken. Leave to cool slightly. Remove the skin from the peppers. Slice the flesh into thin strips.

Heat the oil in a large frying pan over a medium heat. Add the onion and fry for 5 minutes until soft. Add the garlic and fry until just beginning to colour. Stir in the roasted pepper strips, parsley and thyme. Season with salt and pepper. Stir until heated through.

Cook the pasta in plenty of boiling salted water until al dente. Drain well and transfer to a warm serving dish.

Pour the sauce over the pasta and toss well to mix. Sprinkle with the breadcrumbs and serve with Parmesan.

roasted garlic & red pepper sauce

very easy   serves 4

10 minutes   30 minutes

ingredients

6 large garlic cloves, unpeeled
400 g/14 oz bottled roasted red peppers,
    drained and sliced
200 g/7 oz canned chopped tomatoes
3 tbsp olive oil
¼ tsp dried chilli flakes

1 tsp chopped fresh thyme or oregano
salt and pepper
350 g/12 oz dried spaghetti, bucatini
    or linguine

freshly grated Parmesan cheese, to serve

Place the unpeeled garlic cloves in a shallow, ovenproof dish. Roast in a preheated oven at 200°C/400°F/Gas Mark 6 for 7–10 minutes until the cloves feel soft.

Put the peppers, tomatoes and oil in a food processor or blender, then purée. Squeeze the garlic flesh into the purée. Add the chilli flakes and oregano. Season with salt and pepper. Blend again, then scrape into a saucepan and set aside.

Cook the pasta in plenty of boiling salted water until al dente. Drain and transfer to a warm serving dish.

Reheat the sauce and pour over the pasta. Toss well to mix. Serve at once with Parmesan.

marinated artichoke sauce with onions & tomatoes

ingredients

very easy   serves 4

10 minutes   50 minutes

280 g/10 oz marinated artichoke hearts
  (in jar)
3 tbsp olive oil
1 onion, chopped finely
3 garlic cloves, chopped very finely
1 tsp dried oregano

¼ tsp dried chilli flakes
400 g/14 oz canned chopped tomatoes
salt and pepper
350 g/12 oz dried conchiglie
20 g/¾ oz freshly grated Parmesan cheese
3 tbsp chopped fresh flat-leaved parsley

Drain the artichoke hearts, reserving the marinade. Heat the oil in a large saucepan over a medium heat. Add the onion and fry for 5 minutes until translucent. Add the garlic, oregano, chilli flakes and the reserved artichoke marinade. Cook for 5 more minutes.

Stir in the tomatoes. Bring to the boil, then simmer over a medium–low heat for 30 minutes. Season generously with salt and pepper.

Cook the pasta in plenty of boiling salted water until al dente. Drain and transfer to a warm serving dish.

Add the artichokes, Parmesan and parsley to the sauce. Cook for a few minutes until heated through.

Pour the sauce over the pasta. Toss well to mix. Serve at once.

asparagus & gorgonzola sauce with cream

extremely easy

serves 4

10 minutes

20 minutes

ingredients

450 g/1 lb asparagus tips
olive oil
salt and pepper

225 g/8 oz Gorgonzola cheese, crumbled
175 ml/6 fl oz double cream
350 g/12 oz dried penne

Place the asparagus tips in a single layer in a shallow ovenproof dish. Sprinkle with a little olive oil. Season with salt and pepper. Turn to coat in the oil and seasoning.

Roast in a preheated oven at 230°C/450°F/Gas Mark 8 for 10–12 minutes until slightly browned and just tender. Set aside and keep warm.

Combine the crumbled cheese with the cream in a bowl. Season with salt and pepper.

Cook the pasta in plenty of boiling salted water until al dente. Drain and transfer to a warm serving dish.

Immediately add the asparagus and the cheese mixture. Toss well until the cheese has melted and the pasta is coated with the sauce. Serve at once.

spaghetti with garlic & oil sauce

extremely
easy

serves 4

10 minutes   25 minutes

ingredients

450 g/1 lb dried spaghetti
salt
125 ml/4 fl oz extra-virgin olive oil

4 garlic cloves, chopped very finely
¼ tsp dried chilli flakes
3 tbsp chopped fresh flat-leaved parsley

Cook the pasta in plenty of boiling salted water until al dente. Drain and transfer to a warm serving dish. Season with salt to taste and keep the dish warm.

Heat the oil in a small saucepan over a medium–low heat. Add the garlic and chilli flakes. Cook for 1–2 minutes until the garlic is just beginning to colour. Immediately pour the contents of the saucepan over the pasta. Toss thoroughly to mix.

Sprinkle with the parsley and toss again. Serve immediately.

roasted garlic cream sauce

easy   serves 4

10 minutes   20 minutes

ingredients

2 large heads garlic
600 ml/1 pint double cream
3 thin strips lemon peel
salt and pepper

350 g/12 oz dried fettuccine or tagliatelle
35 g/1¼ oz freshly grated Parmesan cheese

2 tbsp chopped fresh flat-leaved parsley,
    to garnish

Separate the garlic cloves, removing as much of the papery skin as possible, but leaving a thin layer intact. Place the cloves in a shallow ovenproof dish. Roast in a preheated oven at 200°C/400°F/ Gas Mark 6 for 7–10 minutes until the cloves feel soft.

When the garlic is cool enough to handle, remove the skin. Put the cloves in a small saucepan with the cream and lemon peel. Bring to the boil, then simmer gently over a low heat for about 5 minutes until thickened. Push the sauce through a fine-meshed sieve, pressing with the back of a wooden spoon. Return to the saucepan. Season with salt and pepper and set aside.

Cook the pasta in plenty of boiling salted water until al dente. Drain and transfer to a warm serving dish. Stir the Parmesan into the sauce and reheat gently. Pour the sauce over the pasta and toss well to mix. Sprinkle with the parsley. Serve immediately.

mushroom & spinach sauce with feta

very easy   serves 4

15 minutes   20 minutes

3 tbsp olive oil
225 g/8 oz mushrooms, sliced
2 garlic cloves, chopped very finely
2 tbsp chopped fresh flat-leaved parsley
salt and pepper
450 g/1 lb dried rigatoni
250 g/9 oz trimmed baby spinach,
   chopped roughly
250 ml/9 fl oz hot chicken stock

TO GARNISH
55 g/2 oz feta cheese (drained
   weight), crumbled
1 tsp chopped fresh thyme

Heat the oil in a large frying pan over a medium–high heat. Add the mushrooms and fry for 5 minutes until the moisture starts to evaporate. Add the garlic and parsley, then cook for a few seconds more. Season with salt and pepper. Remove the cooking pan from the heat.

Cook the pasta in plenty of boiling salted water until al dente. Drain and immediately return to the pan.

Add the spinach, hot stock and the mushrooms to the pasta. Toss well until the spinach has wilted. Transfer to a warm serving dish. Sprinkle with the feta and thyme and serve at once.

courgette sauce with lemon & rosemary

very easy   serves 4

10 minutes   20 minutes

ingredients

6 tbsp olive oil
1 small onion, sliced very thinly
2 garlic cloves, chopped very finely
2 tbsp chopped fresh rosemary
1 tbsp chopped fresh flat-leaved parsley
450 g/1 lb small courgettes,
   cut into 4 cm x 5-mm/1½ x ¼-inch strips

finely grated peel of 1 lemon
salt and pepper
450 g/1 lb fusilli
4 tbsp freshly grated Parmesan cheese

Heat the olive oil in a large frying pan over a medium–low heat. Add the onion and gently fry, stirring occasionally, for about 10 minutes until golden.

Raise the heat to medium–high. Add the garlic, rosemary and parsley. Cook for a few seconds, stirring.

Add the courgettes and lemon peel. Cook for 5–7 minutes, stirring occasionally, until the courgettes are just tender. Season with salt and pepper. Remove from the heat.

Cook the pasta in plenty of boiling salted water until al dente. Drain and transfer to a warm serving dish.

Briefly reheat the courgettes. Pour over the pasta and toss well to mix. Sprinkle with the Parmesan and serve immediately.

Fish and seafood are ideal candidates for pasta sauces, especially if you stock up with storecupboard basics such as bottled clams and cans of tuna and anchovies. These need only the briefest of cooking times, allowing you to get a meal on the table in minutes. Prawns can be combined with tomatoes, garlic and chilli for a robust Mediterranean sauce, or sizzled oriental-style with ginger and spices, while smoked salmon, mussels and scallops can form the basis of rich cream or tomato-based sauces that are ideal for entertaining.

fish & seafood sauces

spaghetti with anchovies, olives, capers & tomatoes

very easy   serves 4

10 minutes   35–40 minutes

ingredients

6 tbsp olive oil

4 anchovy fillets, chopped

2 garlic cloves, chopped very finely

800 g/1 lb 12 oz canned chopped tomatoes

1 tsp dried oregano

¼ tsp dried chilli flakes

salt and pepper

350 g/12 oz dried spaghetti

10–12 black olives, stoned and sliced

2 tbsp capers, drained

Heat the oil with the anchovies in a large frying pan over a low heat. Stir until the anchovies dissolve. Add the garlic and cook for a few seconds until just beginning to colour. Add the tomatoes, oregano and chilli flakes, then season with salt and pepper. Bring to the boil, then simmer over a medium–low heat for 30 minutes until the oil begins to separate from the tomatoes.

Cook the pasta in plenty of boiling salted water until al dente. Drain and transfer to a warm serving dish.

Add the olives and capers to the sauce. Pour over the pasta and toss well to mix. Serve immediately.

clam & tomato sauce

very easy   serves 4

10 minutes   35 minutes

ingredients

400 g/14 oz clams or scallops in brine
  (in jar)
4 tbsp olive oil
4 garlic cloves, chopped very finely
800 g/1 lb 12 oz canned chopped tomatoes

3 tbsp chopped fresh flat-leaved parsley
½ tsp dried chilli flakes
salt
450 g/1 lb dried riccioli or fusilli

Drain the clams or scallops, reserving the liquid from the jar.

Heat the oil and garlic in a large saucepan over a low heat. Cook the garlic for a few seconds until just beginning to colour. Add the tomatoes, the reserved clam juice, parsley, chilli flakes and a little salt. Bring to the boil, then simmer over a medium–low heat for 30 minutes until the oil separates from the tomatoes.

Cook the pasta in plenty of boiling salted water until al dente. Drain and transfer to a warm serving dish.

Add the clams to the sauce, stirring until heated through. Pour the sauce over the pasta. Toss well to mix. Serve immediately.

prawn sauce with tomatoes, garlic & chilli

very easy   serves 4

10 minutes   35 minutes

ingredients

4 tbsp olive oil
5 garlic cloves, chopped very finely
400 g/14 oz canned chopped tomatoes
1 fresh red chilli, deseeded and chopped
    very finely
salt and pepper

450 g/1 lb dried linguine or spaghetti
350 g/12 oz raw peeled prawns

2 tbsp chopped fresh flat-leaved parsley,
    to garnish

Heat 2 tablespoons of the oil and the garlic in a saucepan over a medium–low heat. Cook the garlic until just beginning to colour. Add the tomatoes and chilli. Bring to the boil, then simmer over a medium–low heat for 30 minutes until the oil separates from the tomatoes. Season with salt and pepper.

Cook the pasta in plenty of boiling salted water until al dente. Drain and return to the pan.

Heat the remaining oil in a frying pan over a high heat. Add the prawns and stir-fry for 2 minutes until pink. Add the prawns to the tomato mixture. Stir in the parsley. Simmer over a low heat until bubbling.

Transfer the pasta to a warm serving dish. Pour the sauce over the pasta. Toss well to mix and serve immediately.

clam & leek sauce

very easy   serves 4

10 minutes   15 minutes

ingredients

400 g/14 oz clams in brine (in jar)
3 tbsp olive oil
2 large leeks (white part only), sliced
    lengthwise and cut into thin 5-cm/2-inch
    strips
2 garlic cloves, chopped very finely

4 tbsp dry white wine
1 bay leaf
salt and pepper
350 g/12 oz dried spaghetti or linguine
3 tbsp fresh flat-leaved parsley

Drain the clams, reserving the liquid from the jar.

Heat the oil in a large frying pan over a medium–low heat. Add the leeks and garlic, then fry gently for 3–4 minutes until the leeks are tender-crisp. Stir in the wine and cook for 1–2 minutes until evaporated. Add the bay leaf, clams and the reserved liquid. Season with salt and pepper. Simmer for 5 minutes, then remove from the heat.

Cook the pasta in plenty of boiling salted water until al dente. Drain and transfer to a warm serving dish.

Briefly reheat the sauce and pour over the pasta. Add the parsley and toss well to mix. Serve immediately.

prawn & garlic sauce with cream

very easy   serves 4

15 minutes   15 minutes

3 tbsp olive oil

3 tbsp butter

4 garlic cloves, chopped very finely

2 tbsp finely diced red pepper

2 tbsp tomato purée

125 ml/4 fl oz dry white wine

450 g/1 lb tagliatelle or spaghetti

350 g/12 oz raw peeled prawns, cut into
  1-cm/½-inch pieces

125 ml/4 fl oz double cream

salt and pepper

3 tbsp chopped fresh flat-leaved parsley

Heat the oil and butter in a saucepan over a medium–low heat. Add the garlic
and red pepper. Fry for a few seconds until the garlic is just beginning to colour.
Stir in the tomato purée and wine. Cook for 10 minutes, stirring.

Cook the pasta in plenty of boiling salted water until al dente. Drain and return
to the pan.

Add the prawns to the sauce and raise the heat to medium–high. Cook for
2 minutes, stirring, until the prawns turn pink. Reduce the heat and stir in the
cream. Cook for 1 minute, stirring constantly, until thickened. Season with salt
and pepper.

Transfer the pasta to a warm serving dish. Pour the sauce over the pasta.
Sprinkle with the parsley. Toss well to mix and serve at once.

spicy prawn sauce with ginger

very easy   serves 4

10 minutes   10 minutes

ingredients

4 tbsp passata (sieved tomatoes)
300 ml/10 fl oz single cream
1½ tsp grated fresh ginger
¼ tsp cayenne
1 tbsp lemon juice
1 tsp ground cumin
1 tsp salt

¼ tsp pepper
450 g/1 lb dried flat rice noodles
3 tbsp vegetable oil
3 garlic cloves, chopped very finely
450 g/1 lb raw peeled prawns
2 tbsp chopped fresh coriander

Combine the passata, cream, ginger, cayenne, lemon juice, cumin, salt and pepper in a small saucepan, mixing well. Cook the mixture over a medium heat, stirring, until bubbling. Remove from the heat.

Cook the noodles according to the packet instructions. Drain and transfer to a warm serving dish.

Heat the oil and garlic in a large frying pan over a medium–low heat. Cook until the garlic just begins to colour. Add the prawns and raise the heat to medium–high. Stir-fry for 2 minutes until the prawns are pink. Stir in the sauce and 1 tablespoon of the coriander. Cook for another minute.

Pour the prawn mixture over the noodles. Sprinkle with the remaining coriander and serve immediately.

prawn sauce with lemon & herbs

very easy   serves 4

15–20   10 minutes
minutes

ingredients

350 g/12 oz dried spaghettini or vermicelli
4 tbsp olive oil
4 tbsp butter
8 spring onions, green part included,
    sliced thinly
450 g/1 lb raw peeled prawns
juice and finely grated peel of ½ lemon

3 tbsp chopped fresh flat-leaved parsley
3 tbsp shredded fresh basil
1 tbsp chopped fresh marjoram or oregano
2 tsp chopped fresh thyme
250 ml/9 fl oz chicken stock
salt and pepper

Cook the pasta in plenty of boiling salted water until al dente. Drain and return to the pan and cover to keep warm.

Heat the oil and butter in a large frying pan over a medium–high heat. Add the spring onions and prawns. Stir-fry for 2 minutes until the prawns turn pink. Reduce the heat to medium. Stir in the lemon juice and peel, herbs and chicken stock. Season with salt and pepper. Simmer until heated through.

Transfer the pasta to a warm serving dish. Pour the prawn mixture over the pasta and toss well to mix. Serve immediately.

scallops with porcini & cream sauce

very easy   serves 4

10 minutes +   25 minutes
20 minutes
soaking time

ingredients

25 g/1 oz dried porcini mushrooms
500 ml/18 fl oz hot water
3 tbsp olive oil
3 tbsp butter
350 g/12 oz scallops, sliced
2 garlic cloves, chopped very finely

2 tbsp lemon juice
250 ml/9 fl oz double cream
salt and pepper
350 g/12 oz dried fettuccine or pappardelle
2 tbsp chopped fresh flat-leaved parsley

Put the porcini and hot water in a bowl. Leave to soak for 20 minutes. Strain the mushrooms, reserving the soaking water, and chop roughly. Line a sieve with two pieces of kitchen paper and strain the mushroom water into a bowl.

Heat the oil and butter in a large frying pan over a medium heat. Add the scallops and cook for 2 minutes until just golden. Add the garlic and mushrooms, then stir-fry for another minute.

Stir in the lemon juice, cream and 125 ml/4 fl oz of the mushroom water. Bring to the boil, then simmer over a medium heat for 2–3 minutes, stirring constantly, until the liquid is reduced by half. Season with salt and pepper. Remove from the heat.

Cook the pasta in plenty of boiling salted water until al dente. Drain and transfer to a warm serving dish. Briefly reheat the sauce and pour over the pasta. Sprinkle with the parsley and toss well to mix. Serve immediately.

tuna with garlic, lemon, capers & olives

extremely easy

serves 4

10 minutes

10 minutes

350 g/12 oz dried conchiglie or gnocchi
4 tbsp olive oil
4 tbsp butter
3 large garlic cloves, sliced thinly
200 g/7 oz canned tuna, drained and broken
  into chunks

2 tbsp lemon juice
1 tbsp capers, drained
10–12 black olives, stoned and sliced
2 tbsp chopped fresh flat-leaved parsley

Cook the pasta in plenty of boiling salted water until al dente. Drain and return to the pan.

Heat the olive oil and half the butter in a frying pan over a medium–low heat. Add the garlic and cook for a few seconds until just beginning to colour. Reduce the heat to low. Add the tuna, lemon juice, capers and olives. Stir gently until all the ingredients are heated through.

Transfer the pasta to a warm serving dish. Pour the tuna mixture over the pasta. Add the parsley and remaining butter. Toss well to mix. Serve immediately.

mussels with tomatoes, peppers & olives

ingredients

very easy   serves 4

20 minutes   20 minutes

3 litres/5¼ pints mussels
1 large onion, chopped finely
250 ml/9 fl oz dry white wine
3 tbsp olive oil
3 garlic cloves, chopped very finely
2 yellow peppers, deseeded and diced

400 g/14 oz canned chopped tomatoes
¼ tsp dried chilli flakes
salt and pepper
450 g/1 lb riccioli or fettucine
10–12 black olives, stoned and sliced
6 tbsp shredded fresh basil

Clean the mussels by scrubbing the shells and pulling out any beards that are attached. Rinse well and discard any with broken shells and any that do not close when tapped. Put the mussels in a large saucepan with the onion and white wine. Cover and cook over a medium heat for 3–4 minutes, shaking the pan, until the mussels open. Remove from the heat. Lift out the mussels with a perforated spoon, reserving the liquid. Discard any that remain closed. Remove the rest of the mussels from their shells.

Heat the olive oil and garlic in a frying pan over a medium–low heat. Cook until the garlic is just beginning to colour. Add the peppers, tomatoes, chilli flakes and 4 tablespoons of the mussel liquid. Bring to the boil, then simmer over a medium heat for 15 minutes until slightly reduced. Season with salt and pepper. Cook the pasta until al dente. Drain and transfer to a serving dish. Add the mussels and olives to the sauce; stir until heated. Pour onto the pasta. Add the basil and mix well. Serve at once.

mussels with white wine, garlic & parsley

ingredients

very easy   serves 4

20 minutes   10 minutes

3.5 litres/6 pints mussels, scrubbed
1 large onion, chopped
3 garlic cloves, chopped very finely
500 ml/18 fl oz dry white wine
1 bay leaf
2 sprigs of fresh thyme

5 tbsp chopped fresh flat-leaved parsley
1 tbsp chopped fresh rosemary
4 tbsp butter
salt and pepper
450 g/1 lb dried tagliatelle or other broad-
  ribboned pasta

Clean the mussels by scrubbing the shells and pulling out any beards that are attached. Rinse well, discarding any with broken shells or that remain open when tapped. Put the onion, garlic, white wine, herbs and 2 tablespoons of the butter in a saucepan. Bring to the boil, then reduce the heat. Add the mussels. Season to taste. Cover and cook over a medium heat for 3–4 minutes, shaking the pan, until the mussels open. Remove from the heat. Lift out the mussels with a perforated spoon, reserving the liquid. Discard any that remain closed. Remove most of the others from their shells, reserving a few in their shells to garnish.

Cook the pasta until al dente. Drain and put the pasta into bowls. Spoon the mussels over the pasta. Strain the mussel liquid and return to the pan. Add the remaining butter and heat until melted. Pour over the pasta, garnish with the mussels in their shells and serve immediately.

smoked salmon, soured cream & mustard sauce

extremely easy

serves 4

10 minutes

10 minutes

ingredients

450 g/1 lb tagliatelle or conchiglie
300 ml/10 fl oz soured cream
2 tsp Dijon mustard
4 large spring onions, sliced finely
225 g/8 oz smoked salmon, cut into
 bite-sized pieces

finely grated peel of ½ lemon
pepper

2 tbsp chopped fresh chives, to garnish

Cook the pasta in plenty of boiling salted water until al dente. Drain and return to the pan. Add the soured cream, mustard, spring onions, smoked salmon and lemon peel to the pasta. Stir over a low heat until heated through. Season with pepper.

Transfer to a serving dish. Sprinkle with the chives. Serve warm or at room temperature.

hot cajun seafood sauce

very easy   serves 4

15 minutes   20 minutes

ingredients

500 ml/18 fl oz whipping cream
8 spring onions, sliced thinly
55 g/2 oz chopped fresh flat-leaved parsley
1 tbsp chopped fresh thyme
½ tbsp freshly ground black pepper
½–1 tsp dried chilli flakes
1 tsp salt
450 g/1 lb dried fusilli or tagliatelle

40 g/1½ oz freshly grated Gruyère cheese
20 g/¾ oz freshly grated Parmesan cheese
2 tbsp olive oil
225 g/8 oz raw peeled prawns
225 g/8 oz scallops, sliced

1 tbsp shredded fresh basil, to garnish

Heat the cream in a large saucepan over a medium heat, stirring constantly. When almost boiling, reduce the heat and add the spring onions, parsley, thyme, pepper, chilli flakes and salt. Simmer for 7–8 minutes, stirring, until thickened. Remove from the heat.

Cook the pasta in plenty of boiling salted water until al dente. Drain and return to the pan. Add the cream mixture and the cheeses to the pasta. Toss over a low heat until the cheeses have melted. Transfer to a warm serving dish.

Heat the oil in a large frying pan over a medium–high heat. Add the prawns and scallops. Stir-fry for 2–3 minutes until the prawns have just turned pink.

Pour the seafood over the pasta and toss well to mix. Sprinkle with the basil. Serve immediately.

index

Renault 16 1965-79 Autobook

By the Autobooks Team of Writers and Illustrators

Renault 16 1965-72
Renault 16L 1972-76
Renault 16TL 1970-79
Renault 16TS 1968-76
Renault 16TX 1974-79

Autobooks Ltd. Golden Lane Brighton BN1 2QJ England

The AUTOBOOK series of Workshop Manuals is the largest in the world and covers the majority of British and Continental motor cars, as well as the majority of Japanese and Australian models.

Whilst every care has been taken to ensure correctness of information it is obviously not possible to guarantee complete freedom from errors or omissions or to accept liability arising from such errors or omissions.

CONTENTS

Introduction

Acknowledgement

ISBN 0 85147 903 0

First Edition   1970
Second Edition, fully revised   1971
Third Edition, fully revised   1971
Fourth Edition, fully revised   1972
Reprinted   1972
Fifth Edition, fully revised   1973
Sixth Edition, fully revised   1974
Seventh Edition, fully revised   1975
Eighth Edition, fully revised   1975
Ninth Edition, fully revised   1977
Tenth Edition, fully revised   1978
Eleventh Edition, fully revised   1979

755

Certain illustrations reproduced by kind permission of
the manufacturers © Régie Nationale des Usines
Renault

Printed in Brighton England for Autobooks Ltd by G. Beard and Son Ltd
Bound in Hove England for Autobooks Ltd by Jilks Ltd

G

INTRODUCTION

This do-it-yourself Workshop Manual has been specially written for the owner who wishes to maintain his vehicle in first class condition and to carry out the bulk of his own servicing and repairs. Considerable savings on garage charges can be made, and one can drive in safety and confidence knowing the work has been done properly.

Comprehensive step-by-step instructions and illustrations are given on most dismantling, overhauling and assembling operations. Certain assemblies require the use of expensive special tools, the purchase of which would be unjustified. In these cases information is included but the reader is recommended to hand the unit to the agent for attention.

Throughout the Manual hints and tips are included which will be found invaluable, and there is an easy to follow fault diagnosis at the end of each chapter.

Whilst every care has been taken to ensure correctness of information it is obviously not possible to guarantee complete freedom from errors or omissions or to accept liability arising from such errors or omissions.

Instructions may refer to the righthand or lefthand sides of the vehicle or the components. These are the same as the righthand or lefthand of an observer standing behind the vehicle and looking forward.

Unconventional design proved in a long production run – the Renault 16

CHAPTER 1

THE ENGINE

1 : 1 Description

Model designations:

Full technical details are given in the Appendix at the end of this manual and included are capacities, bore, and stroke of the various engines.

As different engines are fitted to different models it will clarify the position if the designations and types are given in the form of the following table:

Model	Type	Engine
16	R.1150	697.01 or 697.02
16TS	R.1151	807.01, 807.02, 807.03 or 807.04
16 and 16TL	R.1152	821.02 or 821.03
16TA	R.1153	821.01 or 821.04
16TSA	R.1154	807.05 or 807.06
16 (North America)	R.1155	841.04
16TX	R.1156	843.01 or 843.02

Construction:

Much of the design is very similar on all models and extensive use is made of aluminium-alloy castings. The 697, 821 and 841 engines are very similar and are treated in exactly the same manner. Sectioned views of the 697, 821 and 841 type engines are shown in **FIG 1 : 1**, while sectioned views of the 807 and 843 engine are shown in **FIG 1 : 2**. The main and most obvious difference between the two types of engine is in the design of the cylinder head. On the 697, 821 and 841 models the valves are in-line while on the 807 and 843 model the valves are fitted in two banks and two rocker shafts and associated parts are fitted.

The crankshaft runs in five main bearings which are fitted with renewable steel-backed bearing shells. Thrust is taken at the centre main bearing by thrust washers fitted on either side and these also control the end float of the crankshaft. The big-ends of the connecting rods rotate about the crankshaft using renewable bearing shells. The gudgeon pins at the little-ends are a shrink fit into the connecting rod and a free fit in the piston.

A timing chain at the rear end of the engine connects the crankshaft sprocket to the camshaft sprocket so that the camshaft is driven at half engine speed. On the front end of the camshaft is the pulley which drives the water pump and alternator by belts. Pushrods, cam followers and rocker arms in the cylinder head operate the valves from the cams of the camshaft. On all models a single camshaft is fitted into the cylinder block but on the 807 and 843 engines, with their double bank of inclined valves, the valve train is divided between two rocker shafts.

Gears on the camshaft also supply the drive to the oil pump and distributor. The oil pump draws the oil from the sump, through a strainer, and then passes it through a fullflow filter before the oil goes into the main oil gallery running along the side of the crankcase. Lubricating oil is fed to the main bearings by internal passages and from the main bearings it passes to the big-end bearings through drillings in the crankshaft.

Torque settings and thread repairs:

A number of special tools are required for working on the engine but the tool most often required is a torque wrench. Aluminium-alloy is much softer than steel and the correct tightening of bolts is therefore all the more essential. If the bolts or fastenings are overtightened the threads can easily be stripped from the alloy casting while if the bolts are not sufficiently tightened they can work loose, causing failure or damage to parts. These difficulties will be obviated if a torque wrench is used to tighten all fastenings correctly. Torque wrench settings are given throughout the text and also in Technical Data.

Before refitting a bolt or fastener make sure that the threads in both the casting and fastener are clean and undamaged. If necessary run the fastener in and out to check that the threads are free. Normally bolts are refitted with dry threads but bolts which are immersed in oil are usually oiled before tightening.

If a thread does strip or wear it can be rectified by drilling it out oversize, tapping it and then fitting a steel insert thread, such as Helicoil. Such repairs are best left to an agent who will have all the taps and tools required as well as a selection of inserts.

1:2 Removing the engine

The engine cannot be removed separately and the gearbox must be removed with it. Once the power unit is out of the car the gearbox can be separated from the engine.

The manually operated gearbox is dealt with in **Chapter 6** and full details of disconnecting the linkage are given in that chapter. Similarly the automatic transmission is dealt with in **Chapter 7**.

The cooling system is dealt with in **Chapter 4. Draining, filling and bleeding are not straightforward as a sealed system is fitted and if the operations are not carried out correctly damage can be caused.**

On cars fitted with air-conditioning do not disconnect any system pipes. Remove the compressor, base plate and mounting bracket as an assembly, and place out of the way. There are two assemblies, the first, recognised by standard securing bolts and a stud with centralising cones requires alignment with tool MS 516 on refitting, the second assembly is self aligning.

There are slight differences between models but these will be dealt with in the text.

1 Drain the cooling system, engine and gearbox. Disconnect the battery and remove the spare wheel. Either disconnect the bonnet retaining cable and lift the bonnet fully open or else remove the bonnet completely. Remove the radiator (see **Chapter 4**) together with its hoses and expansion bottle. Remove the spare wheel mounting crossmember, and the ignition coil if it is mounted on it.

2 Disconnect the controls to the carburetter and remove the air cleaner. Disconnect the inlet pipe at the fuel pump and the return pipe to the fuel tank. Details of the fuel system are given in **Chapter 2.**

3 Disconnect the heater hoses at the water pump. Disconnect the parts of the emission control, if fitted. The disconnection points for 1152 (16TL) are shown in **FIGS 1:3** and **1:4**. Disconnect the vacuum pipe to the Master-Vac brake servo.

4 Disconnect all electrical leads to the engine, labelling them if there is any doubt as to the correct reconnections. These include the leads to the starter motor, alternator, temperature transmitter, oil pressure transmitter, and engine earth strap. Remove the alternator. The alternator attachments and fuel pipes on the 1150 and 1152 models are shown in **FIG 1:5**.

5 Disconnect the exhaust pipe from the manifold and free any brackets or clamps that secure it to the transmission. Free the steering rack from the steering column and disconnect it from the steering linkage so that it can be removed (see **Chapter 10**).

6 Disconnect the speedometer drive cable from the transmission and also disconnect the selector linkage. On models with manual transmission disconnect the clutch control cable (see **Chapter 5**). If a reverse light switch is fitted on top of the gearbox disconnect the wires and remove the switch.

7 Free the front mounting. On type 336 gearbox the mounting is as shown in **FIG 1:6**. The attachments of the automatic transmission, and type 385 gearbox are shown in **Chapter 7**. On the manual transmission models with type 336 gearbox unscrew the two bolts that secure the pad so that the two anchor washers can be freed, and then remove the two bolts that secure the pad to the front housing so that the pad and its bracket can be removed. If necessary lightly support the gearbox with a jack and pad of wood from underneath. On automatic models and type 385 gearbox refer to **Chapter 7**.

8 Drive out the pins that secure the drive shaft using a suitable drift, preferably No. B.Vi.31.01 as shown in **FIG 1:7**. Fit clips onto the drive shafts to prevent the couplings from falling apart. Special clips are supplied with new drive shafts but if these cannot be obtained hold the parts together with a length of soft wire.

9 Remove the front brake calipers and free the upper suspension ball joints so that the steering knuckles can be swivelled outwards to free the joints from the transmission (see **Chapter 7** and also **Chapter 9** for details of the front suspension).

10 On manual transmission models fit a jack between the gearbox and lefthand sidemember. Use pads of wood to protect the member and casing. Open the jack so that the gearbox is pushed over to the right and the lefthand side drive shaft can then be freed from the sun wheel in the transmission. Slacken the jack and fit it to the righthand side so that the righthand drive shaft can be freed in a similar manner.

11 Check that the only attachments between the engine/gearbox and car are the two engine mountings. **The engine must not be lifted using any form of attachment on the cylinder head bolts or the manifolds.** The only safe and effective sling for lifting out the engine is No. Mot.367.01 and it will be necessary to remove the upper starter motor attachment bolt to fix the sling as shown in **FIG 1:8**. On the TS and TX models (1151, 1154 and 1156) a spacer must be fitted between the sling and boss on the crankcase to make

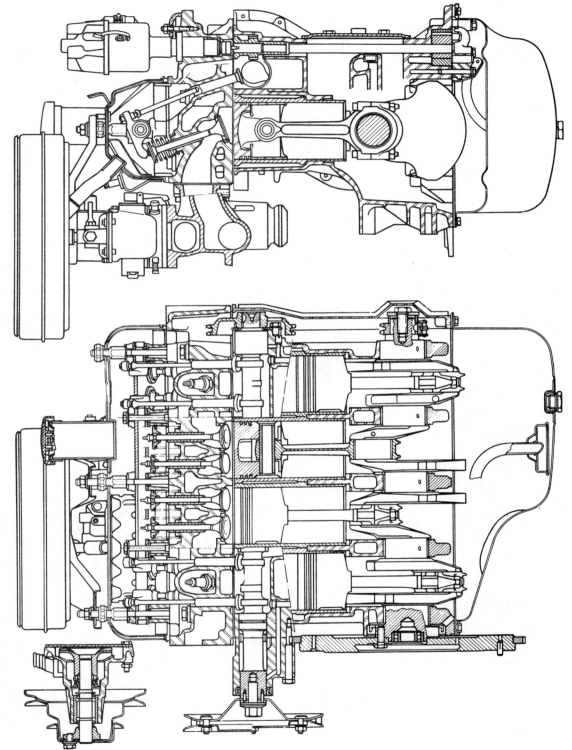

FIG 1:1   Sectioned views of the 697, 821 and 841 type engines

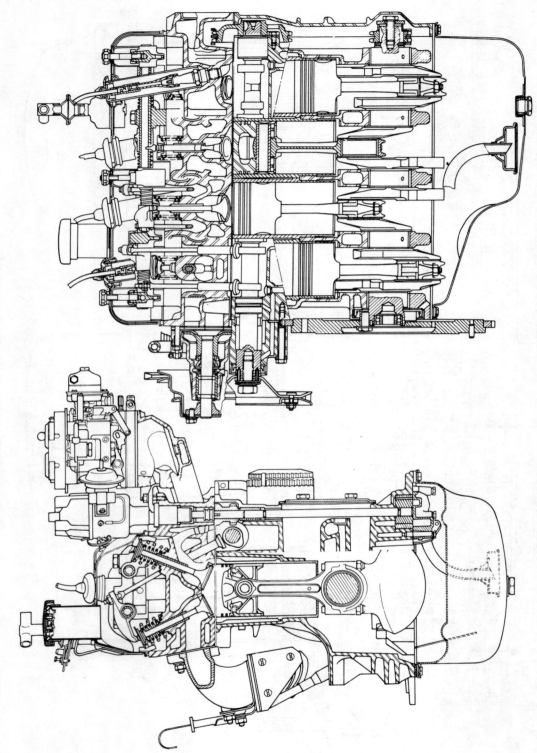

FIG 1:2 Sectioned views of the 807 and 843 type engine

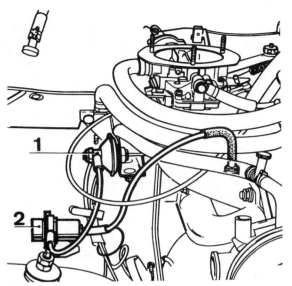

FIG 1:3 The emission control vacuum capsule and solenoid valve

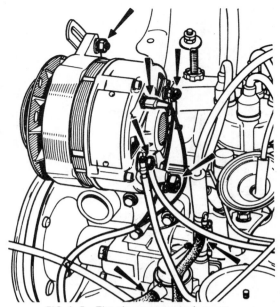

FIG 1:5 The alternator attachments

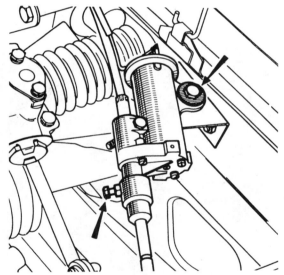

FIG 1:4 The emission control centrifugal switch

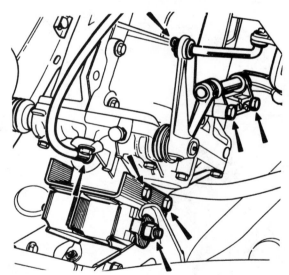

FIG 1:6 The manual gearbox front mounting assembly

sure that the hook does not foul on the water outlet from the cylinder head.

12 Take the weight of the engine using a hoist and the special sling and take out the bolts that secure the engine mountings, arrowed in **FIG 1:9**. Raise the power unit slightly and pull it forwards. Lift up the gearbox so that the power unit makes an angle and keep it up using a chain as shown in **FIG 1:10**. The power unit can then be lifted up and out of the car.

Dismantling:

Remove the lifting hook, starter motor, camshaft pulley

outer flange with its adjusting shims and drive belt, and the water pump pulley. Take off the clutch protective shield and remove the bolts that secure the clutch housing to the engine. Withdraw the transmission, taking great care not to allow its weight to hang on the input shaft in the clutch.

Refitting:

The power unit is refitted in the reverse order of removal. The input shaft splines on the gearbox should be lightly greased and the sun wheel splines should also be greased

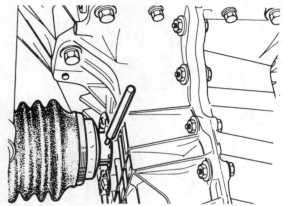

FIG 1:7   Removing the drive pins from the drive shaft

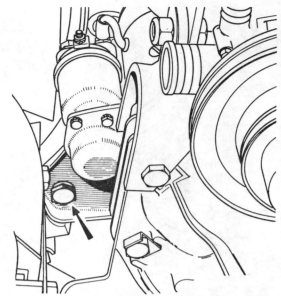

FIG 1:9   The engine mounting bolts

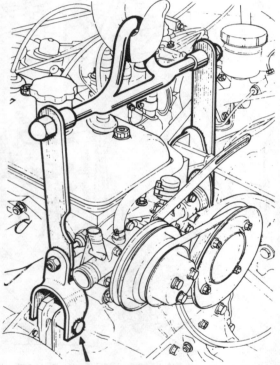

FIG 1:8   Attaching the lifting hook to the engine

FIG 1:10   Lifting out the power unit

with Molykote BR2 grease. Use an elbow drift to align the holes for the drive shafts before driving in new rollpins and then seal the ends of the rollpin holes with Rhodorsil.

The bolt for the starter motor is fitted from the front, with a spring washer under the head followed by a plain washer. A nut and washer then secures the bolt in place.

It will be necessary to re-tension the water pump drive belt by adjusting the shims between the pulley flanges. While doing this the engine must be turned as the pulley bolts are being slowly tightened. **Do not turn the engine using a spanner on the camshaft pulley**

except on automatic models with the spark plugs removed and then only in a clockwise direction. The best way on manual transmission models of turning the engine is to chock the rear wheels, jack-up a front wheel and with top gear engaged turn the road wheel so that the engine is slowly driven round.

1:3 Removing the cylinder head

Wet liners are fitted and these are set to a small protrusion so that the cylinder head presses them down and ensures an effective seal.

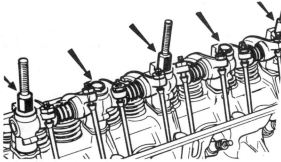

FIG 1:11   697, 821 and 841 rocker assembly attachments

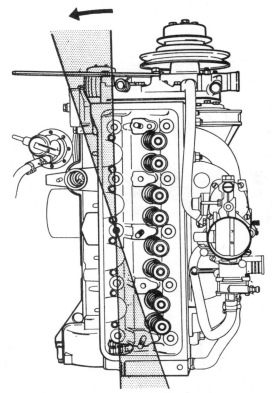

FIG 1:14   Turning the cylinder head about the location dowel to break the seal

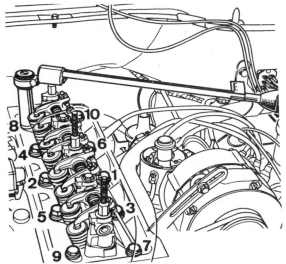

FIG 1:12   The sequence for tightening the cylinder head bolts on 697, 821 and 841 engines

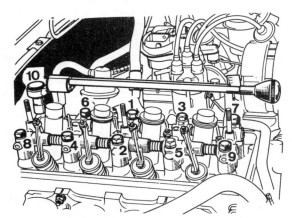

FIG 1:13   The sequence for tightening the cylinder head bolts on 807 and 843 engines

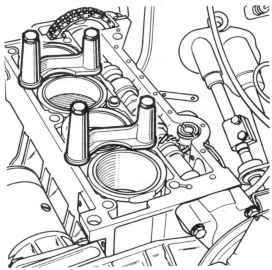

FIG 1:15   Fitting clamps Mot.12 to hold the liners in position. These have been superceded by Mot.521 clamps

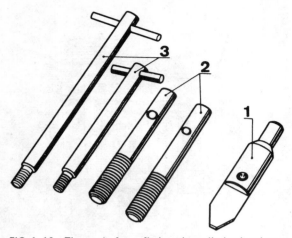

FIG 1:16 The tools for refitting the cylinder head on 807 and 843 engines. The studs 2 and short remover 3 are used on the remaining engines

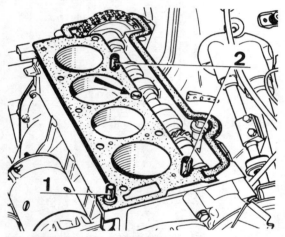

FIG 1:17 The gaskets and tools in place ready for refitting an 807 and 843 cylinder head

Special self-sealing cylinder head gaskets are fitted and once the cylinder head has been lowered into place the gasket must not be in any way disturbed. If the cylinder head is not correctly aligned then the cylinder head must be removed and a new gasket fitted before again refitting the cylinder head.

The alignment of the cylinder head is important as it controls the positioning of the distributor drive shaft and therefore special tools must be used when refitting the cylinder head.

The cooling system must be drained before removing the cylinder head and then correctly refilled after the cylinder head is in place. **As a special sealed cooling system is fitted care must be taken to follow the instructions given in Chapter 4 otherwise air will remain trapped in the system or damage will be caused to parts.**

Removal:

1 Drain the cooling system. Remove the spare wheel and disconnect the battery. Disconnect leads, pipes and wires as required to give access room, and to free the carburetter controls.

2 Remove the alternator, distributor, rocker cover, drive belts and outer flange and shims of the camshaft pulley. Free the exhaust pipe from the exhaust manifold.

3 **697, 821 and 841 engines only.** Evenly slacken and remove the nuts and bolts that secure the rocker assembly in place, arrowed in **FIG 1:11**. Lift off the rocker assembly and then take out the pushrods, storing the pushrods in the correct order for reassembly.

4 **807 and 843 engines only.** Remove the rubber washers and cups from the spark plug tubes. Slacken off the locknuts and valve adjusters so that the pushrods can be removed and stored in the correct order for reassembly. On these models the same bolts that secure the cylinder head also secure the rocker assembly.

5 Evenly and progressively slacken the bolts that secure the cylinder head in the same order as they are tightened after reassembly. The order for 697, 821 and 841 engines is shown in **FIG 1:12** while that for 807 and 843 engines is shown in **FIG 1:13**. When all the bolts are slack take them out and free the cylinder head. **The cylinder head must not be lifted direct otherwise the wet liners may be lifted with it.** Use a rubber mallet to swivel the cylinder head about the locating dowel on the distributor side so that it moves horizontally and breaks the seal, as shown in **FIG 1:14**.

6 Partially lift the cylinder head when it is free and take out the cam followers from underneath it, storing them in their correct order for reassembly. Fully lift off the cylinder head and remove the old cylinder head gasket and tappet chamber seal. On the 807 and 843 model engines it will be found that the rear pair of bolts cannot be fully removed so withdraw them as much as possible and then hold them up by wrapping an elastic band around them.

As soon as the cylinder head has been removed the liners should be held firmly down with clamps as shown in FIG 1:15. They may be omitted provided that the engine is not turned from its original position until the cylinder head has been refitted. If the engine is turned without the clamps in place there is a serious risk of the liners being lifted out of their bottom seals.

Cleaning and examination:

Servicing the components of the cylinder head will be dealt with in the next section but the parts must be cleaned and checked for distortion. The liner protrusion is dealt with in **Section 1:8**.

The faces of the block and cylinder head must not be scraped with sharp metal tools. Use a stick of hardwood or sharpened stick of solder to remove most of the old gasket. The remainder of the sealing can then be softened with trichlorethylene or special fluid No. 77.01.390.107. Allow to soak for ten minutes and then gently wipe or scrape away the residue.

Lay a steel straightedge across the cylinder head and use feeler gauges to measure the maximum distortion. If the distortion exceeds .05 mm (.002 inch) the cylinder head must be sent away for specialist grinding to true it up. The maximum metal that can be removed is .3 mm (.012 inch) and if more metal has to be removed then a new cylinder head must be fitted.

Reassembly:

The cylinder head gasket is a 'one-shot' and once the cylinder head has been laid in place any movement of the cylinder head will destroy the gasket. Special tools must be used to align the cylinder head correctly. It is most advisable for the owner to carry out a dry run, if he has not refitted a cylinder head before, without using any gaskets so as to give familiarity with the tools. If a mistake is made with the gaskets in place then the cylinder head must be removed and the gasket discarded.

The special tools for refitting the 807 or 843 cylinder head are shown in **FIG 1:16** and the tools and gasket in place are shown in **FIG 1:17**. On all other models the tool No. Mot.446 (item 1) is not required and instead a positioning bracket Mot.412 or Mot.412.01 is used instead. The tools and bracket in place on 697, 821 or 841 engines are shown in **FIG 1:18**.

1 Fit the cylinder head gasket into place, locating it on the dowel, after removing the liner holding down clamps. Screw in the two special studs until their balls just hold down the cylinder head gasket in place.

2 Refit the tappet chamber seal, **making sure that its ends do not foul on the cylinder head gasket.** On the 697 engine only there are two types of tappet chamber gasket. The gasket with 9 pips must only be fitted to cylinder blocks with 5 holes and the gasket with 13 pips only to cylinder blocks with 9 holes. The timing cover will either have 2 or 4 holes and if it has only 2 holes then cut off the 2 surplus pips in either case.

3 Fit the cam followers back into their correct locations and give them a light tap to hold them in place. On the 807 and 843 models fit the two rearmost bolts to the cylinder head and hold them in place with an elastic band so that they do not protrude below the cylinder head. Note that on all models the rearmost bolts are also the shortest. Fit the location tool into place as shown in the figures, making sure that the lugs on the tool for the 697, 821 or 841 engines are parallel to the line of the engine.

4 Lower the cylinder head back into place. Before it fully reaches the bottom make sure that it aligns onto the special tool. The face for the manifold must be pressed firmly against both lugs on the special bracket. When aligned lower the cylinder head fully into place. **Once the cylinder head is in place it must not be moved.** Remove the aligning tool and unscrew the special studs using the T-piece handles.

5 Make sure that the cylinder head bolt threads are clean and lubricate them with tallow. Smear the washer under the bolt heads with engine oil. Screw all the bolts back in so that they are finger tight. On the 807 and 843 engines the rocker assembly must be refitted at the same time as refitting the cylinder head bolts. With the rocker adjusters slackened right off refit the pushrods into their correct locations, noting that the exhaust pushrods are longer than the inlet ones for this model. On the other models the cylinder head bolts are

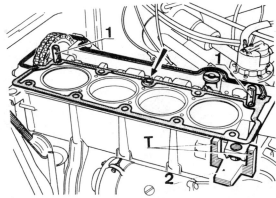

FIG 1:18 The tools and gaskets in place ready for re-fitting a 697, 821 or 841 cylinder head. Note the special bracket 2

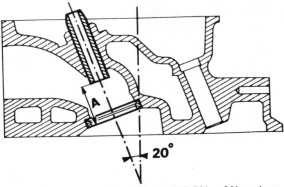

FIG 1:19 Fitting valve guides to 697, 821 or 841 engines

fitted and the rocker assembly fitted afterwards. Tighten all the cylinder head bolts to a torque of 4 kg m (30 lb ft) progressively and in the order shown in **FIGS 1:12** and **1:13**. On 697, 821 or 841 engines refit the rocker assembly, complete with pushrods, and tighten the nuts and bolts to a torque of 2 to 2.75 kg m (15 to 20 lb ft). Again progressively tighten the cylinder head bolts, in the correct order, to a torque of 7 to 7.5 kg m (50 to 55 lb ft) for 697, 821 or 841 engines. For 807 and 843 engines the correct torque is 7.5 to 8.25 kg m (55 to 60 lb ft).

6 Set the valve clearances as described in **Section 1:5** then reconnect the carburetter controls and fill the cooling system so that the engine can be run.
Start and run the engine for 10 minutes, then stop it and allow to cool for 50 minutes. Unscrew each cylinder head bolt by a quarter-turn and retighten to a torque of 8.25 to 8.75 kg m (60 to 65 lb ft), following the recommended sequence.

7 Final tightening of the cylinder head bolts is carried out after the car has been run for 500 km (300 miles). Allow the engine to cool for 50 minutes from normal operating temperature, slacken each bolt in sequence by a quarter-turn and re-torque to 8.25 to 8.75 kg m (60 to 65 lb ft). Alternatively the engine may be

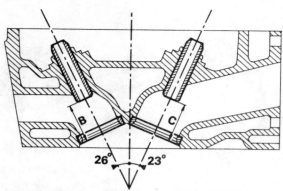

FIG 1:20 Fitting valve guides to 807 and 843 engines

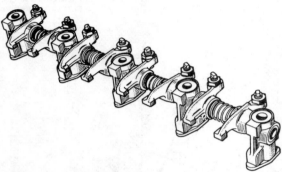

FIG 1:21 The 697, 821 and 841 engine rocker assembly

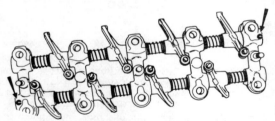

FIG 1:22 The 807 and 843 rocker assembly

allowed to stand for 2½ hours until cold, then the tightening torque will be 7.5 to 8.25 kg m (55 to 60 lb ft).

On 697, 821 and 841 engines check the torque tightening of the rocker arm mounting bolts. Recheck all rocker arm clearances as described in **Section 1 : 5**.

1 : 4 Servicing the cylinder head

Remove the cylinder head from the engine as described in the previous section. If not already done take off the water pump pulley. Remove the water pump, alternator bracket and support and the temperature switch.

Remove the valves, after the carbon has been cleaned from the combustion chambers, by compressing the valve springs with a suitable special tool, lifting out the split collets and slowly releasing the valve spring compresser. Once the tool is released the cap can be lifted off

and the spring removed so that the valve itself can be slid out through the combustion chamber. Store the valves in the correct order for reassembly.

Decarbonizing:

Leave the valves in place so that they protect the valve seats in the cylinder head. Scrape out most of the carbon from the combustion chambers with a stick of hardwood or solder sharpened to a chisel point. **Do not use any other form of tool as it will score the materials of the cylinder head. Similarly do not use rotary wire brushes.** Final polishing and cleaning can be carried out using worn emerycloth dipped into paraffin as a lubricant.

Once the combustion chambers are clean remove the valves. The ports can then be cleaned in a similar manner to the combustion chambers, but taking great care not to damage or score the valve seats or valve guides. Special rotary brushes, with the ends of the wire trapped in collars at either end, can be used to clean the valve guides. Failing the special brushes pull pieces of rag soaked in petrol or paraffin through the guides to clean them. When all carbon has been removed thoroughly wash the cylinder head to remove all traces of dirt or abrasive.

Make sure that the liners are clamped down as shown in **FIG 1 : 15**. Smear a little grease around the top of each bore and turn the engine until one pair of pistons is nearly at TDC. **The engine must be turned by jacking up a front wheel and engaging top gear or on automatic models with the spark plugs removed use the camshaft pulley retaining bolt and turn in a clockwise direction only.** Spring an old piston ring into the bore above the piston to protect the ring of carbon around the periphery of the piston. The ring of carbon acts as an additional oil seal as well as protecting the top piston ring from heat. Plug the passages in the cylinder block with pieces of rag to prevent dirt from falling into the block. Scrape away the carbon from the piston crowns with a sharpened stick of solder or hardwood. **Do not use any abrasive to clean the pistons as particles will remain to work their way between piston and bore to cause scoring.** When one pair of pistons has been cleaned turn the engine and clean the other pair in a similar manner. Blow away loose carbon and then wipe out the grease from the bores which will have the remainder of the dirt and carbon sticking to it.

Take great care not to scratch or mark the mating faces of the cylinder head and cylinder block. Use solvent to soften any parts of the old gasket.

Pushrods:

Keep the pushrods in the order in which they were removed. Check the ball ends for wear and make sure that the pushrods are perfectly straight. Renew any defective pushrods.

Valves:

Clean the valves by scraping off the carbon and deposits. If a suitable lathe or drill is available mount the stems in the chuck and use emerycloth to remove the deposits from the valves as they spin. **Take great care not to mark or damage the seat face.**

Check the valves for excessive wear. The stems must be smooth and free from scoring or pick-up marks. The heads must have sufficient depth of metal to ensure that the seat face does not make a sharp edge with the face of the valve inside the combustion chamber. Check that the valve stems are straight using a steel straightedge. Renew any valves that are defective.

Valve springs:

Special rigs are available for testing valve springs but they can be tested using a modified spring balance to apply the load and measuring the length with a steel ruler. The data is given in Technical Data at the end of this manual.

If a rig is not available mount a new and old valve spring end to end and compress the pair between the jaws of a vice. If the old spring is weak this will be shown by it being appreciably shorter than the new one. Renew the complete set of valve springs if any are more than 10 per cent outside the limits given.

Valve guides:

If these are worn they should be renewed otherwise they will allow oil to pump past them and cause high oil consumption. Check for wear using a new valve or a piece of turned steel which is 8 mm (.315 inch) in diameter.

A press and special tools are required for renewing valve guides. Press the old guide down into the combustion chamber using the special drift No. Mot.356. Check the size of the valve guide as oversize valve guides can be fitted. The sizes are as follows and they are identified by the markings given:

Standard   13 mm (.512 inch) external diameter.
First oversize   13.10 mm (.516 inch) external diameter,
                       one annular groove
Second oversize   13.25 mm (.522 inch) external diameter,
                       two annular grooves

Fit valve guides of the next oversize. Before fitting them ream out the bore in the cylinder head with the appropriate reamer from the special tools No. 357. Press the new valve guide back from the combustion chamber using the guide stop to set the protrusion of the valve guide. The correct positioning for valve guides on 697, 821 or 841 engines is shown in **FIG 1 : 19** and the dimension **A** is 29 mm (1.142 inch). The equivalent settings for the 807 and 843 engines are shown in **FIG 1 : 20** and the dimension **B** for exhaust valves is 31 mm (1.220 inch) while **C** for inlet valves is 32 mm (1.260 inch).

Once the valve guide has been refitted ream it out to a diameter of 8 mm (.315 inch) using the appropriate reamer from the set. The valve seat in the cylinder head must be recut using garage equipment to ensure concentricity.

Tappets (cam followers):

If the cam followers are worn or stick in the bores try fitting new standard size cam followers. Standard size cam followers are 12 mm (.473 inch) in diameter but oversize ones—+.2 mm (.008 inch)—are available. If oversize tappets have to be fitted the tappet bore in the cylinder head must be reamed out using reamer No. Mot.366. There is a counterbore at the top end of the tappet bore and if this is less than 13 mm (.512 inch) in diameter it must be reamed out to this dimension.

FIG 1 : 23   The valve split collets

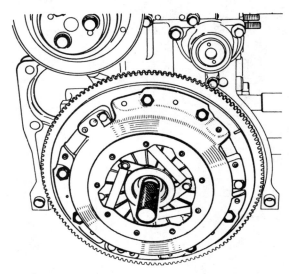

FIG 1 : 24   Refitting the clutch using a mandrel to centralize the driven plate

Valve seats:

Once the valves have been ground in the width of the valve seats in the cylinder head must be checked. The seat width on all exhaust valves should lie between the limits of 1.7 to 2 mm (.067 to .079 inch). The inlet seats for 807 and 843 engines should be 1.5 to 1.8 mm (.059 to .071 inch) while those for 697, 821 and 841 engines should be 1.3 to 1.6 mm (.051 to .063 inch). If the seats are too wide after grinding-in they should be reduced using 20 deg. and 70 deg. cutters, using the cutters to ensure that the seat meets centrally on the valve seating face.

If the seat width cannot be obtained or the seat is so worn that the valve sinks into it then new valve seat inserts should be fitted by an agent.

Grinding-in valves:

If the seats are excessively pitted they should be recut or ground using garage equipment.

Fit the valve back into its correct guide with a light spring fitted between it and the cylinder head. Smear a little grinding paste evenly around the seat face. Normally medium-grade paste should be used first but if the seats are in good condition start off immediately with fine-grade paste.

Press the valve down with a suction cup tool and grind with a semi-rotary motion. Allow the valve to rise up

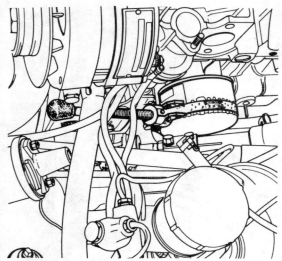

FIG 1:25 Removing or refitting the oil filter using a strap spanner

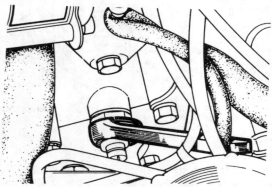

FIG 1:26 Removing or refitting the oil pressure switch

at frequent intervals and turn it through a $\frac{1}{4}$ turn before pressing it down and continuing grinding. When the majority of the pits have been removed wipe away all traces of paste and change to fine-grade. Repeat the grinding operation until both seat faces are matt grey with no pits in them.

Remove the valve and grind-in the next valve. When all the valves are ground-in clean all the parts and wash them thoroughly to remove all traces of abrasive from the cylinder head, ports and valves.

Rocker assembly:

The assembly on the 697, 821 and 841 engines is shown in FIG 1:21. If the parts are dismantled take great care to keep them in order and do not remove the concave plugs from the ends of the shaft. The bearing pedestals were modified but the new type of pedestal can be fitted to all engines. The older type of pedestal cannot be fitted to later cylinder heads.

The assembly on the 807 and 843 engines is shown in FIG 1:22 and the parts can be dismantled after removing the rollpins arrowed in the figure, with a suitable

drift. Take great care to keep the parts in the correct order as there are three differing assembly variations. The bearing pedestals must always be fitted with their machined faces towards the clutch. Note also that the inlet rockers are shorter and more angled than those for the exhaust. Do not remove the concave plugs from the ends of the shafts.

The parts are cleaned by washing in petrol or paraffin. Check the parts for wear. If the operating faces of the rocker arms are lightly worn or scored they can be smoothed down with an oil stone but if they are excessively worn new rockers should be fitted.

Reassembly:

The parts are reassembled in the reverse order of removal. All bearing surfaces should be liberally lubricated with clean engine oil or graphited oil. Note that when refitting the valves the split collets are different and they are shown in FIG 1:23. Check that the ridge pattern inside the split collet matches the valve pattern. The valve springs should be fitted with the larger coil gaps nearest the cylinder head.

1:5 Setting the valve clearances

Before adjusting the valve clearances remove the rocker cover from the engine. Jack up the front of the car so that a road wheel is clear off the ground and securely chock the rear wheels. Select top gear and the engine can then be turned by rotating the front wheel. The engine must not be turned using a spanner on the camshaft pulley bolt except on automatic models and then only with spark plugs removed and only in a clockwise direction.

Special tools are made for adjusting the valve clearance and these consist of a wrench with a built-in central screwdriver (Mot.233 for all 697, 821 and 841 engines, Mot.433 for 807 and 843 engines).

Slacken off all the locknuts on the adjusters as then it will be obvious which valves have been adjusted.

Turn the engine until the valve to be adjusted is fully closed. Give the adjuster a light tap with a plastic hammer so as to drive the pushrod down in case it is sticking and to break any oil film. Slacken off the adjuster with a screwdriver, while applying downward pressure, until the correct size feeler gauge can easily be inserted between the end of the rocker arm and valve stem. Turn the adjuster until the feeler gauge is just lightly nipped and there is light drag on it as it is moved. Hold the adjuster firmly with the screwdriver and tighten down the locknut. Check that the adjustment has not altered and then turn the engine until the next suitable valve is fully closed.

When all the valves have been adjusted refit the rocker cover and any parts that have been removed. Lower the car back to the ground.

The correct clearance for all inlet valves is .20 mm (.008 inch) and the correct clearance for all exhaust valves is .25 mm (.010 inch).

A convenient method for determining which valve to adjust is given in the table below:

Exhaust valve fully open	Adjust
No. 1 cylinder	No. 3 Inlet and No. 4 Exhaust
No. 3 cylinder	No. 4 Inlet and No. 2 Exhaust
No. 4 cylinder	No. 2 Inlet and No. 1 Exhaust
No. 2 cylinder	No. 1 Inlet and No. 3 Exhaust

1:6 The clutch and flywheel

Full details of the clutch and its controls, servicing and repair are given in **Chapter 5**. This section only deals with clutch removal and refitting as removal is necessary to free the flywheel.

The engine does not need to be removed from the car but the gearbox and steering gear must be taken out (see **Chapter 6**) in order to gain access to the parts.

On the models with automatic transmission there is no clutch fitted and a drive plate is used instead of the conventional flywheel. Again it will be necessary to remove the automatic transmission (see **Chapter 7**) in order to gain access to the drive plate.

Removal:

With the gearbox removed, lightly mark across the clutch cover and flywheel to ensure that the clutch will be refitted in its original position. Evenly and progressively slacken the bolts that secure the clutch cover to the flywheel and then take them out. **The bolts must be slackened progressively otherwise there is a danger of straining the cover.** When all the bolts are out lift off the cover assembly and collect the driven plate.

Unlock and unscrew the bolts that secure the flywheel to crankshaft and withdraw the flywheel from the crankshaft. Discard the old lockwasher and flywheel securing bolts as they are of a special type that cannot be re-used.

Reassembly:

Scrupulously clean and degrease the mating surfaces of the crankshaft and flywheel. Make sure that the operating face on the flywheel is clean, oil-free, and not scored. Even light scoring cannot be skimmed off in a lathe so if it is present a new flywheel must be fitted.

Fit the flywheel back into position and secure it using new self-locking bolts. The threads of the bolts should be degreased and a few drops of Locktite applied to them. Progressively tighten the bolts to a torque of 5 kg m (40 lb ft) and then lock the bolts by bending the lockwasher over one flat of each bolt with a pair of pliers.

Refit the driven plate, so that its hub offset faces the gearbox, and hold it in place on the centralising mandrel Emb.257. Lift the cover assembly back into position and align the previously made marks, securing it with the attachment bolts finger tight. The centralising mandrel must be used as shown in **FIG 1:24** when tightening the bolts otherwise the driven plate will be out of line and it will be impossible to pass the gearbox input shaft through it. Progressively and evenly tighten up the clutch attaching bolts and when they are all tight remove the mandrel and refit the gearbox.

Ring-gear:

The starter ring fitted around the flywheel is shrunk-fit into place and can be renewed if it is defective. It is advisable to take the flywheel to an agent as the new ring must be heated to the correct temperature, which lies between narrow limits, for it to be fitted in place. The old ring can be removed by partially drilling through the root of a tooth and then using a cold chisel to split it. If the old ring is removed take great care not to damage or mark the flywheel itself.

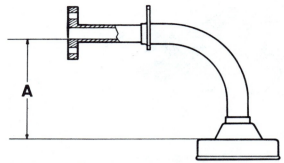

FIG 1:27   The oil pump strainer and inlet assembly

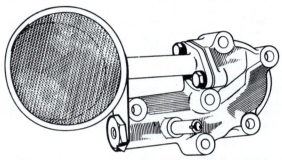

FIG 1:28   The oil pump fitted to early 697 engines

Spigot bearing:

A ballbearing is fitted into the end of the crankshaft to support the spigot of the gearbox input shaft. This bearing should be examined whenever the clutch or flywheel is removed. If the bearing is worn or runs noisily it must be renewed after removing the flywheel.

Withdraw the old bearing using a suitable extractor. Extractor No. Mot.11 is made specially for the task. Press the new bearing back into place exactly as it is received. The bearing is greased on manufacture.

1:7 The sump, oil pump and oil filter

Oil filter:

The element must be renewed at regular intervals otherwise it will choke and fail to filter the oil through the engine.

It is advisable to disconnect the battery before changing the filter. Unscrew and discard the old filter element. A strap spanner will be required to obtain a grip on the case and the special strap spanner Mot.445 is shown in **FIG 1:25**.

Check that the rubber seal on the new filter element is in good condition and smear it with a little engine oil. Screw the new filter back into position until the seal just touches the crankcase and then tighten the filter by $\frac{1}{4}$ turn. Slacken back the filter until the seal is free and then tighten it until the seal again touches and tighten it by a further $\frac{1}{2}$ to $\frac{3}{4}$ turn.

Start the engine and check for oil leaks around the filter, after having wiped away any spillage, and when

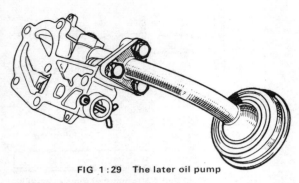

FIG 1 : 29   The later oil pump

satisfied stop the engine and leave the car on level ground. Leave it for five minutes to allow the level to settle and then top up to the full mark on the dipstick to replace any oil lost when changing the filter.

Oil pressure:

An oil pressure gauge is required to check the oil pressure. Disconnect the lead from the oil pressure switch and lay it safely out of the way to avoid shortcircuits. Unscrew the switch. The switch is awkward to get at and the method using special spanner Mot.452 is shown in **FIG 1 : 26**. In place of the switch screw in an adaptor and pressure gauge (Mot.73 is specially made for the task). Start the engine and check the minimum oil pressure. The minimum at 650 rev/min should be 2 to 2.5 kg/sq cm (30 to 35 lb/sq in) while at 4000 rev/min it should be a minimum of 4 to 5.5 kg/sq cm (60 to 80 lb/sq in).

When the check is completed, stop the engine, remove the gauge and refit the switch and its lead.

Sump:

A drain plug is fitted to the sump for draining out the engine oil. The oil is best drained when the engine is hot after a run as the oil will flow easier and dirt will be held in suspension and therefore removed with the oil. It is recommended that the engine oil should be changed at intervals of 5000 km (3000 miles) and the filter renewed at the same time. 4.25 litres (7.5 pints) of 10W30 oil will be required.

The sump is removed by taking out the attachment bolts. When refitting the sump use new gaskets and note that the two shortest bolts for the sump screw into the front main bearing.

Make sure that the sump drain plug is refitted and refill the engine to the top mark on the dipstick with fresh engine oil. A small amount of overfilling is not important at this stage. Run the engine for a few minutes and then stop it. Check the level with the car standing on level ground and with the engine having been stopped for at least five minutes. Top up to the upper mark on the dipstick but do not overfill. Overfilling will cause a high oil consumption.

On the 697 engines only, two different types of sump are fitted. The earlier sump was flat-bottomed but this type is now replaced by a dome-bottomed sump, which is the only one available as a spare. If the old flat-bottomed sump has to be renewed the inlet and strainer for the oil pump must also be renewed. The strainer is shown in **FIG 1 : 27**. On the earlier strainer the dimension A is 70 mm ($2\frac{3}{4}$ inch) but on the later strainer it is 75 mm

($2\frac{31}{32}$ inch). The attachment bolts for the strainer must also be changed.

Oil pump:

A different type of oil pump from standard model pumps is fitted to some earlier 697 engines and this type of pump is shown in **FIG 1 : 28**. The strainer is secured by two bolts and a stay that passes under the threaded plug for the relief valve. On later models the relief valve is held in place by a splitpin and the strainer secured by three bolts. The later type of pump is shown in **FIG 1 : 29**.

The pump cover can be removed, once the sump has been taken off, by taking out the bolts that secure it to the crankcase. The outer rotor can be removed once the cover is off but if the inner rotor needs removal the engine must be taken out of the car and partially dismantled.

Dismantle the pump body by taking out the bolts and removing the plug or splitpin. On the earliest models a ball valve is fitted but the parts of the later pump are shown in **FIG 1 : 30**. Wash the parts in clean fuel and check them for wear or damage. The blanking plug fitted to the body should be of the threaded type shown in **FIG 1 : 30** though some of the early pumps of the later type fitted to the 697 engines did not have this type of blank. If a pump is found without the correct type of blank it should be taken to an agent for modification.

Leave the outer rotor in place and check the clearances shown in **FIGS 1 : 31** and **1 : 32** with feeler gauges. The dimension A must lie between .04 and .29mm (.002 to .012 inch) and the dimension B between .02 and .14mm (.001 to .006 inch). If the clearances are incorrect new rotors must be fitted. The inner rotor is supplied attached to the drive shaft and cannot be changed without removing and partially dismantling the engine.

Make sure that all the parts are clean and that the strainer gauze is undamaged. Lubricate the parts with clean engine oil and reassemble and refit the pump in the reverse order of removal.

The early type of pump on the 697 engine can be replaced with the later type of pump but the engine must then have a dome-shaped sump fitted.

1 : 8 The pistons, connecting rods and liners

The complete assemblies should be removed from the engine for servicing or examination of the components. It is not necessary to remove the engine, though it will be better, as both the cylinder head and sump can be removed with the engine fitted to the car.

Big-end bearings:

These can be attended to after the sump has been removed. If the crankpins are found to be worn or scored then the engine must be taken out of the car and the crankshaft removed so that it can be sent away for specialist regrinding. If the cylinder head has been removed but it is not intended to remove the pistons or connecting rods it is essential that clamps are fitted to hold the liners in place, as shown in **FIG 1 : 15**.

1 Remove the sump as described in the previous section. Check that the connecting rods and big-end caps are numerically marked in order, as shown in **FIG 1 : 33**. No. 1 is nearest the clutch end of the engine and all the numbers must face towards the camshaft side of the engine.

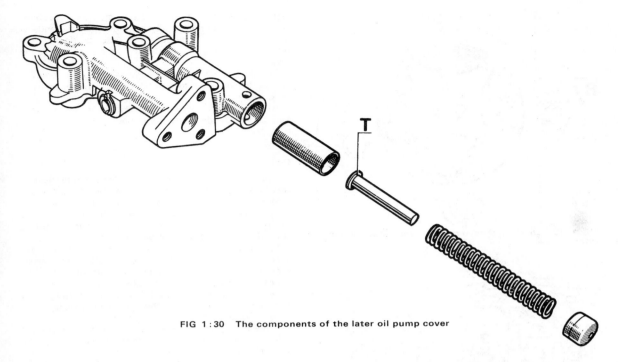

FIG 1:30 The components of the later oil pump cover

2 Turn the engine until the big-ends are in a convenient position for working. Evenly slacken the nuts that attach the caps to the connecting rods and remove the nuts and caps. As each connecting rod is freed push it up the bore so that the big-end clears the crankpin. If the cylinder head has been removed take care not to push the piston rings out through the top of the bore. **Take care when turning the engine that the big-ends are not trapped between the crankcase and crankshaft.**

3 Remove the bearing shells from the caps and connecting rods, keeping all the parts in the correct order for reassembly.

4 Clean all the parts paying particular attention to the crankpins. Measure the crankpins at several points on each using a micrometer gauge. If the pins are worn oval, tapered or are badly scored then the crankshaft must be removed and sent away for specialist regrinding and new oversize bearing shells must be fitted. **Never attempt to take up wear in a bearing by filing the connecting rod or bearing cap.** If the parts are filed the bearings will not be circular so rapid failure can be expected, even after fitting new shells.

5 Check all the shell bearings for wear, pitting, scoring or any other damage. If the shells are damaged a complete new set should be fitted. Make sure that the shells are perfectly clean and wipe them over with a piece of leather or lint-free cloth. New shells are fitted as received, apart from cleaning off any protective, and do not require scraping or boring.

6 Refit the bearing shells to their correct connecting rods and bearing caps. Liberally oil the crankpins with clean engine oil and pull the connecting rods down

into position. Refit the bearing caps, making sure that the numbers are in order and face the camshaft side of the engine. Refit the nuts and tighten them to a torque load of 4.5 kg m (32 lb ft). Make sure that the engine still turns freely and refit the sump.

697 Engines:

Some 697 engines are fitted with liners which are .1 mm greater in internal diameter than standard liners, 76.1 mm (2.996 inch), as opposed to the standard 76 mm (2.992 inch). The upper compression ring is identified by 'GOECRO +0.1' etched on one side and the lower compression ring is identified by 'GOETOP +0.1' etched on the upper face.

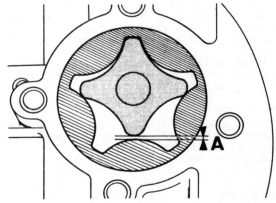

FIG 1:31 Checking the clearance between the oil pump rotors

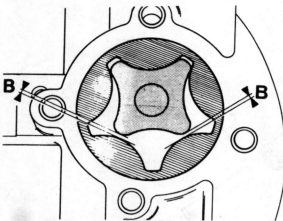

FIG 1:32 Checking the clearance between the oil pump rotors

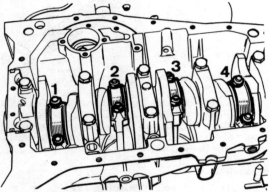

FIG 1:33 The big-end identification marks

Removing parts:

Remove the cylinder head and sump and then disconnect the big-ends as described previously. Mark the top face of each liner lightly so that it will be refitted the same way round. Gently drive each liner up and out through the top of the cylinder block and then draw the pistons and connecting rods out through the bottom of the liners.

The gudgeon pins are an interference fit in the connecting rods so the pistons should not be separated unecessarily from the connecting rods.

Piston rings:

A special ring clamp is best for removing and refitting piston rings as it grips the ends and then gently parts them so that the ring can be lifted off the piston.

Failing the special clamp use three shims, such as discarded feeler gauges. Gently lift one end of the ring out of its groove, starting with the top compression ring, and slip one shim under it. Work the shim around the ring while carefully pressing the ring onto the piston land above it as it comes free. When all the ring is on the land

slip the other two shims under it and space the three shims equidistantly around the piston. Gently part the ends of the ring with the fingernails and slide the ring off the piston, taking great care not to allow the ring to score the piston.

The ring is refitted in the reverse order of removal. Handle the rings gently as they are very brittle and will snap easily.

New rings are fitted as received because the gaps between the ends of the rings have been adjusted on manufacture.

Pistons:

Once the piston rings have been removed the pistons should be cleaned. Use an old broken ring to scrape out carbon from the ring grooves and clear carbon from the oil return holes with a blunt-ended piece of wire. **Take great care not to remove metal from the piston or the oil consumption will be increased.**

Lacquering on the side of the piston, indicative of gas blow-by past the rings, can be cleaned off with a solvent such as methylated spirits or trichlorethylene but no abrasive may be used on the sides of the pistons. The crown of the piston may be lightly polished using worn emerycloth dipped in paraffin but great care must be taken to wash away all traces of abrasive.

If the ring grooves are excessively worn new pistons should be fitted as this is one of the causes of high oil consumption.

Gudgeon pin:

Gudgeon pin renewal is best left to an agent as special tools are required both for removing it and refitting the new one. On reassembly the connecting rod must also be heated. The special tools required are shown in **FIG 1:34**.

Rest the piston in the V of the block **A** with the centre line of the gudgeon pin in line with the V-block marks. Press out the pin with the mandrel **B** in conjunction with a press. Check the connecting rod for twist or bend. Heat the small-end to 250°C (482°F).

Slide the gudgeon pin onto the assembly mandrel **D** of the correct size and screw on the guide up to the gudgeon pin but do not tighten, leave the gudgeon pin free. Lubricate the pin and guide. Fit the thrust pad **C** of the correct size to the support block **A** and clamp the piston to the pad with the clip, the spot facing on the piston resting on the pad. Take the connecting rod out of the oven when it is hot, using rags to hold it, and fit it into the boss of the piston so that the number is nearest the operator, as shown in **FIG 1:35**. As quickly as possible to avoid the connecting rod cooling, press the refitting assembly back through the piston and connecting rod until the guide **D** bottoms in the base **A**. Hand pressure should be sufficient but the press may be used if required. Leave the assembly to cool and then remove the special tools. Check that the piston swivels freely about the gudgeon pin with no tight spots.

Liner bores:

Whenever the cylinder head is removed the bores should be examined for wear or scoring. A guide to the wear is given by the depth of the unworn ridge around the top of the bore.

The accurate method is to use a special gauge and measure the bores at several points. If the bores are excessively worn, out of round, or tapered, then new pistons and liners should be fitted.

If the oil consumption is sufficient to warrant fitting new piston rings but the wear is not yet sufficient to require new pistons and liners then the unworn ridge around the top of each bore should be removed using garage equipment. If the ridge is left then the new upper compression rings will hit the ridge and they will rapidly break up.

Fitting liners:

The protrusion of the liner above the top face of the cylinder block is critical as it controls the sealing of the liner. On all models, except the 841 and 843, the correct protrusion is .15 to .20 mm (.006 to .008 inch) **with** the liner base seal in position. The protrusion can be checked by laying a steel straightedge across the liner and measuring the gap at either side with feeler gauges but a more accurate method is to use a DTI and accurate blocks (such as Mot.252 and support Mot.251). Different bottom seals are available to alter the protrusion.

Clean the base of the liner with a wire brush to remove all dirt, scale or particles. Clean the inside of the block by a less drastic method as it is aluminium.

Fit the thinnest seal marked with a blue spot (seal details are given in Technical Data) and refit the liner to its correct position so that the previously made mark is again in line. Press the liner down firmly by hand and measure the protrusion. If the protrusion is incorrect selectively fit the seal until the protrusion is within limits. Check the protrusion at both sides and if the reading varies by more than .02 mm (.001 inch) turn the liner through 180 degrees and try again. When the correct seal has been fitted mark the front of the liner lightly and remove it ready for refitting the piston. Make sure that the liners are also marked for order so that they will not be interchanged.

On 841 and 843 engines the projection X of the liner above the cylinder block face must be between .10 and .17 mm (.0039 and .0066 inch) **without** the bottom seal J in position. In the event of an incorrect projection dimension, a check must be made to determine whether the error arises from a fault in the liner or in the cylinder block, this can best be done by fitting new sleeves and making a second set of measurements. Refer to **FIG 1:35A** and confirm the following dimensions:

H Distance between the top of the liner and the lower sealing face = 92.58 to 92.61 mm (3.645 to 3.646 inch).
K Height of the top face of the block above the sealing face of the liner = 92.44 to 92.48 mm (3.639 to 3.640 inch).

Reassembly:

Turn the piston rings on each piston until the gaps are spread at an angle of 120 degrees from each other and no gap aligns with the gudgeon pin. Lightly oil the rings.

Special sleeves are made for refitting the piston into the bottom of the liner, as shown in **FIG 1:36**. Sleeve No. Mot.227.01 is for 697 engines and Mot.442 for 807 and

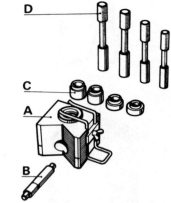

FIG 1:34 The special tool set for removing or refitting the gudgeon pin

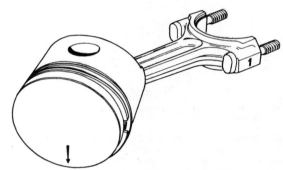

FIG 1:35 The correct assembly of the piston to the connecting rod

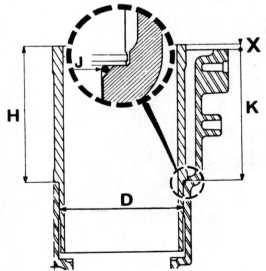

FIG 1:35A Sectional view of a liner in the cylinder block on 843 engines

Key to Fig 1:35A X = .10 to .17 mm H = 92.58 to 92.61 mm K = 92.44 to 92.48 mm J = Circular seal

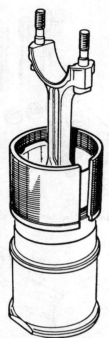

FIG 1:36 Refitting the piston and connecting rod into the cylinder liner

821 engines. For 841 and 843 engines use Mot.557. If care is taken, a large worm-driven hose clip can be used instead of the special sleeves. Compress the rings into the piston with the tool and enter the crown of the piston into the bottom of the liner as shown. Make sure that the piston mark, connecting rod number and mark made on the liner are all correctly orientated for refitting the parts to the engine. Gently press the piston down into the bore letting the tool slide off each ring as it enters the bore. Do not force the rings or allow them to escape before they are in the bore.

When the piston is fully in the liner fit the assembly back into the crankcase and clamp pairs of liners down

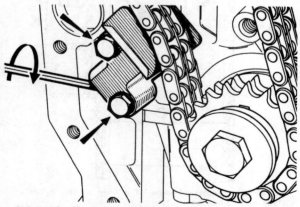

FIG 1:37 Slackening or adjusting the timing chain tensioner. The Allen key must always be turned in a clockwise direction as shown

with the clamps as shown in **FIG 1:15**. Reconnect the big-ends as described previously and reassemble the engine in the reverse order of dismantling.

1:9 The camshaft and drive

In order to remove the camshaft, check the timing chain or remove the distributor and oil pump drive it will be necessary to remove the engine from the car and then dismantle it to a considerable extent.

Preparation:

With the engine out of the car and the gearbox removed take off the cylinder head (see **Section 1:3**) and then remove the sump (see **Section 1:7**). From the end of the engine opposite to the clutch take out the bolts and remove the timing cover.

Remove the pulley flange from the front end of the camshaft, noting that it is held on by a bolt and two roll-pins. Once the pulley has been removed take out the three bolts and remove the front bearing of the camshaft from the front face of the crankcase. Remove the oil pump cover (see **Section 1:7**) and withdraw both rotors and the distributor drive gear.

Timing gear removal:

The timing chain and sprockets are at the rear end of the engine and accessible when the timing cover has been removed.

Take out the bolt in the end of the timing chain tensioner housing and insert a 3mm (.118 inch) Allen key into the aperture as shown in **FIG 1:37**. Turn the key **clockwise** in the socket until the chain tension is released. **The Allen key must never be turned anti-clockwise or an attempt made to force the slipper pad back into the body.** Take out the two bolts arrowed that secure the unit and remove it.

Take out the bolts that secure the guide shoe(s) which prevent the chain from flailing and remove the guide shoe(s).

Remove the bolt that secures the crankshaft sprocket as well as the thrust washer and washer fitted under the bolt. Turn the engine until the two bolts that secure the camshaft flange are accessible through the holes in the camshaft sprocket and then remove the bolts.

Withdraw the crankshaft sprocket from the crankshaft using the special extractor No. Mot.49, as shown in **FIG 1:38**. The special tool must be used as an ordinary two-legged puller would damage the timing chain. While the crankshaft sprocket is being removed pull out the camshaft so that the chain is kept straight between the sprockets and not misaligned.

Remove the chain and completely withdraw the camshaft.

Examination:

Wash all the parts in clean fuel. Check the timing chain for wear and renew it if it is badly worn. At the same time check the teeth on the sprockets and renew them if the teeth show any hook-shaped wear. Note that the camshaft sprocket must be renewed if it is removed from the camshaft.

Check the cams on the camshaft for wear or chipping and the distributor drive gears for wear. If wear is found the camshaft and distributor drive must be renewed as a complete set.

It is advisable to fit new seals into the camshaft front bearing unless the old seals are in very good condition.

Camshaft end float:

Use feeler gauges to check the end float as shown in **FIG 1 : 39**. If the end float is outside the correct limits of .05 to .12 mm (.002 to .0047 inch) then a new flange must be fitted, as well as a new camshaft sprocket as once the sprocket has been removed it cannot be refitted.

To change the flange, remove the rollpins from the end of the camshaft and then use a press and suitable mandrel to remove the sprocket from the camshaft. Lift off the flange and fit a new one in its place. Press the new sprocket back into place while supporting the camshaft under the first camshaft journal.

If the end float is still incorrect yet another new flange and sprocket will have to be fitted.

Leave the rollpins out at this stage.

Reassembly:

Lubricate the bearing surfaces and chain with clean engine oil as the parts are being refitted.

1 Slide the camshaft back into place but do not yet press it fully home. Turn the crankshaft until the key for its sprocket is vertically up. Refit the timing chain over the camshaft sprocket and turn the camshaft until the timing mark on the sprocket lies on the line joining the centres of the camshaft and crankshaft.

2 Lightly push on the crankshaft sprocket, with the chain around it so that both timing marks lie on the line joining the centres, as shown in **FIG 1 : 40, when the chain is hanging freely.** It should be noted that the line through the timing marks will not lie exactly on the line joining the centres when pressure is applied to the chain to bring it into its normal running position, though the line will pass through the centre of the crankshaft.

3 When the timing marks are correct push the crankshaft sprocket back into position with a suitable piece of tube, while pressing the camshaft back so as to keep the chain aligned between the sprockets.

4 Refit the thrust washer, washer and bolt to the crankshaft and tighten the bolt to a torque load of 6 to 8 kg m (45 to 58 lb ft). Refit and tighten the bolts that secure the camshaft flange.

5 Refit the chain tensioner, with its thrust plate and filter, and use an Allen key, **in a clockwise direction,** to adjust the tensioner until the slipper pad is just touching the chain and takes up the slack. Refit the bolt to the tensioner housing and lock it with a new lockwasher.

6 **697 engine.** Only one guide shoe is fitted, as shown in **FIG 1 : 41**, and it should be adjusted until it is parallel to the chain and the gap **D** correct at .8 mm (.032 inch).

7 **Other models.** Two guide shoes are fitted to these. Fit the gauge Mot.420 onto the chain and then refit the shoes so that they are against the gauge, as shown in **FIG 1 : 42**, and then tighten their attachment bolts. Remove the gauge.

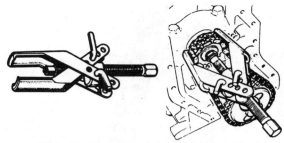

FIG 1 : 38   Removing the crankshaft sprocket

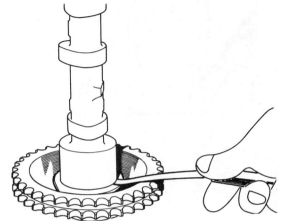

FIG 1 : 39   Checking the camshaft end float

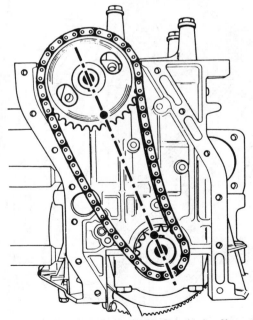

FIG 1 : 40   Aligning the valve timing marks. Note that the chain is allowed to hang freely

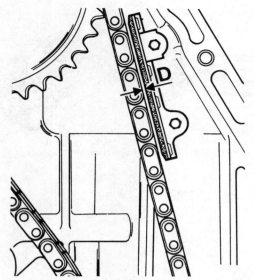

FIG 1:41   Setting the guide shoe on the 697 engine

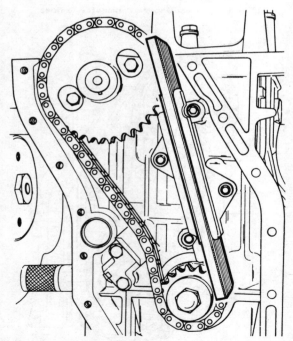

FIG 1:42   Using the gauge to set the double guide shoes

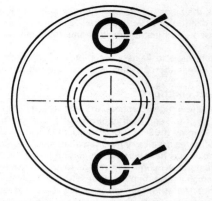

FIG 1:43   The correct positioning of the slots of the roll pins in the camshaft

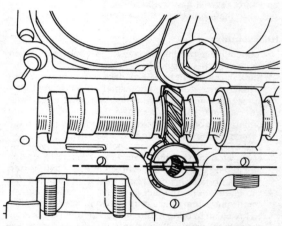

FIG 1:44   The alignment of the distributor drive for 697, 821 and 841 engines

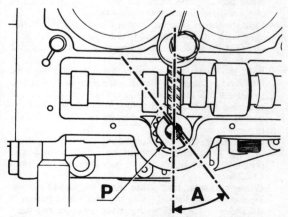

FIG 1:45   The alignment of the distributor drive for 807 and 843 engines

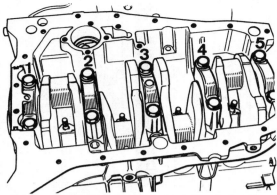

FIG 1:46   The main bearing cap identification numbers

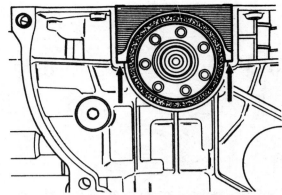

FIG 1:47   Removing the front main bearing cap

8 Refit the timing cover using a new gasket. Make sure that top of the timing cover aligns with the top of the cylinder block before fully tightening the bolts.

9 Fit the special sleeve Mot.258 to the front of the camshaft, using a bolt to secure it. The sleeve protects the seal in the front bearing from damage as the bearing is slid back into place. Make sure that the O-ring and oil seal are fitted to the housing and slide the bearing housing, with a new impregnated paper gasket, back into position along the camshaft. Secure it in place with the three bolts. Remove the special sleeve.

10 Refit the rollpins to the camshaft so that they are positioned as shown in **FIG 1:43** and then refit the pulley.

Distributor and oil pump drive:

Turn the engine until it is in the firing position for No. 1 (front) cylinder. The cams for No. 1 cylinder will both be at their lowest positions and the cams for No. 4 (rear) cylinder will be at the point of balance, where both valves would be opened by an equal amount.

On the 697 and 821 engines refit the drive parts so that smallest offset is towards the camshafts and the slot is parallel with the engine axis, as shown in **FIG 1:44**, after the gears have fully meshed.

On the 807 and 843 engines the smallest offset must still be towards the camshaft but the slot must make an angle **A** of 53 degrees, as shown in **FIG 1:45**. A flat **P** is fitted to give an accurate measuring point. Before refitting the cylinder head fill the chamber under the camshaft with engine oil.

Once the drive parts are in place the remainder of the oil pump can be refitted as well as reassembling and refitting the engine in the reverse order of removal.

1:10 The crankshaft and main bearings

The engine must be removed from the car and dismantled before the crankshaft is taken out.

If only the main bearing shells require renewal it is possible to change them after taking off the sump with the engine out and inverted. After the main bearing caps have been removed slide the shells in the crankcase around the crankshaft so that they can be removed and new bearings slid back. **This should only be attempted**

by the skilled owner as damage can easily be caused by semi-skilled hands and it may also be found after all the effort that the crankshaft will have to be removed anyway for specialist grinding.

For the average owner changing the main bearings should be taken as an opportunity for a major engine overhaul.

Removing the crankshaft:

1 Remove the engine from the car and dismantle it so that the timing gear and camshaft are removed (see previous section). Disconnect the big-end bearings (see **Section 1:8**) and remove the clutch and flywheel (see **Section 1:6**).

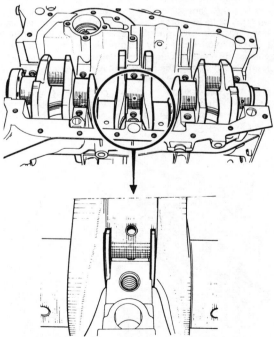

FIG 1:48   The crankshaft thrust washers

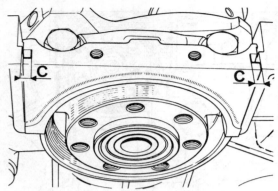

FIG 1:49 Measuring the sealing gap on the front main bearing cap

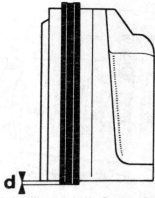

FIG 1:50 Fitting the seals to the front main bearing cap

2 Turn the engine over and support it safely. Make sure that the main bearing caps are marked for order, as shown in **FIG 1:46**, and if they are not then do so with a code of centre punch dots on the camshaft side.

3 Progressively and evenly slacken all the bolts that secure the main bearing caps in place and then remove the bolts. Lift out the main bearing caps except for the front one (No. 1). Gently remove the front bearing cap by tapping lightly and evenly on the lower corners, as shown in **FIG 1:47**. Remove the seal and the two side seals.

4 Lift out the crankshaft and thrust washers. Keep the bearings shells in the correct order for reassembly.

Examination:

Measure the journals at several points with a micrometer gauge and if they are excessively worn, oval or tapered, or have scores, then the crankshaft must be sent away for specialist grinding and oversize new bearing shells fitted on reassembly. All models, except some of the earliest 697 engines, have roll-hardened crankpins and journals. This limits the depth that can be ground off.

Check the bearing shells for wear, scoring, pitting or any other damage and renew the complete set if any are defective. New shells are fitted as received, apart from cleaning off protective, and do not require boring or scraping.

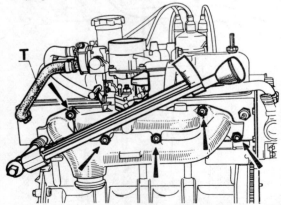

FIG 1:51 The 697 and 821 manifold attachments

Under no circumstances file the bearing caps or bearing shells in an attempt to take up wear in the bearings. Filing the caps will make the bores non-circular and cause rapid failure of all future bearing shells.

Clean all the parts thoroughly. The crankshaft oil passages should be blown through with paraffin (from a syringe) followed by compressed air (from a tyre pump if an airline is not available). This is particularly important if the crankshaft has been reground otherwise particles of swarf may remain in the oil passages and damage the bearings after running.

On 697 engines only, check the size of the drain hole in the front bearing cap. If the hole is only 8mm (.315 inch) in diameter it must be enlarged to 12mm (.472 inch) and the ends carefully deburred.

Reassembly:

1 Wipe the shell bearings with a piece of leather or lint-free cloth and fit them back into position. The shells with oil holes are fitted to the crankcase. On models where the thrust washers are held by tags refit the thrust washers, making sure that the white-metal side faces the crankshaft. On models where the thrust washers are not located by tags the thrust washers can be slid round into place, as shown in **FIG 1:48**, again with the whitemetal towards the crankshaft.

2 Lubricate the bearings and journals liberally with oil and lay the crankshaft back into place. Fit the front bearing cap back into place and secure it with its bolts. Measure the gaps **C** shown in **FIG 1:49**. If the gap is less than 5mm (.197 inch) select two seals 5.10 (.201 inch) thick but if the gap is greater than 5mm select two seals, marked by a white spot, which are 5.40mm (.213 inch) thick.

3 Remove the front bearing cap from the engine. Slide the seals into the cap so that their grooves are outwards and so that they project .2mm (.008 inch) above the joint face towards the cylinder block, as shown at 'd' in **FIG 1:50**. Screw two 10 x 150mm locating studs into the bolt holes in the crankcase. Slide the front bearing cap into place down the studs, using foil strip (or thin feeler gauges) between the seals and block to protect the seals as they slide. Remove the shims and studs and loosely screw in the correct bolts.

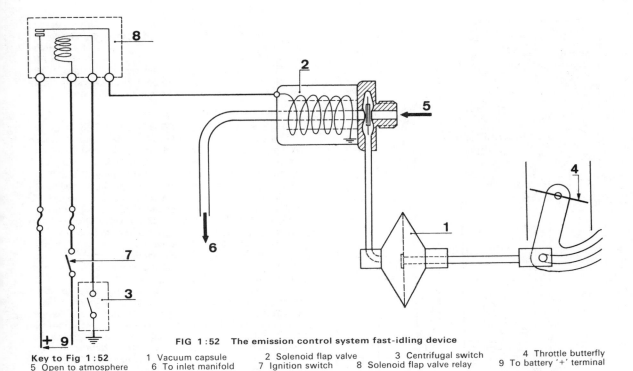

FIG 1:52   The emission control system fast-idling device

Key to Fig 1:52   1 Vacuum capsule   2 Solenoid flap valve   3 Centrifugal switch   4 Throttle butterfly
5 Open to atmosphere   6 To inlet manifold   7 Ignition switch   8 Solenoid flap valve relay   9 To battery '+' terminal

4 Refit the remainder of the bearing caps into their correct positions and progressively tighten all the bolts to a torque load of 6.5 kgm (47 lb ft). Check that the crankshaft revolves freely.

5 Either mount a DTI onto the crankcase so that its stylus rests vertically on the end of the crankshaft or else use feeler gauges to measure the end float between the crankshaft and a main bearing. Lever the crankshaft firmly backwards and forwards and measure the end float. The correct limits are .05 to .23mm (.002 to .009 inch). If the end float is excessive then the crankshaft must be removed again and refitted with new or repair size thrust washers to bring the end float within limits.

6 When the crankshaft is in place refit the oil seal to the front bearing. The seal is very delicate and the only satisfactory method of fitting it is to push it in using the special mandrel No. Mot.259.1. Fit the seal over the tool and lubricate the outside of the seal. Tap the tool and seal gently into the front of the front main bearing until the tool touches the crankshaft. **The tool must always be kept in its box and protected with an old oil seal as any burrs or nicks will damage oil seals and cause oil leaks after reassembly.**

7 Reassemble the engine in the reverse order of dismantling.

1:11   The manifolds

On the 697, 821 and 841 engines both inlet and exhaust manifold are fitted to the same side of the cylinder head and the general attachments of the manifolds are shown in **FIG 1:51**. Note that the hose 'T' for the water-heated choke flap is fitted as shown in the figure. The nuts and bolts are tightened to a torque of 1.5 to 2.5 kgm (11 to 18 lb ft).

On 807 and 843 engines the exhaust manifold can be removed after disconnecting the exhaust pipe and freeing the clip that secures it to the crankcase. Remove the starter shield as well as the dipstick and its tube. The

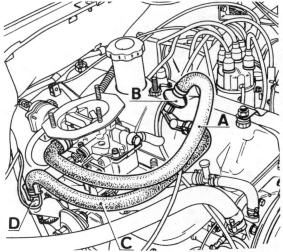

FIG 1:53   The emission control crankcase breathing system

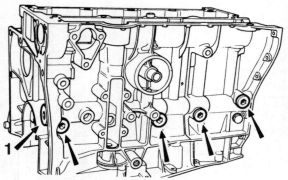

FIG 1:54 The blank plugs on the main oil gallery

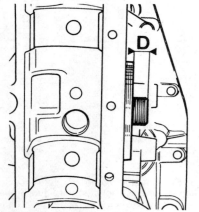

FIG 1:55 The protrusion of the oil filter screw

manifold can then be taken off after the attachment bolts have been removed. Refit the manifold in the reverse order of removal tightening the nuts to a torque load of 2 to 3 kgm (15 to 22 lb ft).

The inlet manifold on 807 and 843 models will vary slightly with type depending on the emission control parts fitted. On models fitted with a water-heated choke, clamp the hoses to prevent coolant leaking out if the carburetter is removed. The nuts are tightened to a torque of 2.5 to 3 kgm (18 to 22 lb ft).

In every case a new gasket must be fitted on reassembly. The mating faces must be carefully cleaned and the parts are refitted dry. There are variations between models, particularly the 697, so make sure that the gasket mates with the cylinder head before refitting the parts.

1:12 Emission control

Special carburetters are fitted. Special pistons running at closer tolerances as well as cylinder head and inlet manifold with individual ports to the cylinders are also fitted to control the emission under all running conditions except deceleration. Crankcase fumes are led to the inlet manifold and carburetter by a system so that they are burnt in the engine.

A system is fitted which holds the throttle valve partially open when decelerating to prevent the emission becoming

excessive. The schematic layout of the early system is shown in FIG 1:52. The vacuum capsule 1 and solenoid flap valve 2 are shown in FIG 1:3. The attachments of the centrifugal switch and its drive cables are shown in FIG 1:4. The idling speed adjustments and details of the carburetters are given in Chapter 2. Later systems were modified for more stringent control of emissions.

Crankcase fumes:

The system is shown in FIG 1:53. A T-piece on the rocker cover extracts the fumes from the engine. The hose A connects the T-piece, via the flame trap B, to the carburetter so that fumes are always drawn in through the carburetter. The flame trap is fitted to prevent any flashback or firing at the carburetter from igniting the oil fumes in the engine. The other hose C connects the T-piece, via the valve D, to the inlet manifold. Under high-vacuum conditions in the inlet manifold the valve D closes and prevents excessive air being drawn into the manifold, the fumes passing through the carburetter. At wide throttle openings the vacuum in the manifold is not so high and the valve D opens to allow the fumes to be drawn in directly to the manifold.

A fume-absorption canister may be fitted to some models, it is located in the engine compartment and connected by breather tubes to the tank vent pipe and the carburetter. Its purpose is to absorb fumes from the tank whilst the engine is stationary and discharge the fumes into the carburetter when the engine is running. The only maintenance necessary is to change the plastic foam pad at intervals of 25,000 miles (40,000 kilometres).

Reassembling a stripped engine:

All the operations have been dealt with in detail in the relevant sections so it is a matter of reassembling the parts in the correct order.

Before starting reassembly operations make sure that all the parts are scrupulously clean and that all old seals and gaskets have been removed and discarded. **The alloy faces must not be scraped with sharp tools and any jointing compound or gaskets should be softened with a suitable solvent and then either wiped off or gently scraped with sticks of hardwood or solder.**

Flush through all oilways and passages with paraffin under pressure (from a syringe if need be) and then blow through them with an airline (or tyre pump). Remove blanking plates and plugs as required. The blanking plugs for the crankcase oil gallery are shown in FIG 1:54. These may be removed but not the concave plugs. The plug 1 is tightened to 8 kgm (58 lb ft) but the other plugs are tightened to a 4.5 kgm (33 lb ft).

Check the protrusion of the screw for the oil filter. The correct protrusion D, shown in FIG 1:55, should be 9.5 to 12.5 mm ($\frac{3}{8}$ to $\frac{1}{2}$ inch). If the protrusion is less than 9.5 mm remove the old screw and fit a repair one in its place and screw it in until the protrusion is within limits. The special repair screw is 41 mm (1$\frac{5}{8}$ inch) long.

The dipstick tube 1 for the 697 and 821 engines is shown in FIG 1:56 and that for the 807 and 843 engines in FIG 1:57. In all cases the dimension A should be 18.5 mm ($\frac{47}{64}$ inch). A 10 mm blanking plug is fitted on righthand side for 697 and 821 engines while an 8 mm blanking plug is fitted on lefthand side for 807 and 843 engines. On the 807 and 843 engines the seam 5 has been eliminated on both the dipstick tube and sealing sleeve on later models. The earlier and later parts are interchangeable as sets.

Small components, nuts, bolts and washers should be tied in bags to the main component on dismantling. Swill them all in petrol to clean the threads.

Lay the parts to be reassembled out in order on a clean paper covered bench.

Start by refitting the crankshaft followed by the camshaft and timing gear. Refit the distributor drive and oil pump followed by the piston, liner and connecting rod assemblies. When these parts have been refitted the sump can then be fitted and the engine stood upright. Refit the cylinder head followed by flywheel and clutch. Leave external accessories and manifolds until last as they can easily be damaged while moving the engine around.

If new pistons and liners have been fitted then the engine must be fully run in as from new. If only new rings or crankshaft bearings have been fitted the running-in is not so stringent but care must still be taken with the engine and it must not be allowed to 'slog' or overspeed for a slightly shorter running-in period.

1:13 Fault diagnosis

(a) Engine will not start

1 Defective ignition coil
2 Faulty distributor capacitor
3 Dirty, pitted or incorrectly set ignition points
4 Ignition wires loose or insulation faulty
5 Water on sparking plug leads
6 Battery discharged, terminal corroded
7 Faulty or jammed starter motor
8 Sparking plug leads incorrectly connected
9 Vapour locks in fuel lines (hot weather only)
10 Defective fuel pump
11 Overchoking or underchoking
12 Blocked fuel filter or float chamber needles
13 Leaking valves
14 Sticking valves
15 Valve timing incorrect
16 Ignition timing incorrect

(b) Engine stalls

1 Check 1, 2, 3, 4, 5, 10, 11, 12, 13 and 14 in (a)
2 Sparking plugs defective or gaps incorrect
3 Retarded ignition
4 Mixture too weak
5 Water in fuel system
6 Petrol tank vent blocked
7 Incorrect valve clearance

(c) Engine idles badly

1 Check 2 and 7 in (b)
2 Air leaks at manifold joints
3 Worn piston rings
4 Worn valve stems or guides
5 Weak exhaust valve springs

(d) Engine misfires

1 Check 1, 2, 3, 4, 5, 10, 12, 13, 14, 15 and 16 in (a) also check 2, 3, 4 and 7 in (b)
2 Weak or broken valve springs

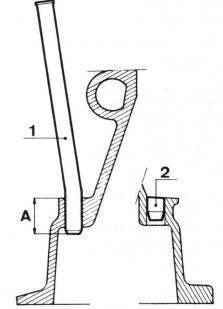

FIG 1:56 The dipstick tube on 697 and 821 engines

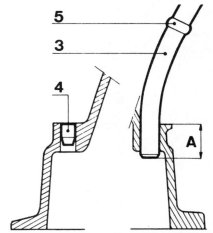

FIG 1:57 The dipstick tube on 807 and 843 engines

(e) Engine overheats (see Chapter 4)

(f) Compression low

1 Check 14 and 15 in (a); 3 and 4 in (c) and 2 in (d)
2 Worn piston ring grooves
3 Scored or worn cylinder bores

(g) Engine lacks power

1 Check 3, 10, 11, 13, 14, 15, 16 and 17 in (a); 1, 2, 3 and 6 in (b); 3 and 4 in (c) and 2 in (d). Also check (e) and (f)
2 Leaking cylinder head gasket
3 Fouled or worn out sparking plugs
4 Automatic advance not operating

(h) Burnt valves or seats

1 Check 14 and 15 in (a); 6 in (b) and 2 in (d). Also check (e)
2 Excessive carbon around valve seat and cylinder head

(j) Sticking valves

1 Check 2 in (d)
2 Bent valve stem
3 Scored valve stem and guide
4 Incorrect valve clearance
5 Gummy deposits on valve stem

(k) Excessive cylinder wear

1 Check 11 in (a) and also check (e)
2 Lack of oil
3 Dirty oil
4 Piston rings gummed up or broken
5 Connecting rods bent

(l) Excessive oil consumption

1 Check 4 in (k) and also check (f)
2 Oil return holes in pistons choked with carbon
3 Oil level too high
4 External oil leaks

(m) Crankshaft or connecting rod bearing failure

1 Check 2 and 3 in (k)
2 Restricted oilways
3 Worn journals or crankpins
4 Loose bearing caps
5 Bent connecting rod
6 Extremely low oil pressure

(n) Low oil pressure

1 Check 2 and 3 in (k) and 2, 3 and 4 in (m)
2 Choked oil filter
3 Weak relief valve spring or dirt under seat in pump cover
4 Faulty gauge, switch or connections

(o) Internal water leakage (see Chapter 4)

(p) Poor water circulation (see Chapter 4)

(q) Corrosion (see Chapter 4)

(r) High fuel consumption (see Chapter 2)

CHAPTER 2

THE FUEL SYSTEM

2:1 Description

Fuel is stored in a tank at the rear of the car and it is drawn from the tank and pressure-fed to the carburetter by a mechanically operated fuel pump, mounted on the engine. The fuel pump is fitted with a strainer gauze for filtering the fuel, and the filter is accessible after removing the fuel pump cover.

Various types of carburetters have been used on the different models, and there are variations in the specification of similar carburetters. Type and mark numbers of Solex and Zenith carburetters are stamped on a tag fitted under one of the float chamber cover screws, and on the base flange on Weber models.

The carburetters have an. engine coolant heated throttle flange on Solex and Zenith and the mounting flange on Weber.

The different types of carburetter normally fitted to the different models are given in the following table. The different jet sizes for the various carburetters are given in Technical Data.

R. 1150

Solex 35 DISA	Swivel operated choke
Solex 35 DISA-2	Swivel operated choke followed by direct operation. Oil vapour breathing.
Solex 35 DISA-3, -4	Directly controlled choke. Oil vapour breathing
Solex 35 DITA	Automatic choke operated by engine coolant

Solex 35 DITA-2	Automatic choke with additional control
Zenith 36 IF	Manual choke
R.1151	
Weber 32-DIR-1, -16, -28	Twin barrel with manual choke
Weber 32 DAR-2, -4, -5, -6	Twin barrel, automatic choke
R.1152	
Solex 26-32 DIDSA-3, -8	Twin barrel, manual choke
Weber 32-DIR-12, -19, -20, -35, -36	Twin barrel, manual choke
R.1153	
Solex 26-32 DIDSA-8	Twin barrel, manual choke
Solex 32-32, SEIEA	Twin barrel, manual choke
Weber 32 DIR-8, -10, -17, -18, -33, -34	Twin barrel, manual choke
R.1154	
Weber 32 DIR-13, -14, -22, -27	Twin barrel, manual choke
R.1155	
Solex 26-32 DIDSA-8	Twin barrel, manual choke
R.1156	
Weber 32 DAR-7, -8	Twin barrel, automatic choke
R1152, 1155 and 1157 (1977)	
Solex MIMAT	Twin barrel, automatic choke

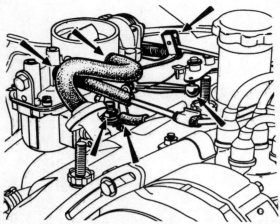

FIG 2:1 The attachments of the carburetter on R.1150 models

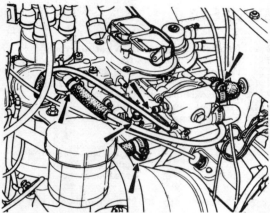

FIG 2:2 The attachments of the carburetter on R.1151 models

2:2 Maintenance

Apart from cleaning the fuel filters and checking that the linkage operates freely, also lightly lubricating the pivot points, there is little required in the way of routine maintenance. On some carburetters a fuel filter is also fitted at the inlet to the float chamber and this filter is accessible after disconnecting the fuel feed pipe or removing its plug. The filters should be washed in clean fuel and then dried with an airline.

If water has entered the fuel tank or there is an excess of dirt in it the tank should be drained and refilled with clean fuel. In extreme cases remove the fuel tank and swill it around with clean fuel and then discard this fuel. Blow through the fuel lines with an airline (after disconnecting both ends) in the reverse direction of normal flow.

A new element should be fitted to the air cleaner at regular intervals. The intervals will depend on the use of the car and the type of area in which it is driven. Very dusty conditions will require the element to be renewed at shorter intervals.

2:3 Carburetter removal

On all models disconnect the vacuum pipe to the distributor and the fuel supply pipe at the float chamber. Remove the air cleaner or disconnect the intake hose, as applicable and any oil vapour rebreathing pipes. Disconnect the throttle linkage and the choke cable (if fitted). As a safety precaution also disconnect the battery.

R.1150:

The attachment points are shown in FIG 2:1. Use clamps Mot.453 on the water hoses to prevent coolant from leaking out when the pipes are disconnected. On all models there is a pipe between the water pump and base of the carburetter and if a manually operated choke is fitted the other pipe also comes from the base of the carburetter. With an automatic choke the pipe comes from the choke housing on the carburetter. Two attachment nuts are fitted and once they are removed the carburetter can be lifted off.

Models with Weber carburetters and manual choke:

The attachments are shown in FIG 2:2. The method is very similar to the R.1150 models except that there is no automatic choke so the coolant hoses are between the base of the carburetter and water pump and the other hose between the reheating housing and inlet manifold. The carburetter is held in place by four attachment nuts.

Emission controlled models:

The attachments are shown in FIG 2:3 and FIG 2:4. In addition to the standard disconnections also disconnect the following: the electrical lead to the idling jet solenoid (sometimes called damper), the vacuum capsule pipe, and the rebreathing pipe on the carburetter. Remove the rebreathing valve by taking off its securing nut and lift off the valve with its hoses. Again clamp the coolant hoses before disconnecting them. The carburetter is attached by four nuts and it should be lifted off complete with the support plate for the vacuum capsule.

Automatic transmission models:

The attachments are shown in FIG 2:5. In addition to disconnecting the standard connections and clamping the coolant hoses before disconnection it is necessary to free the clip holding the transmission computer cable. The carburetter is secured by four nuts.

Refitting:

In all cases the carburetter is refitted in the reverse order of removal. Check the coolant level (see **Chapter 4**). Adjust the accelerator cable, and the idling speed, and on automatic transmission models the governor cable.

It is advisable to use new gaskets between the carburetter and inlet manifold. Check that the flanges are true and flat, using a steel straightedge. A more accurate method of checking is to use engineer's blue on a surface table or plate glass, when high spots will show up deep blue. The flanges can be scraped or filed down but again a more accurate method is to lap them with fine-grade grinding paste spread onto plate glass. Do not use ordinary window glass as this is never truly flat.

2 : 4 Carburetter operation

When an airstream is passed through a constriction the flow speeds up at the constriction and the static pressure drops proportionally to the increase in speed. Carburetters use a venturi, which is a smoothly blended narrowing of the choke tube to increase the velocity of the air flow, and the suction produced then draws the fuel out through the jets. Various jets are fitted to ensure slow-running, high-speed running and a smooth transition between low and high speeds. Compensating jets and air bleeds are fitted to ensure that the mixture strength is correct at all speeds.

As a reasonable example of general carburetter operation a schematic sectioned view of a Solex DITA carburetter is shown in **FIG 2 : 6**. Fuel enters through the inlet pipe, from the pump, and fills the float chamber. The float rises on the fuel until the correct fuel level is reached and the float arm then closes the needle valve **P**, shutting off the fuel supply to the float chamber. As fuel is used the float sinks slightly and allows the valve to open, replenishing the level and keeping it virtually constant.

The throttle valve **V** is connected to the throttle linkage and controls the airflow through the carburetter. At slow-running the mixture is drawn through the port below the throttle valve **V**, controlled by the slow-running volume screw **W**. The fuel is drawn through the pilot jet **g** and the air through the calibrated orifices **u1** and **u2**. The orifice beside the throttle valve allows mixture to be drawn through it as the valve opens slightly to give a smooth transfer from idling to main jets. As the throttle valve is opened further the suction around the valve decreases and the increased airflow causes a reduction of pressure in the throat of the venturi. Fuel for the mixture is then drawn through the main jet **Gg**. An emulsifying tube is fitted to weaken the mixture slightly, by drawing in air through the air bleed jet at large throttle openings. An Econostat is fitted and this allows extra fuel to be drawn from the float chamber only at high speeds and when the suction reaches a predetermined value.

An accelerator pump **M** is fitted to enrich the mixture for acceleration. The pump is linked to the throttle and as the throttle is opened fuel is injected through the tube **I** and non-return ball valve **H2**. When the throttle is released fuel is drawn into the pump from the float chamber, through the ball valve **H1**.

The choke valve is offset on its spindle and is held towards the closed position by the coil spring **r** and the bi-metallic spring **B**. Coolant passes around the chamber 2 so that the temperature is proportional to the engine temperature. When the choke valve is closed there is an increase in suction in the carburetter and excess fuel is drawn through the jets. When the engine is cold the bi-metallic spring exerts a strong closing force on the choke valve and the cam **C** and link **T** open the throttle slightly to increase the idling speed. When the engine fires the airflow acting on the offset tends to open the valve and thus reduce the very rich mixture. A vacuum piston and lever 3 also exert an opening influence on the choke valve so that if the engine is speeded up the valve will open further. As the engine heats up the bi-metallic spring weakens and allows the opening forces to take control, so that the valve gradually opens until when the engine is hot the valve is fully open, and the idling speed is reduced to normal. On models fitted with a manual choke a cable operates the choke valve and the valve must be set by

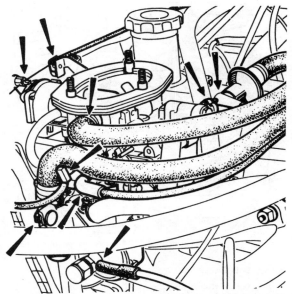

FIG 2 : 3   The attachments of the carburetter on R.1152 models

FIG 2 : 4   The attachments of the carburetter on R.1152 models

hand. When starting a model with an automatic choke, depress the accelerator pedal fully and then release it so that the linkage takes up.

Weber:

The Weber carburetter is a dual-barrel unit where each barrel can be considered as a separate carburetter but they share a common float chamber assembly. Differential throttle action is used.

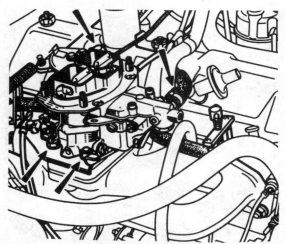

FIG 2:5 The attachments of the carburetter on R.1153 models

Solex DIDSA:

This carburetter is fitted to emission controlled vehicles (such as those for the North American market). The carburetter is made to much closer tolerances than normal and the adjustments and repairs that can be carried out are strictly limited. The carburetter is dual-barrelled. For slow-running and moderate throttle openings only the first barrel is used. At larger throttle openings the linkage opens the throttle valve of the second barrel so that it comes into action. The design ensures good economy at moderate speeds and, more to the point, ensures full vaporization and therefore better combustion and less emission throughout the range.

The fuel system is fitted with a fast-idle device which holds the throttle open slightly (1350 to 1450 rev/min

fast-idle speed) when the car is running at a road speed between 27 km/hr (16 mile/hr) and 37.5 km/hr (23 mile/hr) on R.1152 models where the solenoid flap valve 2 (see **FIG 1:52**) has only one terminal. Where two terminals are used and no relay in the later system the acceleration speed is 32 km/hr (19 mile/hr) and deceleration 27 km/hr (16 mile/hr). On automatic transmission models the fast-idle speed is 1300 to 1400 rev/min between road speeds of 25 km/hr (15 mile/hr) and 33 km/hr (21 mile/hr). This will not affect acceleration or steady running as the throttle is opened further than this point but when the car is decelerating the throttle will be held open slightly between these speeds and this helps to cut down emissions from the exhaust. The components are shown in **FIG 1:52**. The centrifugal switch opens between the speeds given and actuates the solenoid so that vacuum from the manifold can operate the capsule to open the throttle.

A progressive linkage is fitted to bring the second barrel into operation when required by the demands of the engine. The linkage is shown in **FIG 2:7**. The capsule in the bottom righthand corner is the one for the fast-idle and the semicircular slot in which its linkage travels and operates can be seen. **a** is the first throttle valve spindle and the lever **b** is attached to it. When the lever and spindle move in the direction shown by the arrow 1 the first throttle valve opens, and the lever **b** pushes the plate **j** in the direction of arrow 2. The lung **l** is a vacuum capsule taking its suction from both barrels of the carburetter. When suction is applied it draws the linkage **k** in the direction of the arrow 4 and this pull tries to pull the plate **g** in the direction of the arrow 3. The plate **g** is connected to the throttle spindle **h** and movement as shown opens the secondary throttle valve. The peg **f** on the plate **j** fits into the slot in the plate **g** and the amount of movement of the plate **g** is therefore limited by the position of the peg in the slot. Movement of the first throttle therefore frees the linkage to allow the secondary throttle to move

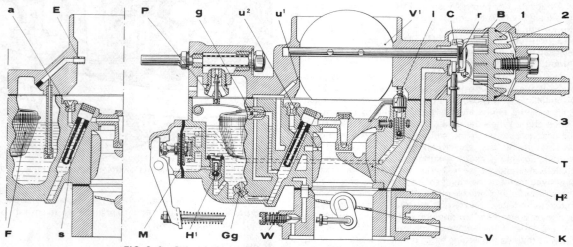

FIG 2:6 Schematic sectioned view of a Solex 35.DITA carburetter

Key to Fig 2:6   **a** Correction jet   **B** Bimetal coil   **C** Cam   **E** Econostat   **F** Float   **Gg** Main jet   **g** Pilot jet
H1/H2 Accelerator pump valves   **i** Pump injector   **K** Venturi   **M** Accelerator pump   **P** Needle valve   **r** Spring
s Emulsion tube   **T** Control rod   **u1/u2** Calibrated orifices   **V** Throttle valve   **V1** Choke valve   **W** Volume control
screw   **1** Body   **2** Chamber   **3** Lever

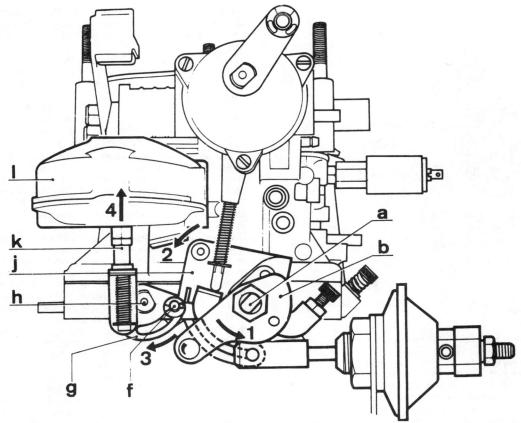

FIG 2:7 The progressive throttle linkage fitted to the Solex 26-32.DIDSA carburetter

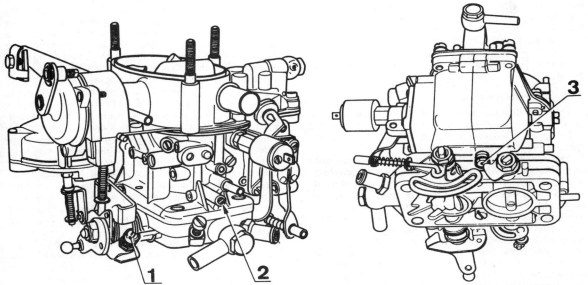

FIG 2:8 The adjustments 1, 2 and 3 are set only at the factory and must under no circumstances be altered, they are sealed and marked with yellow paint

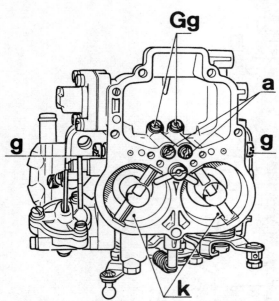

FIG 2:9 The jet positions on Solex 26-32.DIDSA carburetters

and the secondary throttle is opened by suction on the lung.

This type of carburetter is also fitted with a solenoid-controlled idler jet. When the ignition is switched on the solenoid is energized and it draws a needle out of the jet to allow fuel to pass. As soon as the ignition is switched off the needle seals the jet, preventing any fuel being drawn through as the engine stops. The solenoid is fitted with a screw which is normally used to set the needle, so that the engine cuts out immediately the lead to the solenoid is disconnected. The screw can also be used to hold the needle open so that if the solenoid fails the car can still be driven home. Check the solenoid by disconnecting its lead, switching on the ignition and brushing the lead across the terminal when the solenoid should be heard to chatter as the current makes and breaks.

2:5 Carburetter servicing

The general principles of carburetter servicing apply to all the models covered by this manual and so the details will be given in general only making reference to a specific carburetter when required.

The servicing operations that can be carried out to the Solex DIDSA carburetters (emission control) are strictly limited. The adjustment screws shown in FIG 2:8 are set at the factory, sealed with yellow paint and must under no circumstances be altered. The only work that may be carried out is as follows. The carburetter float chamber cover may be removed, jets cleaned or renewed or new float, needle valve and accelerator pump parts fitted. The choke spindle in the cover may be renewed as may the complete vacuum capsule (lung for the progressive linkage) and the pilot jet solenoid may also be renewed (tighten to a torque of .25 kg m, 2 lb ft). If the carburetter shows any other faults

a complete new carburetter must be fitted. This applies not only to the owner but also to garages and agencies. The jet positions on the Solex DIDSA carburetter are shown in FIG 2:9.

The most likely cause of faults in the carburetter is dirt, either in the jets or in the needle valve. If rough running or poor performance starts suddenly then the carburetter should be partially dismantled and cleaned. Fuel starvation or flooding can be caused by dirt in the needle valve, so again cleaning may effect a cure. Wear at the throttle spindle and housing or leaking gaskets will cause poor running which is not curable by cleaning.

The components of a Solex 35.DITA.2 carburetter are shown in FIG 2:10 and the components of all the other single-barrel Solex carburetters are very similar so the figure can be used for these as well. The components of a Zenith 36.IF carburetter are shown in FIG 2:11. The components of a Weber 32.DAR carburetter are shown in FIG 2:12.

When dismantling or reassembling a carburetter it is essential to use well-fitting tools. The castings and jets are made of soft metal and badly fitting tools will quickly tear the slots in screws and cause general damage. Many special tools are made for reconditioning the Weber carburetter and though most owners will not have access to them it is as well to know that they exist.

On all the models the jets, float and needle valve are accessible after the float chamber cover has been removed from the top of the carburetter. As a quick field test take out the screws that secure the cover and swing it to one side. Crank the engine over on the starter motor and at every other revolution of the engine there should be a good spurt of fuel through the needle valve. Take care to direct the fuel safely away from the hot exhaust, preferably into some container. If fuel does not spurt out then either the lines are blocked or the pump is defective. This test will also help to wash out any dirt causing the needle valve to stick. Lift out the float and check it for damage or leaks. A leaking float can be detected by the loose fuel swishing in it or otherwise it can be found by immersing the float in hot water, whereupon the leak will be shown by a stream of bubbles. The weight of the float is one of the controlling factors in the fuel level, so if the float is flooded the fuel level will be too high and the carburetter will flood. For the same reason a float should not be repaired by soldering the leak, even after the fuel has been driven or shaken out, as this will alter the weight of the float.

If flooding is persistent make sure that the spillage is not caused by leaking gaskets or loose unions. Remove the float chamber cover and unscrew the needle valve assembly from it. At the same time remove the inlet filter and clean it. On the models where the needle can be removed from the valve withdraw it and check the tapered seat of the needle. If there is a step worn on it the complete needle valve assembly must be renewed. On the other models hold the needle closed with a finger and try to blow through the valve. If the valve leaks it must be renewed.

If misfiring is persistent and cannot be traced to flooding it can be caused by dirt in the jets. Remove the float chamber cover and unscrew the jets. Lay the jets out in order to avoid any confusion when refitting them, or else do one jet at a time and refit it before cleaning the next. **Do not poke through the jets with wire as this will**

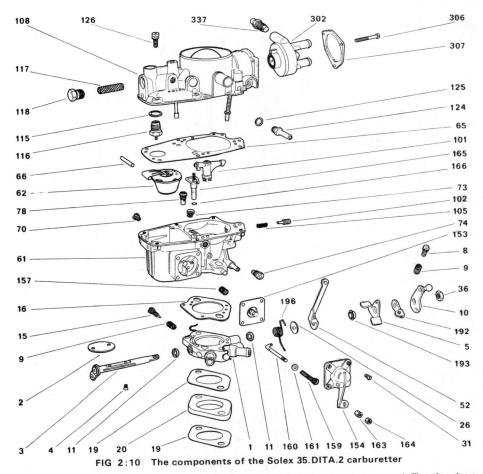

FIG 2:10 The components of the Solex 35.DITA.2 carburetter

Key to Fig 2:10   1 Heated throttle casing   2 Throttle valve   3 Throttle spindle   4 Throttle valve securing screw
5 Abutment for fast-idle   8 Slow-running adjustment screw   9 Spring   10 Throttle lever   11 Seal   15 Volume control screw
16 Gasket   19 Gaskets   20 Flange   26 Washer   31 Screw   36 Nut   61 Float chamber   62 Float   65 Gasket 66 Float spindle
70 Main jet   73 Correction jet   74 Pilot jet   78 Accelerator inlet valve   101 Sprayer   102 Screw for sprayer   105 Spring
108 Float chamber cover   115 Washer   116 Needle valve   117 Strainer   118 Plug   124 Fuel inlet   125 Washer   126 Screw
153 Accelerator pump diaphragm   154 Accelerator pump cover   157 Spring   159 Spring   160 Operating rod
161 Retaining washer   163 Adjustment nut   164 Locknut   165 Calibrated pump injector with spring   166 Washer
192 Intermediate lever   193 Lever ring   196 Spring   302 Water casing and bi-metal spring   306 Screw   307 Retaining ring

damage the calibrated orifices. Flush the jets in clean fuel and then blow through them to remove any dirt. Gum or difficult deposits may be softened by soaking in methylated spirits, trichlorethylene or special carburetter cleaning fluid.

If there is an excess amount of dirt in the carburetter remove it from the engine and completely dismantle it. On some carburetters the passages are sealed at the ends with lead balls. Carefully drill out the lead balls and then soak the components in special cleaning fluid. Blow through all the internal passages with an airline or use the special tools to clear the passages. New lead balls should be driven back into place using a drift with a slightly concave face. Wash the parts in solvent before reassembly.

The most likely points of wear are around the throttle and choke spindles. Dismantle the linkage parts and hold the butterfly to prevent it being strained when undoing the nuts holding the linkage. Take out the screws securing the valve to the spindle and then slide the valve out of the spindle so that the spindle can be withdrawn. Try fitting a new spindle but if the wear is still excessive a new housing or carburetter must be fitted. On Weber carburetters oversize spindles are available and the housing should be reamed out with a special reamer. When refitting the valve leave the screws just tight enough to hold it and then check that the valve moves through its full range of movement without binding in the bore. Adjust the position of the valve as required and then fully tighten the screws. Support the spindle on a block of metal, through the bore, and stake the threads of the screws to prevent them from loosening.

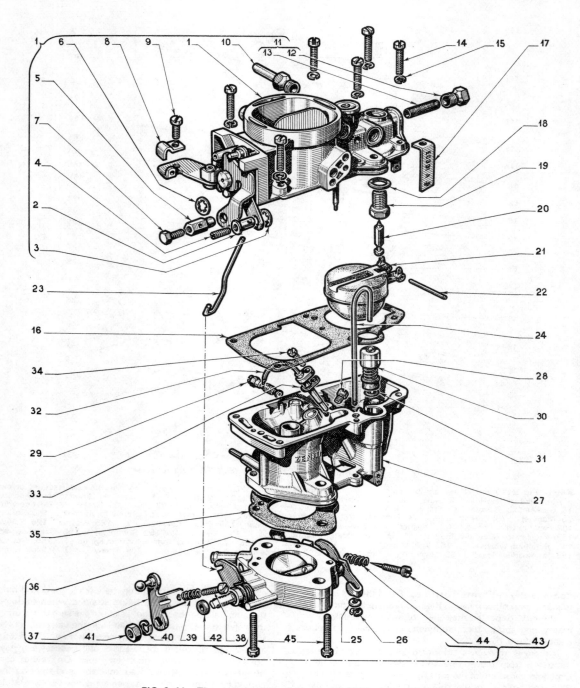

FIG 2:11   The components of the Zenith 36.IF carburetter

Key to Fig 2:11   1 Float chamber cover assembly   2 Fast-idle rod trunnion   3 Spring clip   4 Fast-idle rod adjustment screw   5 Choke cable clamp   6 Clip   7 Clamp screw   8 Outer cable clamp   9 Screw   10 Fuel inlet   11 Strainer assembly   12 Plug   13 Strainer   14 Screw   15 Spring washer   16 Gasket   17 Number tag   18 Seal   19 Needle seat   20 Needle valve   21 Float   22 Float spindle   23 Fast-idle rod   24 Accelerator pump operating rod   25 Washer   26 Spring clip   27 Float chamber   28 Main jet   29 Slow-running jet   30 Accelerator pump   31 Washer   32 Accelerator pump nozzle   33 Washer   34 Screw   35 Gasket   36 Throttle casing   37 Throttle lever   38 Slow-running screw   39 Spring   40 Spring washer   41 Nut   42 Seal   43 Volume control screw   44 Spring   45 Screws

Weber fuel level:

The method of checking the fuel level on Weber carburetters is shown in **FIG 2:13**. Special gauges are made for the check but if care is taken a steel rule can be used to take the measurements. Hold the cover vertical so that the float arm 3 just rests against the needle valve 1 when it is closed, without compressing the ball 2 into the needle. Measure the distance **A** between the float and cover. The distance should be 5mm ($\frac{13}{64}$ inch). If the distance is not correct carefully bend the arm 3 making sure that the tongue 4 still makes a right angle with the needle until the setting is correct. When the dimension **A** is correct check that the travel of the float **B** is correct at 8mm ($\frac{5}{16}$ inch). If the travel is incorrect carefully bend the tongue 5 to bring the travel within limits.

2:6 Carburetter adjustment

The Solex DIDSA carburetters fitted to emission controlled models will be dealt with separately in the next section.

Before adjusting the carburetter make sure that the ignition is correctly set and working correctly. If the engine or carburetter are generally worn difficulty will be found in obtaining a smooth and accurate idle speed. In such cases where it is impractical to carry out full overhaul it will assist by increasing the idling speed slightly and though this will make idling better and help to prevent stalling it will not increase efficiency.

Run the engine until it has reached its normal operating temperature, indicated by the cooling fan switching on.

The engine idling-speed is controlled by a spring-loaded screw on the throttle linkage acting against a stop on the carburetter body. A rough adjustment for starting and running the engine is 1 to 1½ turns screwed in from the position at which the end of the screw just touches the stop when the throttle valve is fully closed. The best method of checking the speed is to borrow an electronic tachometer and connect it in as instructed by the maker of the instrument. The correct idling speeds for the various models are given in **Technical Data**.

The slow-running mixture is controlled by the volume screw. Before starting the engine screw the volume screw fully in so that it gently touches its seat while counting the number of turns required. Remove the screw completely and check the tapered end. **If the taper has a step worn in it the screw must be renewed as the adjustment will not be accurate and smooth. Turning the volume screw tightly onto its seat is the commonest cause of a step so always make sure that the screw is not tightened too firmly, but only touches its seat lightly.** Refit the volume control screw to its original position, normally 1½ to 2 turns out from its seat.

With the engine running and hot adjust the slow-running screw until the idling speed is correct. If a vacuum gauge is available it should be connected to the inlet manifold and the volume control screw adjusted to give the highest vacuum reading with the idling speed correct. If a vacuum gauge is not available adjust the volume screw until the engine is running at its highest idling-speed with an even beat. Readjust the slow-running screw to bring the idling speed back within limits and then carry out further small adjustment to the volume screw to make the exhaust beat

even. It may be necessary to readjust the idling speed again but after this further adjustments will be so small as to be negligible.

2:7 Adjusting Solex DIDSA and SEIEA carburetters

On these models it is essential to use a tacho-meter as the emissions from the exhaust depend on the accuracy of the settings. It is also advisable to have the emissions checked with an exhaust gas analyser. On these models the engine, carburetter and ignition must all be in first-class order and all other settings correctly made, otherwise no amount of carburetter adjustment will bring the emissions within limits.

The settings of the screws shown in FIG 2:8 must not be altered. The slow-idling speed is adjusted by an air bleed screw **A** and the mixture at slow-running by the volume screw **B**, shown in **FIG 2:14**. The fast-idle adjustment is carried out at the vacuum capsule of the fast-idle circuit (not the 'lung' of the carburetter).

Adjusting slow-running:

1 Run the engine until it has reached its normal operating temperature, indicated by the cooling fan operating. Connect a tachometer.
2 Adjust the air screw **A** until the engine is running at the desired idling speed for the engine type as given in **Technical Data**. Turn the fuel screw **B** until the engine speed has increased to a maximum. Readjust the idling speed using the screw **A**, and then again obtain the highest idling speed by adjusting screw **B**. Repeat these adjustments until the highest possible idling speed obtainable when turning the fuel screw **B** is no more than 25 rev/min above the desired speed.
3 When operation 2 has been finished accurately, turn the **fuel screw B** in a clockwise direction until the engine speed drops up to 25 rev/min. **Make sure that the speeds are accurately set as the emission depends on this accuracy.**

Adjusting fast-idle:

The adjustment point on the vacuum capsule is shown in **FIG 2:15**. Set the slow-running idle speed correctly and leave the tachometer in place.

1 Disconnect the electrical lead to the solenoid flap valve. Hold the nut **C** with a spanner, unscrew the protective cover and slacken the locknut **D**. Start the engine, making sure that the end of the lead cannot accidentally earth.
2 Insert a 3mm Allen key into the adjusting screw **E** and turn the screw until the engine is idling at the recommended speed (see **Section 2:4**). With the Allen key still holding the adjusting screw, hand tighten the locknut **D**. Hold the nut **C** with a spanner and fully tighten the locknut **D**.
3 Stab the accelerator pedal a few times and check the fast-idle speed each time to ensure that the setting has not altered when tightening the locknut and that the fast-idle speed is constant after operation of the throttle linkage.

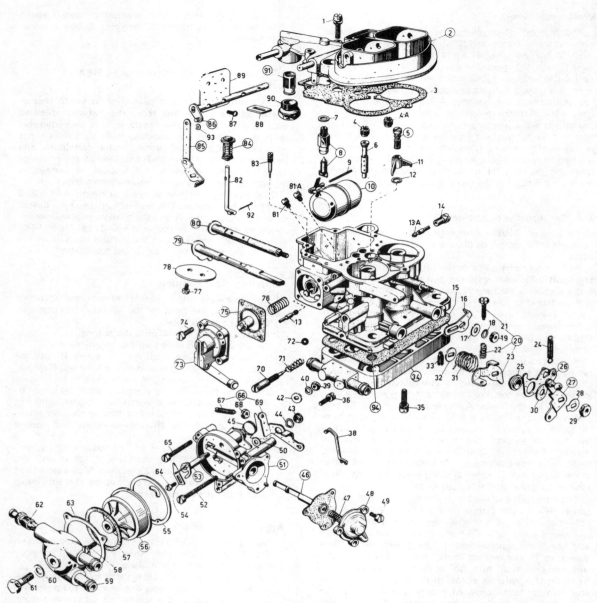

FIG 2:12   The components of the Weber 32.DAR.2 carburetter

Key to Fig 2:12   1 Screw   2 Float chamber cover   3 Gasket   4 Primary air correction jet   4A Secondary air correction jet   5 Non-return valve, for accelerator pump jet   6 Emulsion tube   7 Washer   8 Needle valve   9 Float spindle   10 Float   11 Accelerator pump jet   12 Washer   13 Primary slow-running jet   13A Secondary slow-running jet   14 Plug   15 Gasket   16 Secondary throttle lever   17 Washer   18 Wave washer   19 Nut   20 Fast-idle adjustment set   21 Screw   22 Spring   23 Lever   24 Spring   25 Bush   26 Operating lever, secondary throttle   27 Throttle control lever   28 Tabwasher   29 Nut   30 Washer   31 Throttle return spring   32 Washer   33 Adjustment screw, secondary throttle   34 Flange   35 Screw   36 Screw   38 Fast-idle rod   39 Nut   40 Spring washer   42 Washer   43 Bush   44 Wave washers   45 Spring   46 Diaphragm and spindle economy valve   47 Spring   48 Cover   49 Screw   50 Washer   51 Body, automatic choke control   52 Screw   53 Shaft and lever   54 Adjusting plate   55 Gasket   56 Thermostat assembly   57 Gasket   58 Screw   59 Water chamber   60 Washer   61 Screw   62 Bleed valve   63 Ring securing   64 Screw   65 Screw   66 Fast-idle lever assembly   67 Screw   68 Locknut   69 Lever   70 Volume control screw   71 Spring   72 O-ring   73 Accelerator pump cover   74 Screw   75 Diaphragm   76 Spring   77 Screw   78 Throttle valve   79 Primary throttle spindle   80 Secondary throttle spindle   81 Main jet primary   81A Main jet secondary   82 Valve rod   83 Plug for pump discharge   84 Float chamber vent valve   85 Operating lever for choke valve   86 Choke valve spindle   87 Screw   88 Dust seal   89 Choke valve   90 Strainer plug   91 Strainer   92 Splitpin   93 Spring clip   94 Carburetter body

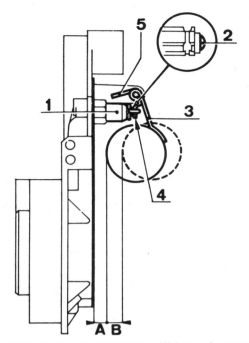

FIG 2:13 Setting the fuel level on Weber carburetters

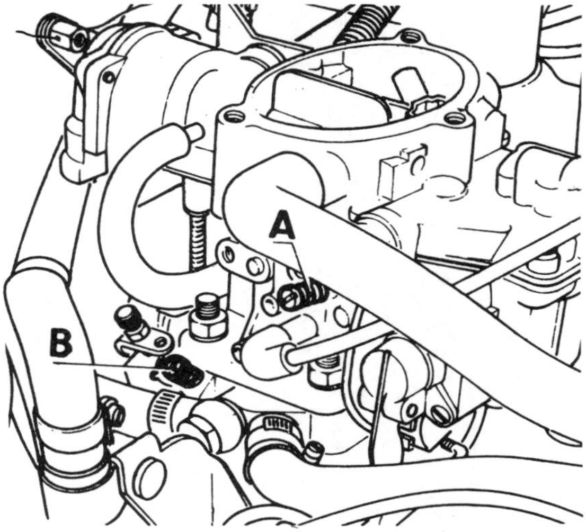

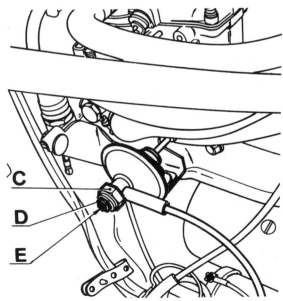

FIG 2:14 The slow-running adjustment points on Solex 26-32.DIDSA carburetters

4 Refit the protective cover to the vacuum capsule. Reconnect the lead to the solenoid flap valve, noting that the idling speed should drop to normal when it is reconnected.

5 The operation can be road tested, or checked with one wheel jacked up and the car securely chocked while in gear. Connect a telltale light between the terminal of the solenoid valve and a good earth, taking great care to prevent shorts, and fit the lamp so that it can be seen readily. Check that contact is made and broken at the recommended acceleration and deceleration speeds for the vehicle concerned. Automatic transmission models require special equipment for testing and is beyond the resources of the owner driver.

2:8 Fast-idle circuit faults

Engine sticks in fast-idle:

Connect a telltale light between the terminal of the solenoid flap valve and a good earth. Start the engine and check that the telltale comes on. If the lamp does not come on, first check the wiring to see that there are no breaks or defects and if this is satisfactory renew the relay if fitted. If the lamp still does not light renew the centrifugal switch. The relay should be changed first as this is the most likely component to fail. If it is found that the centrifugal switch is at fault then refit the original relay and check the circuit again.

If the telltale light does come on then disconnect the vacuum pipe from the capsule, clamping it to prevent air entering the engine. If slow-running idling speed is now restored then change the solenoid valve.

Check that the setting of the vacuum capsule is such that the clearance between the end of its fork and the quadrant on the carburetter is 1.6 mm ($\frac{1}{16}$ inch).

Make sure that the idling speed is not increased by sticking throttle linkage.

FIG 2:15 Adjusting the fast-idle on Solex 26-32.DIDSA carburetters

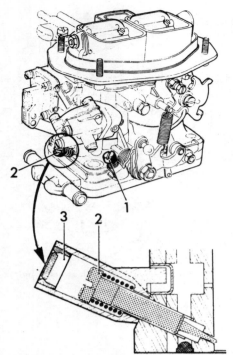

FIG 2:16 Adjusting the idle speed and mixture and sealing the mixture screw (Weber 32 DIR)

Key to Fig 2:16 1 Idle speed screw 2 Idle mixture screw 3 Seal

Fast-idle does not select:

Jack up one front wheel of the car clear off the ground and securely chock the rear wheels with the handbrake firmly applied. Start the engine and engage second gear. Have an assistant watch the vacuum capsule and open the throttle until the speedometer reads approximately 56 km/hr (35 mile/hr). If the vacuum capsule is seen to exert a pull on the linkage then the system is functioning correctly. If no movement takes place disconnect the lead

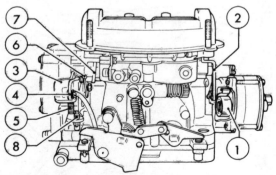

FIG 2:17 Solex carburetter type MIMAT, showing details of the automatic choke

Key to Fig 2:17 1 Bi-metal spring 2 Link rod 3 Link 4 Link 5 Stop screw 6 Lever 7 Rod 8 Stop screw

to the solenoid. If fast-idle is now obtained check the centrifugal switch and relay circuit as described for sticking in fast-idle.

2:9 Weber carburetter type 32.DIR

This is a double-barrelled downdraught type and is fitted to engines with automatic transmission. It is similar in most respects to type 32.DAR except that a hand operated choke is incorporated in place of the thermostatically operated mixture control.

Slow-running adjustment:

With the automatic transmission selector in the P position start the engine and allow it to reach normal working temperature. With the engine running at idling speed proceed as follows:

Turn the volume control screw 70 to obtain the fastest possible running of the engine and then, if necessary adjust the throttle stop screw to bring the speed to that given in **Technical Data** for the type. Repeat the foregoing until the engine is running smoothly at this speed.

Now screw back the volume control screw to weaken the mixture and obtain a reduction in engine speed of up to 25 rev/min without causing it to lose its regularity.

The accuracy of this adjustment is most important in securing the minimum gas emission as required by certain local regulations. No other screws on the carburetter should be touched.

On those carburetters where the mixture control screw is sealed (see 2 in **FIG 2:16**) it may be an offence in certain territories to run the car without a seal in position even if the CO level is correctly adjusted. Make sure that a new seal will be available to fit on the screw after an adjustment has been made.

The old seal is removed by pushing in a screwdriver and levering away. The new seal is fitted by pressing it over the screw as shown.

2:10 Weber carburetter type 32.DAR-7 or 8

This carburetter, which is fitted to the Renault 16TX, is a double barrelled downdraught type with differential opening of the two throttles and an automatic choke, controlled by water circulating in the engines cooling system. It is in most respects, similar to the type 32.DAR-2 shown in **FIG 2:12**.

The description and directions given earlier in this chapter are largely applicable and in normal service it is unlikely that the home operator will need to do any more than adjust the engine slow-running or perhaps check the float level. These operations are quite simple.

Slow-running adjustment:

Ensure first that the components and settings of the ignition system are all in order and that the engine is at full working temperature.

Refer to **FIG 2:12**. Use the screw 21, acting on the primary throttle lever, to obtain the slow-running speed (see **Technical Data**).

Unscrew the volume control screw 70, which regulates the strength of the idle fuel mixture, a couple of turns and then steadily screw it in until the engine starts to run unevenly. Unscrew slightly from this position so that the engine is once more running smoothly.

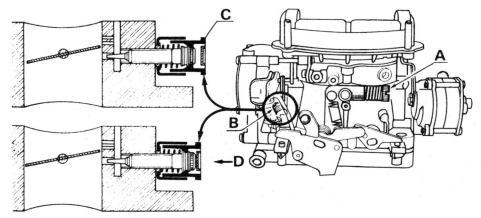

FIG 2:18   Adjusting the idle speed and mixture, Solex MIMAT

Key to Fig 2:18   **A** Idle volume (speed) screw   **B** Idle mixture screw   **C** Sealing cap solid with screw   **D** Sealing cap free of screw

If these adjustments have caused the engine speed to rise above or fall below the set idle speed, use the throttle stop screw 21 to bring the speed back again.

Setting the float level:

Directions for setting the float level on Weber carburetters were given in **Section 2:5** and these apply also in this case, except that the dimension **A** must now be 7 mm.

2:11 Solex carburetter type MIMAT

This is another carburetter of similar design to those already described and was introduced on R1153, R1155 and R1157 models in 1976. In order to comply with emission regulations, cars fitted with these carburetters must be taken to a Renault agent to have the mixture adjusted to ensure a CO content of between 2.5 and 3% and to fit seals on the adjusters after the first 600 miles (1000 km). Any further adjustment will necessitate the breaking of these seals and must be carried out using a CO meter, after which new seals must be fitted.

The operation of the choke is effected through two bi-metal springs and a system of levers and link rods (see **FIG 2:17**). When cold, the spring 1 hold the choke plates closed through the rod 2. Another bi-metal spring, acting through the levers 3 and 4 and the stop screw 5 opens the throttle for a fast-idle setting. As the engine starts running, the depression in the inlet manifold acts on a vacuum capsule and, through the lever 6 and rod 7, opens the chokes against the action of the spring 1 and so prevents strangulation of the engine as the throttle is opened.

As the engine warms up the bi-metal spring permits the choke plates to open and, by means of an internal mechanism, returns the throttle to its idling position, which is pre-set and cannot be adjusted without special tools.

Adjusting the idle speed and fuel mixture:

The idle speed is adjusted only by means of the volume screw **A** in **FIG 2:18** which regulates the amount of a pre-mixed fuel admitted into the inlet duct; the throttle stop position is not adjusted. The specified idle speeds are: 700 ± 25 rev/min with manual or 625 ± 25 rev/min for automatic transmissions in D.

If the use of the volume screw **A** only does not give a smooth idle at the correct speed, it will be necessary to break the seal and use the mixture strength screw **B**. In an emergency when a CO meter is not available or if regional regulations do not demand a strict control on exhaust emissions, the idle mixture can be adjusted as follows:

Start the engine and use the screw **A** to obtain a speed of not more than 700 rev/min on manual transmission models or 625 rev/min on automatics with D selected.

Use the mixture screw **B** to obtain the highest possible engine speed consistent with smooth running, then return to the former speed by using the volume screw **A**.

Repeat these adjustments until the highest speed obtainable with the mixture screw **B** is within the limits 700 ± 25 rev/min or 625 ± 25 rev/min as appropriate.

Finally, screw the volume screw inwards to reduce the speed by 25 rev/min.

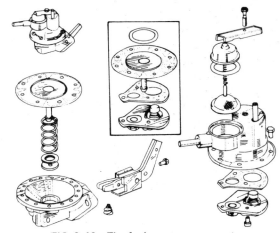

FIG 2:19   The fuel pump components

If a CO meter is available use the two adjusting screws to obtain a CO content of 2.5 to 3% at the specified idle speed.

Sealing the mixture control screw:

The white seal is fitted firstly over the screw as shown at **C** in **FIG 2:18** and is attached solidly to the screw.

After adjusting the idle mixture, press the seal fully in to position **D** which releases it from the screw so that it turns freely and so prevents any further adjustment until it has been forcibly removed.

2:12 The fuel pump

This is driven by an eccentric on the camshaft and may be one of several makes, SEV, Guiot, AC or Sofabex. The pump may also have a rocker operated or reciprocating rod operated diaphragm.

FIG 2:19 shows the components of the more usual type of pump and no difficulty should be experienced in dismantling and reassembling it if required. Care must be taken to mark the sections before separating in order to ensure correct refitting.

2:13 Fault diagnosis

(a) Insufficient fuel delivery or fuel leakage

1 Fuel tank vent restricted or blocked
2 Petrol lines blocked
3 Air leaks at pipe connections
4 Filters blocked
5 Defective fuel pump

6 Defective float in float chamber
7 Worn needle valve or needle valve held by dirt
8 Fuel vaporizing in lines due to excess heat

(b) Excessive fuel consumption

1 Choked air cleaner
2 Carburetter requires adjustment
3 Fuel leakage
4 Idling speed too high
5 Excessively worn carburetter
6 Excessive engine temperature
7 Brakes binding
8 Tyres underinflated
9 Car overloaded

(c) Idling speed too high

1 Rich fuel mixture
2 Carburetter controls sticking
3 Slow-running incorrectly adjusted
4 Worn butterfly valve
5 Fast-idle circuit defective (emission control only)

(d) Noisy fuel pump

1 Mountings loose
2 Air leak on suction side
3 Obstruction in fuel line

(e) No fuel delivery

1 Tank empty
2 Float needle valve stuck closed
3 Blocked fuel lines or filters
4 Defective fuel pump

CHAPTER 3

THE IGNITION SYSTEM

3:1 Description

A distributor is fitted to the engine and it is driven by gears from the engine camshaft at half engine speed. The components of a distributor are shown in **FIG 3:1**. An ignition coil generates the very high voltage required and the HT voltage is led through special heavily insulated HT leads. At the appropriate instant the spark across the sparking plug electrodes ignites the mixture in the cylinder that is firing.

On early models a conventional type of distributor is used (see **FIG 3:1**); in 1977 a new type with encapsulated contact breaker was introduced which will be described separately in **Section 3:5**.

The ignition coil and distributor low-tension circuit are connected in series so that current only flows when the contact points are allowed to be closed by the position of the cam on the distributor shaft. As the contacts open the current flow is sharply cut off, assisted by the action of the capacitor on the outside of the distributor, and the resultant rapid collapse of the magnetic field in the primary coils induces the very high voltage in the secondary coils. An HT lead transfers this high voltage to the central electrode in the distributor cap and from there it passes through the carbon brush and spring to the rotor arm. The distributor is synchronized with the engine and the HT voltage jumps the small gap between rotor arm and appropriate electrode from where it is led to the correct sparking plug by another HT lead.

Combustion takes a certain finite time and to ensure that it is at its maximum at the optimum piston position allowance must be made for the speed of the engine. The spark requires to take place earlier (advanced) when the piston speed is high. Spring-loaded weights are fitted to the distributor shaft. As the engine speed increases these weights are moved out by centrifugal force, against the calibrated springs, and they rotate the cam ahead of the main shaft to advance the ignition with speed.

The combustion time will vary with the amount of mixture drawn into the engine. The manifold suction varies with the quantity of mixture induced at each stroke and use is made of this to adjust the ignition point. The manifold is connected to the vacuum unit on the distributor by a small-bore pipe. The vacuum unit rotates the contact breaker plate in the body to alter the timing.

3:2 Maintenance

The HT leads, distributor cap and ignition coil top should be regularly wiped over with a soft clean cloth to remove any moisture or dirt.

The sparking plugs should be cleaned at intervals of 10,000 kilometres (6000 miles) and renewed at intervals of 20,000 kilometres (12,000 miles). See **Section 3:6** for details.

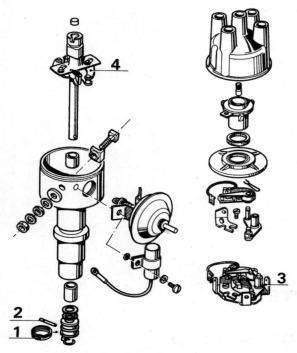

FIG 3:1 The distributor components

Distributor lubrication:

Excessive lubrication must be avoided otherwise lubricant will dirty the points or spread inside the distributor cap.

Free the clips and remove the distributor cap. Firmly and squarely pull off the rotor arm. Pour a few drops of oil onto the felt pad in the top of the cam. Lightly smear the cam lobes with a little grease so that the foot of the moving contact will be lubricated. Occasionally put a single drop of non-spreading oil onto the pivot post for the moving contact. Wipe away all surplus lubricant and make sure that none comes onto the contact points themselves. Wipe the rotor arm and inside of the distributor cap with a soft clean cloth, and then refit the parts making sure that the lug inside the rotor arm fits squarely into the slot in the cam.

Cleaning contact points:

In normal use there will be a build up of metal on one contact and a pit formed in the other. This build up can be left until it has reached .3 mm (.012 inch) without taking any action but when it has reached the limit new contact points should be fitted.

If the points are contaminated with oil, shown by a smudgy black line underneath them on the contact breaker plate, they should be removed and cleaned with an oilstone or fine file, or ground down. Do not use emerycloth as this will leave hard particles imbedded in the metal. Wash the points with methylated spirits or trichlorethylene before refitting them.

Adjusting contact points:

Before setting the gap make sure that the points are clean and fit for further service. Check that the moving contact pivots freely about its post. If the contact sticks make sure that the spring is not weak or broken. Take off the moving contact, lightly polish the pivot post with fine-grade emerycloth and refit the contact after lubricating the post with a single drop of oil.

The best method of setting the contacts is to use a Dwell meter while the engine is running, or the distributor rotated on a test bench. This method can only be done by an agent with the correct equipment. It should be noted that the dwell percentage is 63 ± 3 per cent. When the dwell has been set the gap between the points should be checked with feeler gauges and if it is less than .35 mm (.014 inch) then the points must be renewed.

If a dwell meter is not available then the points can be set using feeler gauges. Turn the engine until the points are fully open. Slacken the clamp screw 2, shown in **FIG 3:2**, and turn the adjusting screw 1 until the correct thickness feeler gauge can be inserted between the points. The correct gap is .4 to .5 mm (.016 to .020 inch). New points should be set to the highest limit to allow for bedding in of the foot of the moving contact. On used points adjust to the lower limit but make sure that the feeler gauge is inserted between the unworn portions of the contacts, otherwise it will bridge the gap and give a false reading. Rotate the adjusting screw until the feeler gauge is just nipped and slight drag can be felt on it as it is drawn between the points and tighten the clamp screw 2. Check that the adjustment has not altered after tightening the clamp screw and check that it is correct at the other three lobes of the cam.

On engines fitted with manual transmission rotate the engine by turning a front wheel with the wheel jacked up and top gear engaged. On those models with automatic transmission remove the sparking plugs and turn the engine using the camshaft pulley. On all models it will be easier to adjust the contacts before refitting the distributor.

3:3 Ignition faults

If the engine has a persistent misfire it can be caused by faulty ignition.

Start the engine and run it until it is hot. Increase the idling speed either by adjustment or else by propping open the accelerator pedal slightly. Use dry rags or thick gloves as insulators and disconnect each HT lead from its sparking plug in turn. Reconnect the lead before disconnecting the next one. If the cylinder is firing correctly the misfire will become more pronounced as the lead is disconnected, but if the cylinder is not firing there will be no difference. Having found the faulty cylinder stop the engine and bare the end of the HT lead. Restart the engine and hold the end of the lead approximately 5 mm ($\frac{3}{16}$ inch) away from a convenient earth point on the engine **(but not the fuel system)**. If a regular stream of good sparks jumps across, the lead and ignition is satisfactory. Stop the engine again and remove, clean, and test the sparking plug. Refit the plug or a new one in its place and repeat the test. If there is no improvement then the fault is other than ignition.

If the sparks are weak and irregular stop the engine and check the ignition. Make sure that the HT lead is not perished, cracking or defective and renew it if required. Remove the distributor cap and rotor arm for checking and wiping clean with soft cloth. Use methylated spirits to wash away dirt if required, paying particular attention to crevices in the cap. Check the cap for cracks or 'tracking' and renew it if either are found. 'Tracking' shows up as thin black lines between electrodes or an electrode and the edge of the cap. Make sure that the carbon brush in the cap is undamaged and moves freely against its spring pressure.

Weak sparks on all four cylinders can be caused by a poor HT lead between coil and distributor, defective ignition coil, or excessively worn or dirty contact points.

Testing the low-tension circuit:

As a quick field test remove the distributor cap and rotor arm, switch on the ignition and push the car in gear until the contact points are closed. Flick the points apart with a fingernail and if the circuit is live there should be a small low-voltage spark between the contacts.

As a more accurate test disconnect the low-tension lead between the ignition coil and distributor and reconnect it with a low-wattage 12-volt test lamp in series. Jack up one front wheel of the car and engage top gear. Turn the engine over slowly by rotating the front wheel. On automatic models it will be necessary to remove the sparking plugs and rotate the engine by the camshaft pulley. As the points close with the ignition switched on the lamp should light and then go out again as they open.

If the lamp fails to light at all use the test lamp to trace back through the circuit until the fault is found.

If the lamp does not go out at all there is a shortcircuit in the distributor. Check the internal wiring for frayed insulation or incorrect assembly. If no fault is found repeat the test with the capacitor disconnected. If the distributor now operates satisfactorily the capacitor is faulty and must be renewed.

Capacitor:

Capacitor failure is usually fairly rare. The unit is made up of foil wrapped with paper insulation and if the insulation fails the foil is eroded away by the spark to make shortcircuits self-healing. A shortcircuit will be detected as described just previously.

Open-circuit is more difficult to detect without special equipment but it may be suspected if starting is difficult and the points are excessively 'blued' or burnt. Substitution with a know satisfactory capacitor is the best test readily available.

3:4 Servicing the distributor

Removal:

Free the distributor cap and leave it attached to the HT leads. Disconnect the vacuum pipe at the vacuum unit and the electrical lead at the low-tension terminal. Remove the clamp screw that secures the distributor and withdraw the distributor with a firm jerk or pull.

The distributor is refitted in the reverse order of removal but it will be necessary to reset the ignition timing afterwards. To make the task easier make sure that the body is refitted so that it points in roughly the same direction as it did before removal. The drive dog and the drive gear have

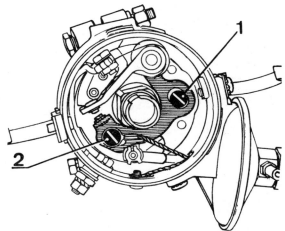

FIG 3:2 Adjusting the distributor contacts

the slot offset, so make sure that the shaft is aligned correctly. The correct positioning of the distributor drive gear, when the engine is at TDC on No. 1 cylinder, is dealt with in **Chapter 1, Section 1:9**.

Dismantling:

With the distributor removed take out the screws that secure the vacuum unit and capacitor. Free the link and remove the vacuum unit. Remove the low-tension terminal parts, carefully noting the position of all washers, and then lift out the contact breaker assembly.

Refer to **FIG 3:1**. Carefully check and note the relation of the offset on the drive dog and the slot in the cam. Remove the retaining spring 1 and take out the pin 2. Remove the drive dog and its associated washers and slide out the shaft assembly 4. **If the cam is separated from the shaft take great care not to twist or distort the weight springs.**

Reassembly:

Wash all the metal parts as well as the felt pad in clean fuel. Lubricate all the bearing surfaces lightly with oil and reassemble the unit in the reverse order of dismantling.

Distributor cap:

Check the cap for cracks or tracking and renew it if it is defective. Swill the cap with methylated spirits and then wipe it out with a soft clean cloth.

If the HT leads have been disconnected turn the engine until it is at TDC after the compression stroke on No. 1 cylinder. The electrode in the cap to which the rotor arm now points is connected to No. 1 sparking plug. The remainder of the HT leads are then fitted clockwise around the cap and in the firing order (1–3–4–2).

3:5 The later type distributor

Description:

In this type of distributor the contact breaker is housed in a detachable cassette which is designed to give more precise operation and easier adjustment as this can be effected from outside the distributor body with the engine running, if necessary.

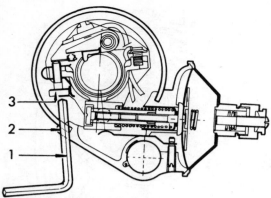

FIG 3:3 Adjusting the contact breaker and dwell angle on later type distributor

Key to Fig 3:3   1 3 mm Allen key   2 Hole in housing
3 Adjusting screw

Adjusting the contact gap and dwell angle:

Refer to **FIG 3:3** which shows a section through the contact breaker mechanism and the method of adjustment, for which the use of a dwell meter is essential as the contacts are fully enclosed and therefore inaccessible.

Connect the dwell meter according to the makers' instructions and run the engine at idling speed.

Insert a 3 mm Allen key 1 through the hole 2 provided in the distributor housing and into the adjusting screw 3.

Note the dwell angle and, if necessary, adjust by turning the screw to obtain the specified angle of 57 deg. ± 3 deg. It will be noted that turning the Allen key in a clockwise direction will increase the dwell angle and vice versa.

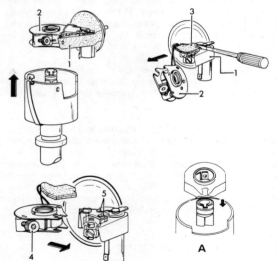

FIG 3:4 Removing and refitting a contact breaker cassette

Key to Fig 3:4   1 Condenser and vacuum capsule
assembly   2 Cassette   3 Connector   4 Adjusting screw
5 Connecting lugs   A Correct alignment for refitting into
the body

It is recommended that the ignition timing should be checked stroboscopically after any adjustment of the contact breaker.

Renewing the contact breaker cassette:

This is a simple operation after removing the distributor cap and lifting out the circular rotor. Refer to **FIG 3:4**.

Withdraw the condenser and vacuum capsule assembly 1 complete with the cassette 2 out of the distributor body.

Pull off the cassette connector 3 from the condenser assembly, using a small screwdriver as shown if necessary.

To refit the cassette, engage the connector on the lugs on top of the condenser and then fit the assembly over the camshaft and into the distributor housing, making sure that the contact and the notch in the shaft are lined up as shown at **A**.

Fit the rotor and make sure that it is pressed fully home, otherwise it will foul the distributor cap.

3:6 Setting the ignition timing

The timing marks are shown in **FIG 3:5**. On models fitted with manual transmission jack up one front wheel and with top gear engaged use it to turn the engine. On automatic models remove all four sparking plugs and turn the engine using the camshaft pulley.

Turn the engine in its normal direction of rotation until the timing point is exactly set. **If the timing point is overshot turn the engine a full revolution on so that the timing point is correctly set or else rotate it back well past the timing point and then rotate it forward again to the point.** This ensures that all backlash is taken up correctly.

The correct timing points are:

R.1150, R.1151 (except distributor 4215 or 4217), R.1152, R.1153 (USA) R.1154 (with distributor 4231 or 4232)	0 ± 1 deg.
R.1151 (with distributor 4215 or 4217)	2 ± 1 deg.
R.1153 (except USA), R.1154 (with distributor 4237, 4238, 4348 or 4349)	6 ± 1 deg.
R.1154 (with distributor 4433 or 4434)	10 ± 1 deg.
R.1155 (automatic transmission)	3 ± 1 deg.
R.1156 (manual transmission)	4 ± 1 deg.

From 1976 the correct timing point for the engine is stamped on a sleeve attached to one of the high-tension cables to the distributor.

Connect a low-wattage 12-volt test lamp to the distributor as shown in **FIG 3:6**. Note that in this case the lamp is in parallel with the distributor and will light as the points open and go out as they close, acting the opposite way to when the lamp is connected in series for testing the ignition.

Slacken the clamp screw that secures the distributor body and turn on the ignition. Lightly press the rotor arm in an anticlockwise direction to take up any backlash and rotate the distributor body slightly in either direction until the point is found where the test lamp has just come on, indicating that the points have just opened. Tighten the distributor clamp screw.

Rotate the engine for a full turn in its normal direction and before the timing marks are approaching, slow down the rate of turning. Stop turning the instant the light comes on and check that the timing marks are again accurately aligned.

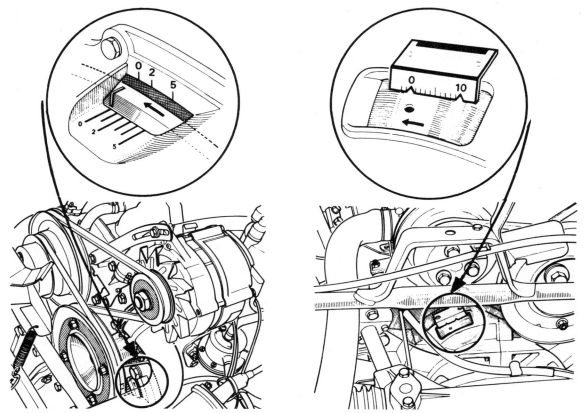

FIG 3:5 The ignition timing marks. Left, manual gearbox; right, automatic transmission. Settings shown are for No. 1 cylinder at TDC on firing stroke

Once the timing is set statically it can be checked at idling speed using a stroboscopic lamp. Connect the lamp as instructed by the maker and set it to shine on the timing marks and disconnect the vacuum advance pipe from the distributor. The timing marks should be made obvious with a thin white line painted on them. **When the engine is running take great care to avoid clothes, hands or tools coming in contact with the drive belts.** Rotate the distributor body until the timing marks appear exactly aligned and then clamp the body in this position. The advance and retard can also be tested empirically by altering the speed of the engine through the range (when the timing should advance smoothly) and disconnecting and reconnecting the vacuum pipe (when the timing should alter by a step).

3:7 The sparking plugs

Removal:

Disconnect the battery before removing or refitting the sparking plugs, as the box spanner can easily short the positive terminal on the alternator when removing No. 1 (front) sparking plug.

Slacken each plug using a well-fitting box spanner and then blow away loose dust or dirt with an airline or tyre pump. This will be more difficult on the 807 engines as

they are recessed in tubes but persevere in order to prevent dirt from falling into the engine. When the dirt has blown away unscrew the plugs by hand.

If the plug is stiff great care must be taken otherwise there is a very real danger of stripping the threads in the cylinder head. Lay a piece of rag around the base of the plug and soak it with penetrating oil or

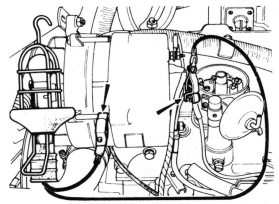

FIG 3:6 Setting the ignition timing with the aid of a lamp

paraffin and then leave it overnight. Unscrew the plug until it becomes too stiff and then run it in and out a few times to that point before unscrewing it a little further.

If the thread does strip then the cylinder head must be removed and steel insert-threads fitted.

Store the plugs in order as they are removed for subsequent examination of the firing ends.

Examination:

The colour of the firing ends will give a good guide to the conditions in the combustion chamber.

If the deposits are light and powdery while ranging in colour from brown to greyish tan, coupled with light wear on the electrodes, then the conditions are normal. Much constant-speed or city driving will leave the deposits white to yellowish. Cleaning and testing is all that is required.

If the deposits are wet and black looking they are caused by oil entering the combustion chamber, either past worn rings and pistons or down valve guides and stems. An engine overhaul is the only effective cure but the problem may be alleviated by fitting a hotter running grade of sparking plug.

Dry black deposits that seem fluffy are caused by incomplete combustion. Excessive idling may be the cause but it may also be traced to defective ignition or running with too rich a mixture.

Overheated sparking plugs have a white blistered look about the central electrode and when lead-based fuels are used there may be glints of metal on the insulator. The electrodes will also be excessively burnt away. Some of the possible causes are poor cooling, weak mixture, mistimed ignition, or running at high-speeds with the car overloaded. Make sure that the correct grade of sparking plug is used.

When examining the sparking plugs reject out of hand any that have cracked insulators or excessively worn electrodes.

Cleaning:

Wash oily sparking plugs in petrol. Clean the plugs on an abrasive-blasting machine and have them pressure tested after attention to the electrodes. If a machine is not available they can be cleaned by scrubbing with a steel-wire brush, though this is not so effective. **Never use a soft-metal brush as this will leave traces of metal on the central insulator.**

Trim the electrodes square with a fine file and adjust the gap by bending the side electrode. **Never bend the central electrode as this will crack the insulator.** On all models the correct gap is .6 mm to .7 mm.

Clean the threaded portion of the plug with a wire brush and if need be lubricate the threads with graphite grease. Clean the external portion of the insulator by wiping it with a piece of cloth dipped in methylated spirits.

Refitting:

If the plug is stiff to turn clean the threads in the cylinder head using a well-greased tap. Failing a tap use an old sparking plug with cross-cuts down the threads.

Check the sealing washers and renew them if they are compressed to less than half their original thickness.

Screw the sparking plugs fully into place by hand. This ensures that any cross-threading or stiffness is immediately apparent. Tighten the sparking plugs to a torque of 3 to 3.5 kgm (22 to 28 lb ft). If a torque spanner is not available tighten the plugs a further half turn from the handtight position with a box spanner. **Do not overtighten the sparking plugs.**

3:8 Fault diagnosis

(a) Engine will not fire

1 Battery discharged or the terminals dirty
2 Distributor contact points dirty or out of adjustment
3 Distributor cap dirty, cracked or tracking
4 Carbon brush in cap not in contact with rotor arm
5 Faulty cable or loose connection in low-tension circuit
6 Distributor rotor arm cracked or omitted on reassembly
7 Weak, broken contact spring or points stuck open
8 Water or dirt on the HT leads
9 Ignition coil defective
10 Defective HT lead between coil and distributor
11 Shortcircuit in distributor

(b) Engine misfires

1 Check 2, 3, 5 and 9 in (a)
2 Weak contact spring
3 Sparking plugs fouled, incorrectly set, loose or insulation cracked
4 Defective HT lead
5 Ignition timing too far advanced

CHAPTER 4

THE COOLING SYSTEM

4:1 Description

The engine is cooled by the passage of coolant through the water passages around the liners and the coolant then gives up the heat as it passes through the core in the radiator, the heat being taken by the passage of air around the fins of the core. Hot water rises and therefore a thermo-syphonic flow is set up around the cooling system as the engine heats. This flow is strongly boosted by the action of a water pump, belt-driven from the camshaft pulley. An electrically driven cooling fan is fitted to increase the airflow through the radiator when the coolant heats up. The fan is controlled by a thermostatic switch and relay. This ensures that power is not being wasted in driving a conventional fan when it is not needed, particularly when the car is moving fast.

A thermostat is fitted into the water pump, and held in position by the hose, and when the coolant is cold the valve remains closed. The coolant then bypasses the radiator and returns directly to the engine, giving a quicker warm-up, as less coolant requires heating and no heat is lost through the radiator. When the coolant heats up the valve opens and allows the coolant to pass through the radiator where it is cooled normally.

The cooling system is sealed in use and should normally only require refilling at two year intervals. A cap is fitted to the radiator and the system is completely filled with coolant, air being bled out. An expansion bottle is fitted and this bottle is vented to atmosphere through a valve, which allows air to escape if the pressure becomes too high. As the system heats up excess coolant passes into the expansion bottle and it is then drawn back as the system cools. The valve in the expansion bottle prevents losses by evaporation.

A mixture of antifreeze and water is always used in the system. The antifreeze serves the triple purpose of preventing freezing, raising the boiling point of the coolant, and supplying the inhibitors necessary to prevent corrosion in the system, and it is for these reasons that antifreeze is used in all climates.

4:2 Maintenance

The sealed cooling system should require no maintenance for two years and at the end of this time it should be drained, flushed and then refilled with fresh coolant.

Topping-up should not be required unless there are leaks in the system. **The level is checked at the expansion bottle, which is marked with a maximum level, and never at the radiator itself.** If the expansion bottle is empty then the system must be correctly refilled and bled. **Never overfill the expansion bottle as coolant passing through the vent valve will damage it.**

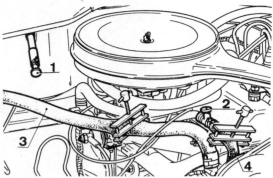

FIG 4:1 Filling the cooling system on 697 and 821 engines

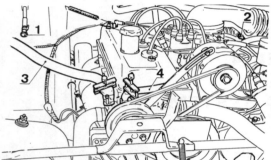

FIG 4:2 Filling the cooling system on 807 and 843 engines

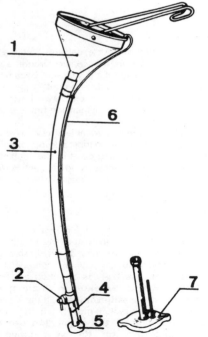

FIG 4:3 The special filling funnel Mot.431

Draining:

Remove the vent valve from the expansion bottle. If the coolant is being drained for any other reason than renewal of coolant, it should be drained into clean containers so that it can be used again after the system has been reassembled. Remove the drain plug from the radiator. At first the flow will be fairly slow but when it speeds up, showing that the expansion bottle is empty, remove the radiator filler cap. At the same time set the heater to hot (Red sector) and open the bleed screws on the heater and water pump as well as opening the drain on the engine. To empty the system completely, blow through the bleed screws with compressed air, but do not use pressures above 3 kg/sq cm (40 lb/sq in). The radiator drain plug or tap is located at the bottom lefthand corner of the radiator, the cylinder block drain plug is situated on the lefthand side below and to the left of the fuel pump. Alternatively, the system can be drained by disconnecting the bottom radiator hose.

Flushing:

The system can be flushed through using clean water from a hose pipe, not forgetting to wash out the expansion bottle. Water should be run through until it comes out clear through the drains. In extreme cases it may be necessary to remove the radiator and invert it so that it can be flushed through in a reverse direction.

The best method is to use a desludging agent, No. 806.542. Mix up the agent with slightly less water than the cooling system holds and then fill and bleed the system with the mixture, topping-up with further water if required. Mask off the bottom part of the radiator with a strip of cardboard measuring 200 mm ($7\frac{7}{8}$ inch) and then run the engine for 10 minutes at a speed of 2000 rev/min to heat it up quickly. Top up the expansion bottle if required. The engine can be run for two hours with the car stationary or the car can be driven for 200 kilometres (120 miles). Leave the heater on hot so that it is also flushed. At the end of the time drain out the desludging mixture, preferably while it is still hot as dirt will be held in suspension. Flush the system and then fill it with clean water. Run the engine for 10 minutes at 2000 rev/min then drain, flush and fill again. Run the engine for a further 10 minutes at 2000 rev/min and drain out this water followed by a final flush through with clean water. Fill the system and bleed it using coolant.

Coolant:

Ready mixed coolant is available in 6 or 8 litre drums. Though antifreeze can be added to water to make the coolant, if it is bought ready mixed the water used will be perfectly pure and soft, ensuring that corrosion and scaling will be limited. The ready-mixed coolant protects the engine to temperatures down to —30°C.

If antifreeze and water is to be used the recommended antifreezes are Glaceol or Sexprot. Glaceol is obtainable in 1 or $2\frac{1}{2}$ litre tins but Sexprot is only obtainable in bulk. 40 per cent of antifreeze will prevent damage down to a temperature of —35°C, though below —27°C the coolant will be pasty. 50 per cent of antifreeze will protect the system down to —45°C.

Never use water alone as the antifreeze raises the boiling point of the coolant and also contains the essential corrosion inhibitors.

Filling:

On later models the cooling system can be filled using two clamps Mot.453. Fill the expansion bottle, using coolant, so that it is 30 mm ($1\frac{3}{16}$ inch) above the maximum mark and then refit the valve and cap. Open the bleed screws 1 and 2 shown in **FIGS 4:1** and **4:2**. Fill the system through the radiator until the radiator is full. Clamp the hoses 3 and 4 as closely as possible to the water pump and start the engine. Run the engine at a fast-idle, approximately 1500 rev/min, and keep on filling through the radiator until only coolant and not a trace of air comes out of the bleed screws. Close the bleed screws as soon as pure coolant is coming out. Remove the two clamps from the hoses, top up the radiator and refit the cap. Run the engine until the cooling fan starts and then switch off the engine and leave it to cool. Check the level in the expansion bottle and top up if required.

On models where the hoses cannot be clamped (early 1150 models) the system must be filled from a head of coolant. This method can be used on all models if desired. A special filling funnel (shown in **FIG 4:3**) is required. A rigid tube 4 and cap fit into the filler orifice of the radiator and the flow can be controlled by the tap 2. The funnel 1 is connected to tap by a length of clear hose 3 and a narrow-bore tube 6 is fitted to bleed out air. Fit the attachment into the radiator and hang the funnel up under the bonnet. Unscrew the bleed screws and fit hoses Mot.413 in their place and loop the other ends of the hoses into the funnel, as shown in **FIG 4:4**. On some models with a bleed screw on the carburetter a needle valve is fitted in place of the screw. The hose can be fitted directly to the needle valve and the valve then opened by unscrewing it partially. Fill the system through the funnel and start the engine. Keep adding coolant to the funnel as the level drops and the system fills, and do not allow the funnel to empty otherwise air will be drawn into the system. When the fan starts to run lift the hoses out of the funnel and allow them to run into a clean container on the ground level. As the level in the funnel falls, shut the tap on the funnel and clip the hoses to prevent coolant from flowing out or in. Pour the coolant in the container back into the funnel and open the tap and clips again. When no more air comes out of the hoses lift them back into the funnel again and allow them to flow for a few minutes. Allow the engine to cool. Close the tap on the funnel and disconnect the hoses. Refit the bleed screws but do not tighten them. Open the tap on the funnel and allow coolant to flow out from the bleed screws to remove any air that might have been drawn in while disconnecting the hoses. Close the bleed screws fully, close the tap on the funnel, remove it, and refit the radiator cap. Fill the expansion bottle to the correct level with coolant.

On all models leave the heater controls on hot when refilling the cooling system.

4:3 The cooling fan

The cooling fan attachments are shown in **FIG 4:5**. A Mosta switch is fitted to the radiator and when the coolant reaches a temperature of 92 ± 1.5°C the switch closes, operating the relay fitted behind the battery and switching on the cooling fan. When the coolant temperature has dropped to 82 ± 1.5°C the contacts open and the fan is switched off. From 1976 the fan motor is operated directly

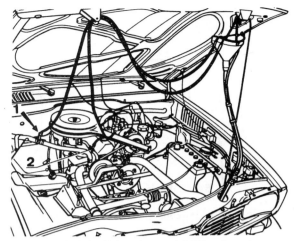

FIG 4:4 Using the special filling funnel

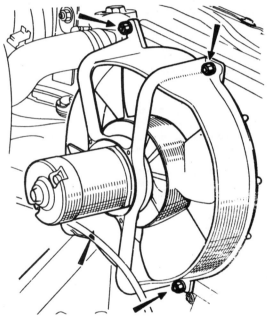

FIG 4:5 The cooling fan attachments

from the thermoswitch on the radiator and the relay is omitted.

Testing the Mosta switch:

The method is shown in **FIG 4:6**. Heat the water and check that the bulb lights up at an indicated temperature of 92 ± 1.5°C, showing that the switch contacts have closed. Allow the water to cool and observe that the switch opens at a temperature of 82 ± 1.5°C.

The warning light switch and temperature bulb, on models fitted with a gauge, is tested in the same manner except that the actual gauge is used instead of the lamp when testing the temperature bulb.

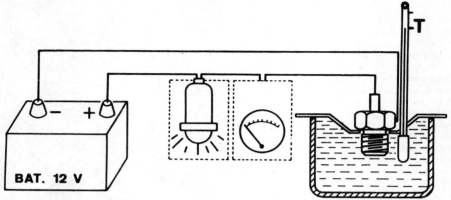

FIG 4:6   Testing the cooling switch. The gauge is fitted in place of the low-wattage bulb when testing the temperature bulb

Dismantling the cooling fan:

Before removing the unit disconnect the battery. Disconnect the leads and then take off the attachment nuts so that the unit can be removed.

The components of the motor are shown in **FIG 4:7**. General details of servicing electric motors are given in **Chapter 12**. It should be noted that the nut securing the actual fan is lefthand threaded. The brush leads are secured by soldering to the brush carrier.

4:4   The expansion bottle

The method of removing the expansion bottle, without having to drain the cooling system, is shown in **FIG 4:8**. Note the clamp on the hose to prevent the coolant syphoning out.

The bottle is refitted in the reverse order of removal. Tighten the attachment screw until it touches the spiral

spring and then back it off by one turn. Fill the bottle with coolant to the 'maximum' mark and then refit the valve with the seal between the valve and bottle.

The valve is only designed to pass air and if the system is over-filled so that coolant passes through the valve then it will be damaged and a new valve must be fitted in its place.

4:5   The radiator and hoses

The radiator attachments are shown in **FIG 4:9**.

Removal:

Drain the cooling system and disconnect the battery. Disconnect the electrical leads for the fan motor at the relay and the leads at the switch on the radiator. Disconnect the water hoses, remove the two attachment bolts and lift out the radiator.

The radiator is refitted in the reverse order of removal.

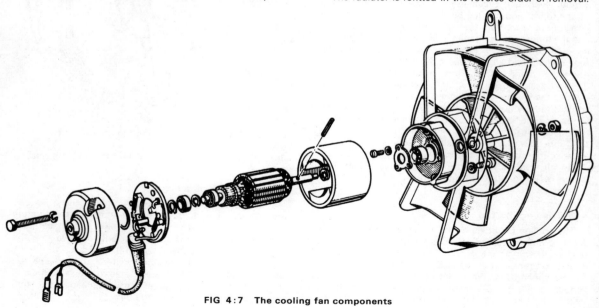

FIG 4:7   The cooling fan components

Maintenance:

At regular intervals check the water hoses and their clips. Make sure that the clips are tight enough to prevent leaks without cutting into the material of the hose. If the hoses are softening, hardening, perishing or cracking they should be renewed as soon as possible. If a hose bursts in use all the coolant will be lost, possibly causing damage to the engine by overheating, and difficulty will be found in filling the system after repairs without the tools being at hand.

If the radiator fins become dirty with mud or insects use an airline or hose pipe to wash out the dirt from the rear of the radiator. In bad cases it will be necessary to remove the radiator so that it can be soaked and scrubbed in a hot weak detergent solution.

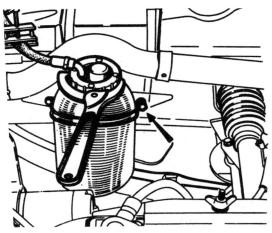

FIG 4 : 8   Removing the expansion bottle

4 : 6 The drive belts

Two drive belts are used to drive the accessories. One belt operates between the camshaft pulley and the smaller pulley on the water pump. The other drive belt then operates between the larger pulley on the water pump and the alternator pulley. Correct tension is essential on both drive belts as if a belt is slack the drive will slip and if it is too tight the bearings will be damaged.

The drive belts can be adjusted individually. The best method of checking the tension is to use the special gauge Ele.346. The tool is fitted with its arm along the drive belt and over the pulleys. When the end is pressed down so that the plunger is level, the internal spring applies a pressure of 6 lb 3 oz (2.8 kg) to the centre of the drive belt run and the deflection can be read off on the scale of the tool. If the tool is not available apply moderate thumb pressure to the centre of the run and note the deflection. Applying a load of 6 lb 3 oz (2.8 kg) the belt tension is correct if the following deflections are obtained.

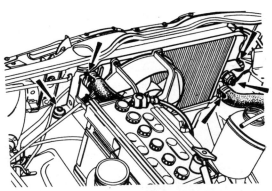

FIG 4 : 9   The radiator attachments

Alternator

New belt	3.5 to 4.5 mm
Used belt	5 to 6 mm

Water pump

New belt	2.5 to 4 mm
Used belt	3 to 5 mm

Adjustment:

The pulley on the camshaft is split into two flanges held together by nuts. Shims are fitted between the flanges to alter the depth to which the drive belt sinks. Spare shims are kept under the nuts on the outside flange and adjustment is by transferring shims. The more shims that are fitted between the flanges the slacker the belt will be. When tightening the nuts on the pulley flanges tighten them evenly and progressively while turning the engine over. On manual transmission models turn the engine by jacking up one front wheel and turning it with gear engaged. On automatic models remove the sparking plug and turn the engine using the camshaft pulley.

The points for adjusting the alternator belt are shown in **FIG 4 : 10**. Slacken both bolts **A** and **B** so that the alternator can be pulled away from the engine until the tension is correct, and then retighten the bolts.

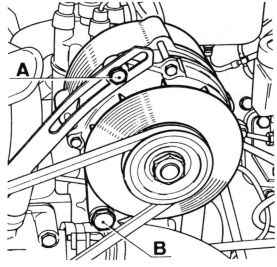

FIG 4 : 10   The alternator adjustment points

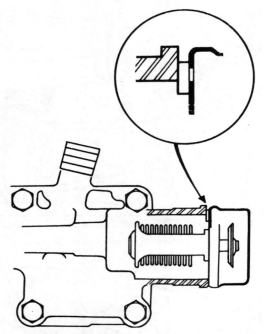

FIG 4:11   The thermostat fitted correctly

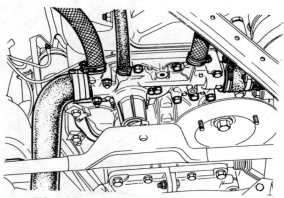

FIG 4:12   The water pump attachments

Removal:

Take off the nuts and outer flange of the camshaft pulley and remove the belt that drives the water pump. Slacken the attachment bolts of the alternator and press it towards the engine. If the belt is still not slack enough to remove from the pulleys remove the bolts that secure the alternator. **Do not lever the belt off with a screwdriver as this will damage it.**

4:7 The water pump and thermostat

The thermostat is fitted into the water pump and held in place by the top radiator hose. The thermostat can be checked by suspending it in water and then heating the water. If the valve does not open or sticks in the open position a new thermostat must be fitted as the unit cannot be repaired.

When refitting the thermostat make sure that the bleed hole is fitted uppermost, as shown in **FIG 4:11**.

The 843 engine (R.1156) is fitted with a modified water pump which can only use a wax type thermostat, do not use the spirit type.

The water pump:

The unit cannot be repaired and if it is defective it must be renewed.

Disconnect the battery, drain the cooling system and remove the spare wheel. Remove both drive belts as described in the previous section. Remove the bolt that secures the alternator stay bracket to the pump. The water pump attachments are shown in **FIG 4:12**. Disconnect the hoses and remove the bolts that secure the pump. Unstick the pump with a plastic mallet so that it and the plate can be removed.

The water pump is refitted in the reverse order of removal. Make sure that the joint faces are clean and use a new gasket. The gasket is fitted dry.

4:8 Fault diagnosis

(a) Internal water leakage

1 Loose cylinder head bolts
2 Defective cylinder head gasket
3 Cracked or distorted cylinder head
4 Defective liner seals

(b) Poor circulation

1 Perished or collapsed water hoses
2 Defective thermostat
3 Radiator or engine water passages blocked

(c) Corrosion

1 Impurities in the water
2 Infrequent draining and flushing

(d) Overheating

1 Check (b)
2 Lack of coolant
3 Defective water pump
4 Radiator cooling fins blocked with dirt
5 Defective cooling fan or fan circuit
6 Low oil level in the engine
7 Sludge in the crankcase
8 Retarded ignition
9 Mixture too weak
10 Tight engine
11 Choked exhaust
12 Binding brakes
13 Slipping clutch

CHAPTER 5

THE CLUTCH

5:1 Description
5:2 Maintenance
5:3 The clutch linkage

5:4 The release bearing
5:5 Servicing the clutch
5:6 Fault diagnosis

5:1 Description

A single dry-plate diaphragm-spring clutch is fitted to transmit the drive between the engine and gearbox. A sectioned view of the early clutch is shown in **FIG 5:1**. The later clutch has a modified release bearing. The clutch is operated by a cable linkage from the clutch pedal.

The cover assembly is bolted to the engine flywheel and rotates with it. The assembly consists of the actual cover, the diaphragm spring, and the pressure plate, and they are linked so that they all revolve together. The driven plate assembly is splined to the input shaft of the gearbox so that they revolve together. The diaphragm in the cover acts between the cover and pressure plate to force the pressure plate forwards so that the driven plate is gripped between it and the flywheel. The driven plate is gripped by its friction linings and the drive is transmitted from the flywheel to the gearbox input shaft.

The release lever is operated by the cable from the clutch pedal. When the pedal is operated the lever moves the release bearing towards the flywheel. The release bearing presses against the fingers of the diaphragm spring. This action pivots the spring so that the outer end releases its pressure and then draws the pressure plate back slightly. The driven plate and gearbox shaft are then free

to revolve independently or even come to a halt with the engine running.

When the pedal is released the pressure on the driven plate builds up gradually so that at first the linings slip between the pressure surfaces and the drive is gradually taken up. Springs on the hub of the driven plate also damp the shock of take-up.

The release bearing fitted to all R.1150 models and early R.1151 and R.1152 models acted in conjunction with a thrust ring to operate the diaphragm spring, on later models the release bearing acts directly on the spring.

5:2 Maintenance

At regular intervals check the clutch adjustment. The release bearing must not be in constant contact with the diaphragm spring otherwise there will be excessive wear. The clearance is checked at the end of the release lever where the cable attaches, shown in **FIG 5:2**. The end of the lever should have a free movement of 2 to 3 mm ($\frac{5}{64}$ to $\frac{1}{8}$ inch) before the release bearing is felt to make contact. To adjust the clearance slacken the locknut 1 and then screw the nut 2 in or out until the clearance is correct. Retighten the locknut 1.

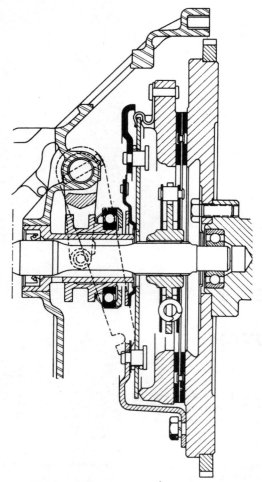

FIG 5:1 Sectioned view of the clutch

On special models fitted with an engine undertray the adjustment can be carried out without removing the tray but special tools will be required. The nut 2 is held with a long open-ended spanner EMB.389 while the nut 1 is slackened with the universal spanner EMB.388, as shown in **FIG 5:3**. Once the nuts are slack the universal spanner is fitted over both of them and the adjustment set by rotating both nuts. When the adjustment is correct hold the nut 2 with the open-ended spanner and tighten the locknut 1 with the universal spanner.

5:3 The clutch linkage

Removal:

The clutch pedal can be removed separately leaving the cable in place, but the complete removal is given.

1 Disconnect the cable from the end of the release lever, by undoing both nuts, and then remove the cable stop fixing shown in **FIG 5:4**. Push the cable out through the stop.

2 Remove the glove compartment and free the return spring 1 from the pedal, shown in **FIG 5:5**. Take off the retaining clip shown in the figure and free the pedal from its shaft and the cable.

3 Remove the cable from the car.

Reassembly:

The parts are refitted in the reverse order of removal. The cable stop must be attached to the clutch housing before the cable is attached to the pedal. Seal the point where the cable passes through the scuttle. The pedal sleeve should be lubricated with Molykote BR.2 grease before reassembly. It should be noted that the type of return spring has been altered and the spring shown at 2 in **FIG 5:6** is the only one available as a spare.

5:4 The release bearing

Early type:

The assembly is fitted into the clutch housing and the gearbox must be removed from the car before the parts are accessible.

The attachments and method of removing the pins are shown in **FIG 5:7**. Withdraw the solid pins **A** using special extractor No. Emb.322 and use the extractor Emb.384 for the grooved pins **B**. Once the pins are out the fork can be pivoted and the release bearing removed.

Renew the release bearing if it runs noisily or is worn. The parts are refitted in the reverse order of removal. Lubricate the guide with Molykote BR.2 and make sure that the protrusion of the pin at **D** is 1 mm ($\frac{1}{32}$ inch).

On early models only check that there is an 8 mm (.315 inch) hole in the bottom of the guide, shown arrowed in **FIG 5:8**. If the hole is not present take the guide to an agent for modification. The hole is drilled using a 7 mm drill and the tool No. Emb.387 as a guide.

Later type:

Proceed in a similar manner until the release bearing is accessible, then unhook the retaining spring (see **FIG 5:9**) and remove the release bearing.

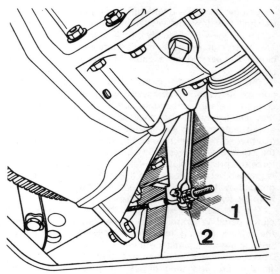

FIG 5:2 Adjusting the clutch cable

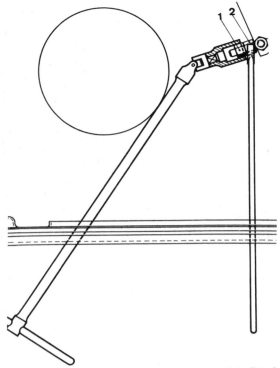

FIG 5:3 Adjusting the clutch cable on models fitted with engine undertray

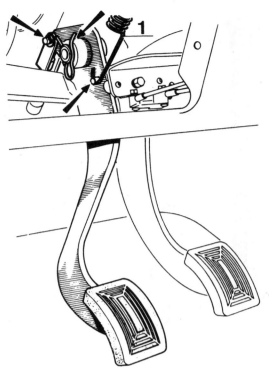

FIG 5:5 Removing the clutch pedal

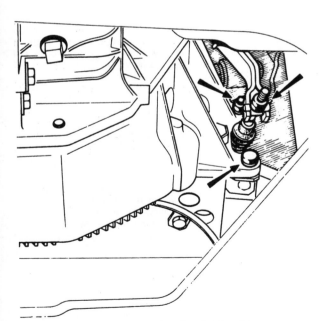

FIG 5:4 Disconnecting the clutch cable

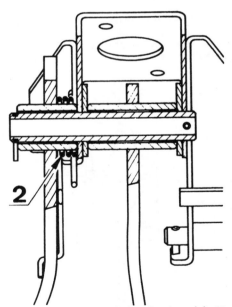

FIG 5:6 Sectioned view of the clutch pedal attachment showing the later type of spring

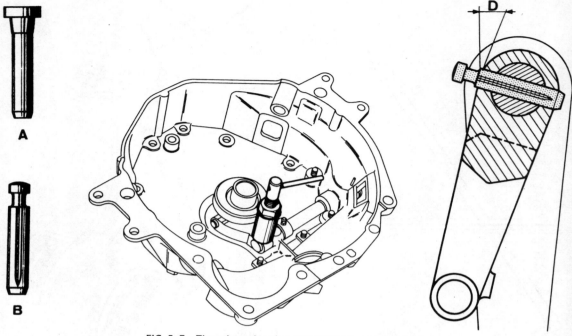

FIG 5:7   The release bearing attachments, early type

If the fork or spring requires renewal proceed in a similar manner to the early type using tool Emb.384 to withdraw the fork pins.

When refitting the pins observe the same dimensions as on the earlier type.

5:5 Servicing the clutch

The removal and refitting of the clutch to the flywheel has been dealt with in **Chapter 1, Section 1:6**. Note that the attachment bolts must be tightened and slackened

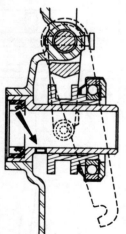

FIG 5:8   Hole in the bottom of the guide on early models

progressively and that a centralizing mandrel must be used to centralize the driven plate when the parts are being refitted. The spigot bearing in the crankshaft should be checked whenever the clutch is removed.

Cover assembly:

The assembly cannot be dismantled and it must be renewed if it is defective. **Do not wash the unit in solvent** but if it is very oily wipe the pressure plate and cover surface with a rag moistened with fuel. Use an air-line and brush to remove loose dirt and dust.

Check the pressure plate surface for wear, scoring or deep burn marks. Check the cover and straps for cracking or distortion, particularly around the attachment holes.

Check the friction surface of the flywheel for scoring or other signs of damage. Unless such are very slight, the flywheel must be renewed as no reconditioning is possible.

Driven plate:

The driven plate must be renewed if the linings are worn nearly down to the rivets or if they are contaminated.

Check the driven plate for mechanical damage such as loose rivets, fractured or loose damper springs or broken linings. Slide the hub back onto the gearbox input shaft and check that it slides freely without excessive rotational play.

When the linings are working at their maximum efficiency they will have a polished finish through which the grain of the friction material is clearly visible. Small amounts of oil will leave dark smears while larger amounts will leave a dark polished glaze. Large amounts of oil will be obvious from the oil-soaked appearance of the linings and the free oil in the clutch housing. Provided that the grain of the friction material is still visible the linings are serviceable but if they have been contaminated so that the grain is hidden then a new driven plate must be fitted. The owner should not attempt to rivet new linings to the driven plate but should use factory reconditioned units.

Oil seal:

Remove the gearbox and separate the clutch housing from the gearbox (see **Chapter 6**).

Prise out the oil seal from the clutch housing.

Fit the new seal with the lip of the seal facing the gearbox.

Refit the clutch housing to the gearbox taking care not to damage the lip of the seal with the splines of the gearbox shaft, covering the splines with adhesive tape would be a suitable precaution (see **FIG 5:10**).

5:6 Fault diagnosis

(a) Drag or spin

1 Oil or grease on driven plate linings
2 Incorrectly adjusted cable
3 Binding spigot bearing in crankshaft
4 Distorted driven plate
5 Warped or damaged pressure plate

(b) Fierceness or snatch

1 Check (a)
2 Excessively worn clutch linings
3 Worn or loose driven plate hub

(c) Slip

1 Check 1 and 2 in (a) and 2 in (b)
2 Weak diaphragm spring
3 Sticking cable

(d) Judder

1 Check (a)
2 Pressure plate not parallel with flywheel face
3 Contact area of linings not evenly distributed
4 Buckled driven plate
5 Faulty or loose engine mountings
6 Defective front suspension or drive shafts

(e) Rattles

1 Broken damper spring in driven plate
2 Worn release mechanism

(f) Tick or knock

1 Worn spigot bearing in crankshaft
2 Badly worn splines on input shaft or hub
3 Loose flywheel

FIG 5:9 Retaining spring shown arrowed on later release bearings

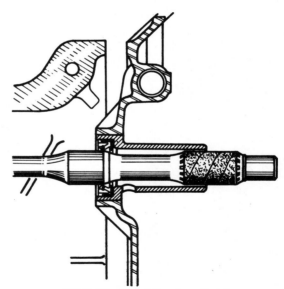

FIG 5:10   Clutch housing oil seal

NOTES

CHAPTER 6

THE TRANSMISSION

6:1 Description
6:2 Removing the transmission unit
6:3 The gearshift mechanism

6:4 Dismantling the transmission unit
6:5 Gearlever adjustment—16TX
6:6 Fault diagnosis

6:1 Description

The combined gearbox and differential assembly is mounted in front of the engine. On 16TX models there are five forward speeds and a reverse, other models have only four forward speeds. **FIG 6:1** gives a sectioned view of the more common four speed box.

An input shaft connects the hub of the clutch driven plate to the primary shaft in the gearbox. This is carried in two roller bearings and has five gears integral with it, plus the fifth gear wheel and synchronizer free on an extension in the case of the TX. The secondary shaft has four gears revolving freely about it and meshing with the gears on the primary shaft, plus an extension with a fixed gear for the fifth speed when fitted.

A Renault synchromesh unit is used for first and second gears and a Borg-Warner for third, fourth and fifth when applicable. The outer sleeve of the third and fourth synchronizer is slid into mesh with an idler gear on a separate shaft for selecting reverse gear. The description which follows is of the four speed box since this is the most common, the five speed unit being similar but having the extra gears added as an extension.

Four main castings are used to contain the parts. A clutch housing surrounds the clutch at the rear end of the unit. At the front end is the casting which takes in the selector as well as having the mounting attached to it. The main parts are enclosed in two castings which join

longitudinally. Separation of these two main castings exposes all the internal parts of the gearbox and differential.

The gearbox is not suitable for the average owner to work on as the two main castings have to be parted to gain access and on reassembly the differential must be correctly set up using special tools. Some parts of the gearbox are heated before reassembling the parts so gearbox reassembly is not straightforward. Probably the best solution for the average owner is to remove the transmission unit from the car and then arrange for an agent to carry out dismantling and reassembly.

The gearbox selector mechanism is shown in **FIG 6:2**. Each selector shaft is held in place by a detent ball and spring acting in slots in the shaft. In addition the disc 1 locks the other two shafts so that they cannot move when the third shaft is moved into a select position.

Lubrication:

The oil should be drained out and the gearbox refilled with 1.64 litres (2.9 pints) of fresh SAE 80 EP oil at intervals of 15,000 km (9000 miles) or every 12 months, whichever is first.

The gearbox is filled to the bottom of the hole for the combined level and filler plug **A**, shown in **FIG 6:3**, with EP.80 oil. A drain plug **B** is fitted under the gearbox. When draining the unit it is best to do so when it is hot after a run as the oil will flow faster.

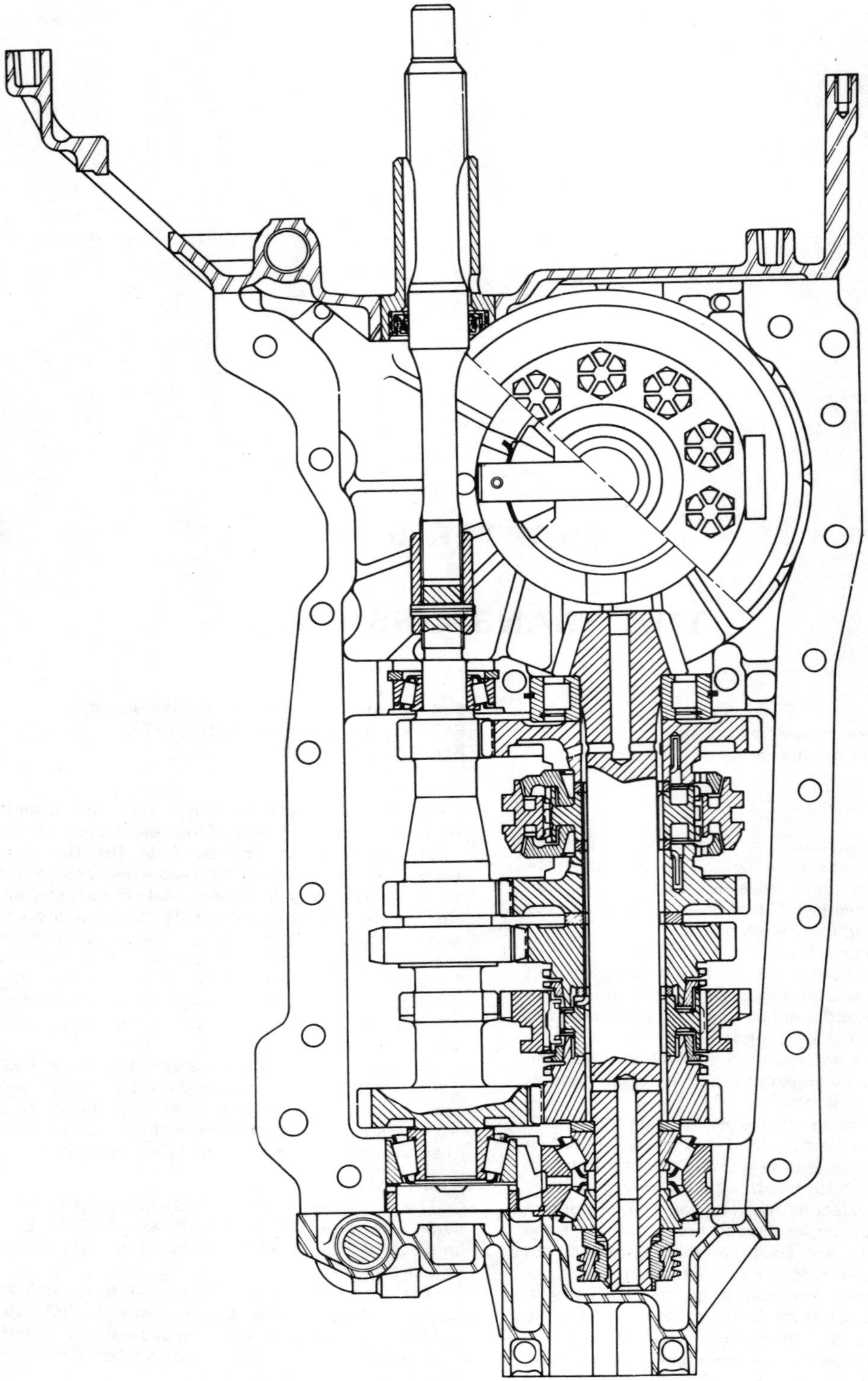

FIG 6:1 Sectioned view of the transmission unit

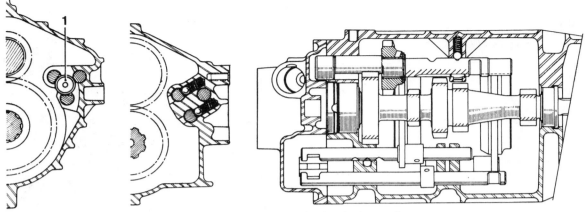

FIG 6:2 The selector mechanism in the gearbox

6:2 Removing the transmission unit

The transmission unit can be removed leaving the engine still fitted to the car.

1 Remove the spare wheel, and spare wheel cross-member if fitted. Disconnect the battery and disconnect the input cable from its clamp on the steering column. On the R.1152 models only, remove the expansion bottle and take out the two bolts that secure the radiator in place (see **Chapter 4**) and then, without disconnecting the water hoses, swing the radiator up and over so that it lies on top of the engine. Still only on the R.1152 models disconnect the tachometer cable from the centrifugal switch and then free the switch by taking out its attachment bolt. On all other models remove the cooling fan. Drain the transmission unit through the drain plug.

2 Remove the steering rack unit as described in **Chapter 10**.

3 Disconnect the reverse light switch wires and if need be remove the switch. Disconnect the speedometer drive cable and the selector linkage, and remove the two bolts securing the control to the side of the gearbox, shown in **FIG 6:4**. Lay the selector rods and linkage safely out of the way.

4 Unscrew the two nuts on either side of the front mounting and remove the lockwashers. Support the transmission with a jack and pad of wood underneath it and take out the two bolts that secure the front mounting to the front housing so that the mounting and its bracket can be removed.

5 Drift out the rollpins that secure the drive shafts to the sunwheels in the transmission. Use loops of soft wire or special clips to hold the inboard joints together so that they do not fall apart. Disconnect the clutch operating cable from the transmission. Place a jack and pads of wood between the gearbox and lefthand sidemember. Extend the jack so that the gearbox is pushed over to the right and the lefthand drive shaft can be disconnected. Remove the jack and fit it between the gearbox and righthand sidemember so that the righthand drive shaft can be disconnected in a similar manner. When the drive shafts have been

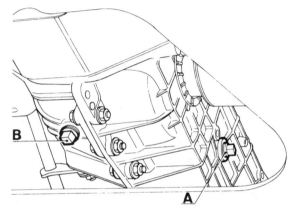

FIG 6:3 The drain and filling plugs

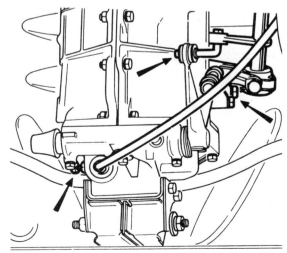

FIG 6:4 Disconnecting the selector linkage

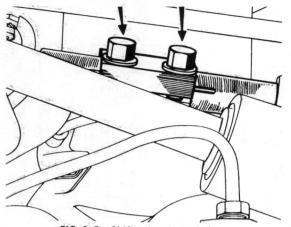

FIG 6:5   Shift tube clamp bolts

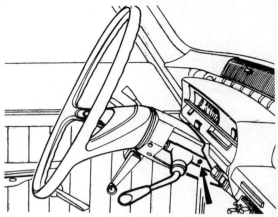

FIG 6:8   Setting the gearlever on all models from 1968 onwards

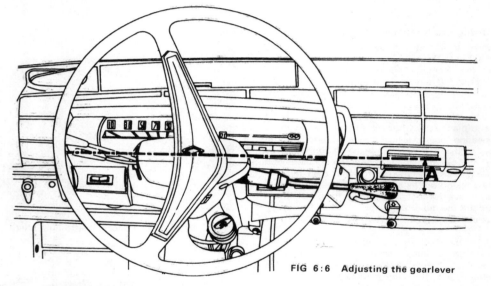

FIG 6:6   Adjusting the gearlever

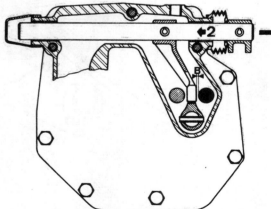

FIG 6:7   Setting the pre 1968 gearbox selector shaft

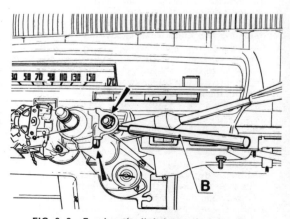

FIG 6:9   Freeing the lighting switch bracket

disconnected use this second jack to support the
engine from underneath to prevent it pivoting about
on its mountings.

6 Remove the bolts that secure the clutch housing to
the engine and also remove the bolts that secure the
starter motor in place. Withdraw the starter motor as
far as possible. Support the transmission and draw it
forwards until the input shaft is well clear of the clutch
and then raise the front end of the transmission and
lift it out, taking care not to damage the radiator. **The
weight of the transmission must not be
allowed to hang on the input shaft otherwise
the clutch will be damaged.**

Refitting:

The transmission is refitted in the reverse order of
removal.

It should be noted that a modified clutch housing is
fitted to later models as standard. The modified housing
is the only one available as a spare and it can be fitted to
earlier engines, provided that 80 mm long starter mounting
bolts are fitted as well as a modified clutch shield.

The clutch input shaft and drive shaft splines should be
lightly greased before reassembly. The ends of the rollpins
for the drive shafts should be sealed with Rhodorsil after
reassembly. Tabwashers may have been used to lock the
starter motor bolts but these should be discarded and
lockwashers used instead.

6:3 The gearshift mechanism

On all models a steering column mounted gearlever is
fitted. The linkage fitted to pre 1968 models is slightly
different from the 1968 onwards models.

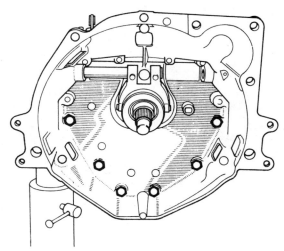

FIG 6:11   The clutch housing internal attachment bolts

Adjusting gearlever:

On the pre 1968 models engage 2nd gear but on all
later models engage top gear. Slacken the clamp bolts on
the shift tube, shown in **FIG 6:5**. Operate the gearlever
several times to free the linkage but then make sure that
the selector lever on the gearbox is in the correct position.

On the pre 1968 models pull the gearlever back so as to
bring the first/second-speed position up against the
reverse stop and then move the lever vertically so that the

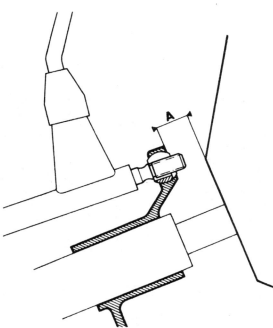

**FIG 6:10   The correct positioning of the lighting switch
bracket**

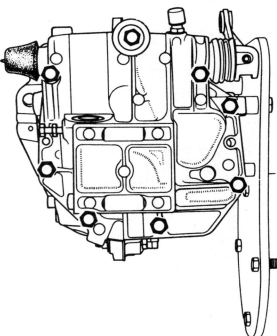

FIG 6:12   The front housing attachments

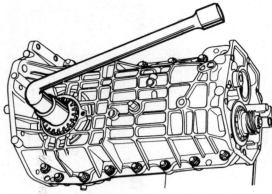

FIG 6:13 Freeing the differential nuts

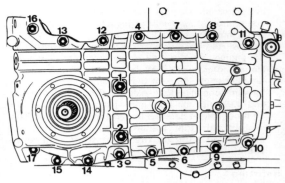

FIG 6:14 The split casing attachment bolts, showing the sequence for tightening

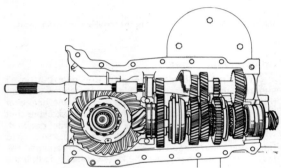

FIG 6:15 The transmission unit with a split casing removed

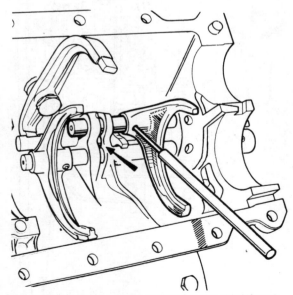

FIG 6:16 Driving out the rollpin for the third/fourth selector fork

dimension **A** shown in **FIG 6:6** is correct at 30 ± 10 mm ($1\frac{3}{16} \pm \frac{25}{64}$ inch). On righthand drive models the correct setting is when **A** is 64 mm ($2\frac{17}{32}$ inch). Hold the lever in this position. Pull the shift fork control lever shaft on the gearbox in the opposite direction to arrow 2 and then move it back in the direction of the arrow so that the clearance at **B** is .5 to 1 mm ($\frac{1}{32}$ to $\frac{3}{64}$ inch), as shown in **FIG 6:7**. Hold the shaft in this position and tighten the clamp bolts shown in **FIG 6:5**.

On all later models set the lever so that the dimension **A** shown in **FIG 6:6** is correct at 46 ± 10 mm ($1\frac{13}{16} \pm \frac{25}{64}$ inch). Move the lever in line with the column until the hole in the tube is opposite to the rollpin, as shown in **FIG 6:8**, and with the gearbox selector correctly in position tighten the clamp bolts.

On all models check that the gears engage smoothly and accurately.

Removal:

Remove the steering wheel, after taking out the wheel embellisher and the nut that secures the wheel to the inner column. Disconnect the battery.

Mark the position of the lighting switch in relation to the steering column and remove the bracket bolt. Fit a drift **B** into the hole in the rod and use this to prevent the rod from turning, as shown in **FIG 6:9**. Remove the (arrowed) ball joint locknut and then use a suitable socket spanner to unscrew the ball joint, gradually drawing back the lighting switch at the same time. Unlock and unscrew the clamp screws holding the ends of the gear control tube. Lift the lighting switch off the end of the control rod and pivot it around the column so that it is out of the way. Lay the tube/lever assembly to one side and free it from the clamp.

Disconnect the control mechanism from the gearbox and remove it. The tube/lever assembly cannot be repaired if it is defective, so a new assembly must be fitted. The rubber cover and rollpins can be renewed on the tube/lever assembly. Different washers are available to take out any end play in the parts of the control at the gearbox end.

The parts are refitted in the reverse order of removal. The ball joint should be lubricated with Molykote BR.2 grease and tightened until it moves freely without end

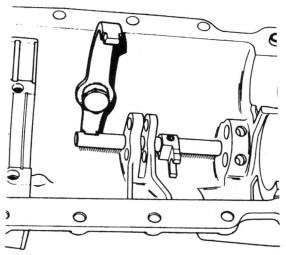

FIG 6:17 The reverse gear swivel lever and its pivot

FIG 6:18 Removing the speedometer worm drive gear

play. If the position for the light switch bracket is lost it should be fitted so that the dimension **A** between the ball joint bracket and underside of the steering wheel, shown in **FIG 6:10**, is correct at 25 mm ($\frac{63}{64}$ inch). Adjust the setting after the parts have been refitted.

6:4 Dismantling the transmission unit

Because of the complexity of the unit and the fact that the differential unit must be removed when dismantling the unit the average owner should not attempt to carry out work on the internals of the unit. The general procedure is given in this section as if nothing else it will give a better understanding of the gearbox.

1 Remove the gearbox from the car. A special stand B.Vi.240 is made for supporting the unit and this is shown in some of the figures. If the special stand is not available then lay the unit onto a clean bench.

2 Remove the clutch housing after taking out the bolts shown in **FIG 6:11**. If necessary remove the reverse light switch and then take off the front housing by removing the bolts shown in **FIG 6:12**.

3 Free the lockwashers and remove the differential adjusting nuts as shown in **FIG 6:13**.

4 Slacken and remove the bolts that secure the two halves of the casting together. The numbered sequence shown in **FIG 6:14** is the order in which the bolts are tightened on reassembly. Separate the castings and the unit will then appear as shown in **FIG 6:15**. Lift out the secondary shaft assembly followed by the primary and input shaft assembly and finally the differential unit.

Selector mechanism:

Drive out the rollpin that secures the fork to the third/fourth selector shaft, as shown in **FIG 6:16**. Withdraw the shaft, collecting the detent ball and spring as well as taking the interlock disc out from between the shafts.

Push the first/second selector into the first-speed position and push the reverse selector as far as possible on the control side. Drive out the rollpin and remove the first/second selector shaft in a similar manner to the third/fourth shaft.

Unscrew the pivot for the swivel lever and remove the pivot pin and lever shown in **FIG 6:17**. Turn the shaft slightly and drive out the rollpin that secures the fork so that the shaft can be withdrawn, collecting the detent spring, ball and fork.

Remove the circlip that secures the reverse gearwheel and then take out the shaft, gearwheel, friction washer and guide, collecting the retaining ball and spring.

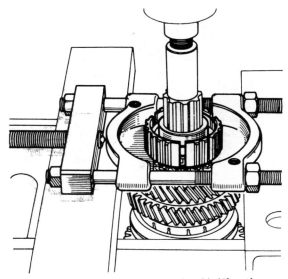

FIG 6:19 Removing the hub for the third/fourth synchromesh hub

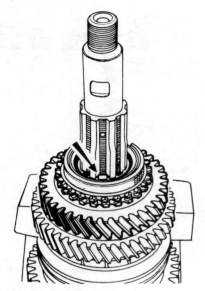

FIG 6:20 The third-speed stopwasher key

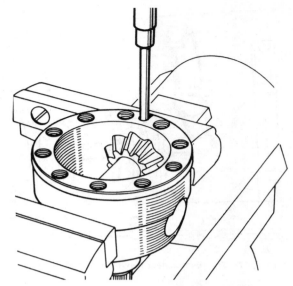

FIG 6:22 Driving out the rollpins for the differential

Primary shaft assembly:

Drive out the rollpin and separate the input shaft from the primary shaft. If required remove the inner races of the bearings with a suitable extractor.

Secondary shaft assembly:

Grip the first-speed gear in the padded jaws of a vice and move the synchromesh unit into the first-speed position. Unlock and unscrew the speedometer worm drive gear, as shown in **FIG 6:18**. Lift off the tapered

bearing. Lift off the double-tapered bearings, the pinion protrusion adjustment washer, and the fourth-speed gear with its baulk ring. Mark the position of the sliding gear in relation to the synchromesh hub and slide off third/ fourth synchromesh, collecting the keys.

Remove the inner hub of the synchromesh unit using the special tool No. T.Ar.65 as a support, as shown in **FIG 6:19**, and a press to remove the hub.

Remove the key arrowed in **FIG 6:20** and then take off the stopwasher and third-speed gear with its baulk ring.

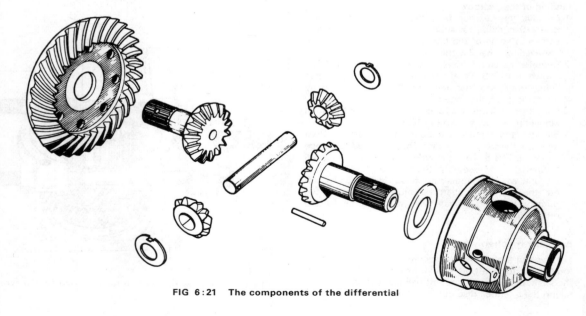

FIG 6:21 The components of the differential

Remove the next stopwasher and second-speed gear with its baulk ring. Mark the position of the first/second synchromesh sleeve in relation to its hub and then slide off the sleeve and the stopwasher.

Withdraw the hub for the synchromesh unit using a press and the special tool in the same manner as removing the first/second synchromesh hub. Slide off the first-speed baulk ring, stopwasher and gear.

It should be noted that on the special reinforced crownwheel and pinion assemblies the inner track of the bearing is bonded to the shaft and cannot be removed. A clip should be fitted to the bearing to prevent the rollers from falling out.

The differential:

The differential components are shown in **FIG 6:21**. If the differential requires dismantling the bearing inner races must be pulled off with a suitable extractor. Take out the bolts that secure the crownwheel to the housing and remove it. Drive out the rollpins as shown in **FIG 6:22** and the internal gears can then be removed.

Reassembly:

Reassembling the unit is the reverse of the dismantling operations, provided that new parts do not have to be fitted. No instructions have been given in this section for removing the outer races or adjusting parts of the differential and if these are removed they must be set up correctly by experienced fitters. The pinion shaft protrusion must also be set up accurately by use of the protrusion shim.

Note that the hub of the first/second-speed synchromesh unit must be heated to a temperature of 250°C (482°F) in an oven before it is pressed back into place, and pressure must be kept on it until it has cooled.

If new parts are to be fitted the assembly should be carried out by an agent. The smooth and quiet operation of the complete unit depends on the accuracy of the settings.

6:5 Gearlever adjustment—16TX

If poor gear selection is due to faulty adjustment of the selector linkage, it should be corrected as follows:

First tighten up the swivel joint to eliminate any looseness and secure the locknut to a torque of 2 kg m.

Loosen the bolts securing the upper support bracket and move it as necessary to obtain the dimension **A** in **FIG 6:23**. This is measured between the selector shaft bearing and the hub of the steering wheel and must be 23 mm. Tighten the support bolts to 3 kg m.

With the lower coupling loosened, move the gearbox selector lever to the fourth gear position.

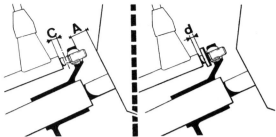

FIG 6:23 Adjusting the gear selector lever on 16TX models

Key to Fig 6:23   A = 23 mm   c = 5.5 mm   d = 3 mm

Move the hand selector lever to the fourth gear position and then move it vertically to obtain the dimension **A** in **FIG 6:6** = 50 ± 10 mm. At the same time move the lever axially to obtain dimension **C** in **FIG 6:23** = 5.5 mm. This latter dimension can most easily be obtained by inserting a 5 mm diameter rod into the hole in the selector shaft and moving the lever as necessary to obtain dimension **d** = 3 mm between the rod and the top of the tube. Secure the lower coupling by tightening the bolts to 2 kg m.

6:6 Fault diagnosis

(a) Noisy or whining operation

1 Insufficient or incorrect lubricant
2 Worn bearings
3 Worn or damaged gears
4 Incorrect end floats
5 Incorrect setting of differential bearings or pinion protrusion

(b) Jumping out of gear

1 Broken or weak detent spring on selector shafts
2 Detent notches in selector shaft excessively worn
3 Worn or defective synchromesh unit
4 Excessive end floats and clearances
5 Incorrectly adjusted gearshift mechanism

(c) Difficulty in engaging gear

1 Check 5 in (b)
2 Clutch defective or incorrectly adjusted
3 Spigot bearing in crackshaft seized
4 Damaged shift mechanism
5 Too thick a grade of lubricant

(d) Oil leaks

1 Defective oil seals
2 Nuts and bolts not correctly torque-loaded
3 Defective gaskets
4 Joint faces on castings warped, chipped or damaged
5 Stripped threads (Use Helicoil inserts to repair)

NOTES

CHAPTER 7

THE AUTOMATIC TRANSMISSION

7:1 Description

The Renault 16TA (R.1153), 16TSA (R.1154) and 16TX(A) (R.1156) are fitted with an automatic transmission in place of the manually-operated transmission fitted to the other models covered by this manual. A steering column mounted selector lever is fitted to give control and a degree of override on the unit, but the speeds are selected using an electronic and hydraulic control system. A computer unit accepts the signals from the various points and integrates them to operate two solenoid ball valves which control the hydraulic selection circuits. A torque converter is fitted in place of the conventional clutch and therefore no clutch pedal is required. The gearbox itself uses epicyclic gearing to give the ratios required. The final drive parts are incorporated with the unit and a sectioned view is shown in **FIG 7:1**. Clutches **E** and brake bands **F** are operated by the hydraulics to release or lock the various components to give the ratio required.

The unit is self-contained for purposes of lubrication, and the oil pump 5 driven by the input shaft provides the necessary pressure for circulation, lubrication and operation. The fluid used has the difficult task of providing lubrication for the gearbox and final drive, operating successfully as a hydraulic fluid both in the controls and fluid flywheel, and cooling the parts as well, all while operating at a high temperature. **The only fluids recommended to meet all these requirements are Elf Renault Matic or Mobil ATF.200.** Standard automatic transmission fluids will not be acceptable as they may not cope with the lubrication of the final drive. It is recommended that the transmission should be drained every 15,000 km (9000 miles) and refilled with the specified oil.

The unit is very complex and internal faults require that it is returned to the factory for repairs. The amount of work that can be carried out is limited and the owner should not attempt to carry out more than is given in this chapter.

Torque converter:

This is a sealed unit and cannot be repaired, so if it is defective a new unit must be fitted.

A sectioned view of the torque converter is shown in **FIG 7:2**. Oil is continuously circulated to ensure that the temperature is kept within its operating range. The oil flows in through the hollow drive shaft and then returns through the centre stator shaft. A calibrated plug, accessible from outside, controls the rate of flow.

The case 13 and impeller 12 are integral and are driven by the drive plate 14 on the engine crankshaft. The turbine 15 is integral with the input shaft to the epicyclic

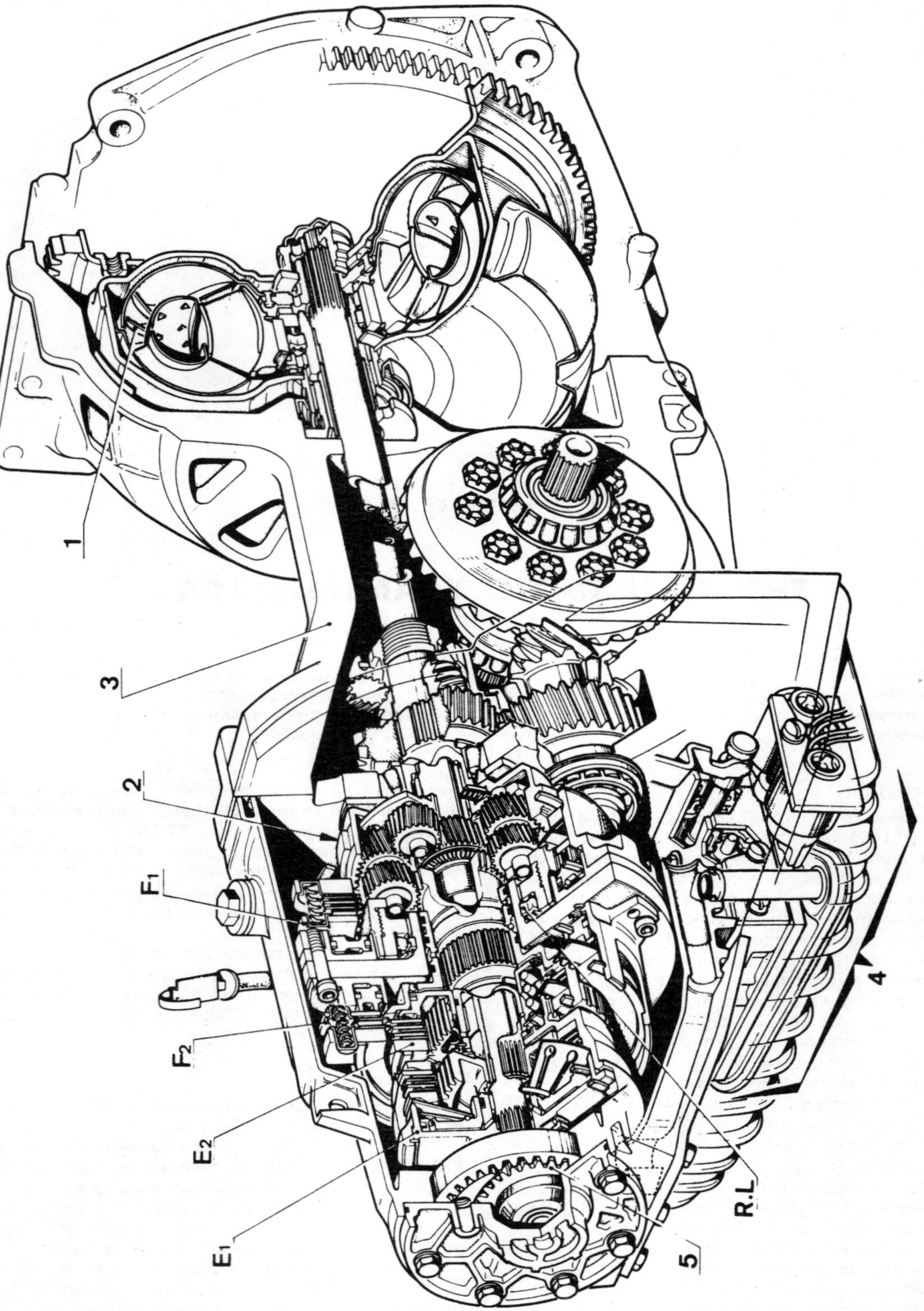

FIG 7:1 Sectioned view of the automatic transmission

gearbox. The space inside the cover is filled with oil. When the impeller is driven by the engine it drags the oil around with it, between the vanes of the impeller and turbine. As the impeller rotates the centrifugal force, being greater on the outer edge than the inner, sets up a circular flow in the plane of the vanes. The combination of these two makes the oil follow a spiral path around the torque converter and this flow transmits torque from the impeller to the turbine. The stator 16 guides the oil flow from the turbine so that it impinges on the vanes of the impeller so as to help the impeller to rotate. The effect of this is to give a torque multiplication factor of up to 2.3:1. As the impeller speeds up the oil flow impinges on the back of the stator vanes. The stator is fitted on a one-way clutch 17 so that the oil flow on the back of its vanes causes it to start rotating and prevents any power loss. There will always be a slight speed differential between impeller and turbine, because of friction losses, but as the impeller speeds up the torque multiplication ratio drops until it is approximately 1:1 and the torque converter acts as a fluid flywheel.

The torque converter therefore acts as an infinitely variable gearbox between the ratios 2.3:1 and 1:1 when the car starts from rest.

Epicyclic gearbox:

A schematic layout of the gearbox is shown in **FIG 7:3**. A complex epicyclic gear train is used and the figure shows the various drives through the gear train and the positions of the clutches, brakes and freewheel RL for the various selections.

Electrical control system:

The parts are shown in **FIG 7:4**. The solenoid ball valves El.1 and El.2 guide the hydraulic selection valve into its required position. When the solenoid is energized the ball and passage is held closed so that oil cannot flow. The ball valves are controlled by the computer **C** and the inputs to the computer are shown in the figure. The governor **G** is a low-wattage alternator. The rotor is made up of a permanent magnet, with three pairs of poles, and it is driven directly from the output shaft so that its speed of rotation is proportional to the road speed of the car. The governor is designed to have a linear output so that the AC current which is produced is therefore also proportional to the road speed of the car. The current is produced in the stator windings. The stator also has three pairs of magnetic poles in it. One pair of poles is fixed but the other two pairs are movable and connected to the throttle by a cable. When the throttle is at idle the poles are in their normal position and at full throttle they are at their maximum offset. When the moving poles are offset the output is still linear but the maximum output is reduced. The dotted line in **FIG 7:5** represents the output at small throttle openings while the heavy line represents the output at full throttle openings. It can be seen that the engine must run to a higher speed at large throttle openings before the output signal reaches sufficient strength to make the computer shift speed.

A kick-down switch is also fitted and this only comes into operation when the acceleration pedal is floored. Within certain limits it automatically selects a lower gear for rapid acceleration.

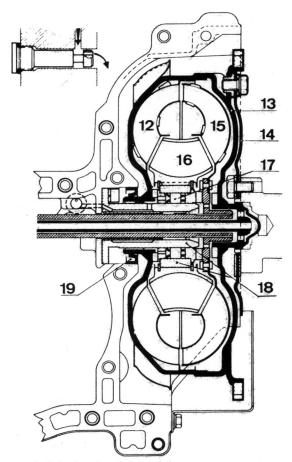

FIG 7:2 Sectioned view of the torque converter

7:2 Operation

Except for pushing around for short distances, such as in the garage, **the car must not be freewheeled without the engine running, nor can the engine be started by towing or pushing the car.** Normally the car should be towed, when this is necessary, with the front wheels raised off the road, but under exceptional circumstances the vehicle can be towed on its wheels if the following precautions are observed:

Add an extra 2 litres (3.5 pints) of fluid to the transmission.

Do not exceed a distance of 50 km (30 miles) or a speed of 30 km/hr (19 mile/hr).

The positions of the selector lever and their uses, are given in case the owner has any doubt about the limits that apply.

P position:

When this position is selected a latch is pushed into one of the recesses in the drive shaft. The latch prevents the drive shaft from rotating and therefore immobilises the car. This selection should be used in conjunction with the handbrake, otherwise difficulty may be found in releasing

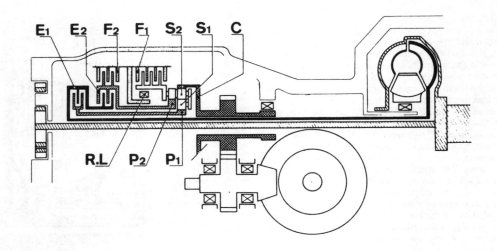

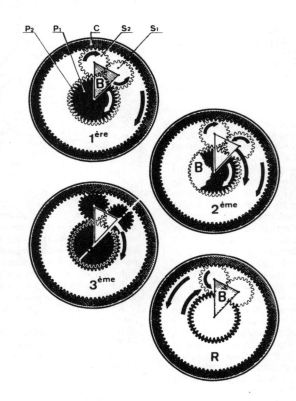

FIG 7:3   Schematic views showing the operation of the automatic transmission

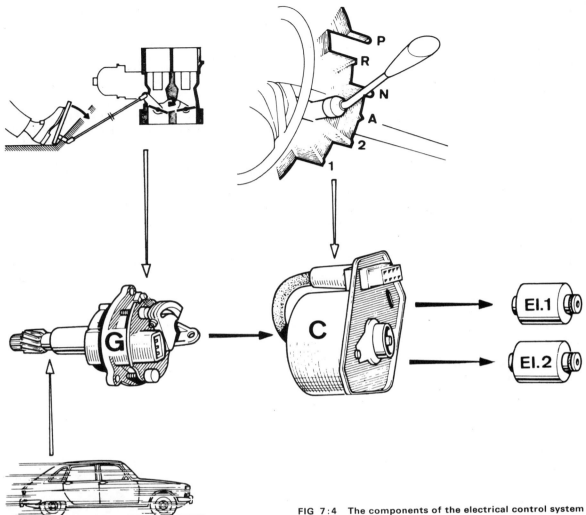

FIG 7:4   The components of the electrical control system

it if the car is tending to roll down a hill. Do not select this position when the car is in motion.

R position:

This is equivalent to the reverse on a normal gearbox. The car is held stationary on the footbrake, or handbrake, with the selection made. The car will then move off backwards when the brake is released and the throttle opened slightly. The car may be stopped and held stationary with the brakes without the selector being moved.

N position:

This is equivalent to the normal neutral and in this selection there is no connection between the engine and front wheels. This selection must be used when starting the engine, as the safety switch prevents the starter from operating in drive selections, and it should also be selected if the car is held stationary with the engine

running for long periods, such as in traffic jams. Leaving the selector in a drive position with the engine running and the car stationary will cause slip in the torque converter, with possible overheating.

A position:

This is the normal selection for all forward driving. The car can be held stationary on the brakes and it will start off in first gear with the up and down shifts made automatically.

2 position:

The gearbox will change up and down automatically between first and second speeds but third-speed is isolated and the gearbox will not change up onto third.

The selection should be made to give increased engine braking, on steep hills or mountain passes or on winding roads, to prevent frequent changes up and down into third.

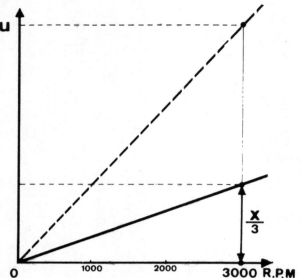

FIG 7:5 The output of the governor at small and large throttle openings

1 position:

This selection locks the gearbox into first-speed and the unit will not change up into second or third speeds. Great care must be taken not to overspeed the engine in this selection and the car should not be driven faster than 35 km/hr (21 mile/hr).

Road test:

This should be carried out by a qualified mechanic unless the owner has recently driven a similar model with transmission known to be in good condition as otherwise the owner may not notice faults as he is accustomed to them.

The average shift points are given in the following table:

	Gearchange (k.p.h.)			
	1 to 2	2 to 1	2 to 3	3 to 2
Light throttle (P.L.)	20 (12 mph)	13 (8 mph)	32 (20 mph)	23 (14 mph)
Full throttle (P.F.)	56 (35 mph)	36 (23 mph)	96 (60 mph)	65 (40 mph)
Kick-down (R.C.)	57 (35 mph)	51 (31 mph)	99 (62 mph)	83 (52 mph)

7:3 Maintenance

Oil:

Only Elf Renault Matic or Mobil ATF.200 should be used in the automatic transmission as other automatic transmission fluids will not be able to cope with lubricating the final drive parts.

Oil level:

The level can be checked with the transmission cold or with it at its normal operating temperature, but not at points in between. **The level must be checked with** the engine running at idling speed and the car standing on level ground.

The dipstick has three marks on it, as shown in **FIG 7:6**. The bottom mark is the minimum level when the transmission is cold and in this case $\frac{1}{4}$ litre ($\frac{1}{2}$ Imp pint, $\frac{3}{4}$ US pint) should be added to bring the level up to mark 2, which is the maximum mark for the transmission cold. The mark 2 is the minimum level when the transmission is hot, after approximately 1 hours running, and the mark 3 is the maximum level when the transmission is hot. **Never exceed the maximum mark as overfilling will cause frothing in the oil and faulty operation of the unit.**

The level is checked by withdrawing the dipstick and wiping it clean on a piece of lint-free cloth. Refit the dipstick and press it fully in and then immediately withdraw it to check the level.

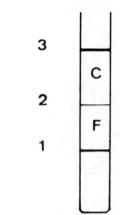

FIG 7:6 The dipstick markings

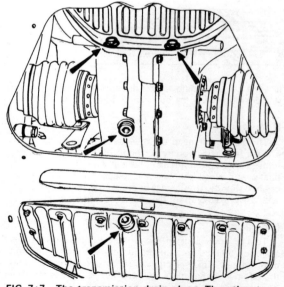

FIG 7:7 The transmission drain plugs. The other two arrows show the torque converter cover attachments

Draining and filling:

The old oil should be drained out at intervals of 30,000 kilometre (18,000 mile) and discarded and the unit then refilled with fresh oil. The quantity of oil required to refill will vary with the amount of work done on the unit and a straight drain and refill will require the least oil for refilling. This is because the torque converter does not empty when draining normally.

Remove the filler plug and the two drain plugs, shown in **FIG 7:7**, and allow the oil to drain out for approximately 5 minutes. Refit the drain plugs and refill using approximately 3 litres (5 Imp pints, 6 US pints) of oil. Check the level on the dipstick after the engine has been started.

If draining has been left running for some time, such as when the lower housing has been removed, then the torque converter will slowly have emptied itself down to half its capacity. In such cases a total of approximately 4½ litres (8 Imp pints, 9½ US pints) will be required to refill. The unit should be filled with 3½ litres first and then topped up with the remainder as necessary after starting the engine.

If the torque converter has been removed and a new empty one has been fitted then approximately 6 litres (10½ pints, 12½ US pints) will be required to fill the unit. Fill up with 5 litres first and then top up as required with the remainder after the engine has been started.

The old oil should be drained out when the unit is at its normal operating temperature as this ensures that dirt is held in suspension. **Take great care when draining as the oil will be hot enough to cause serious scalding.**

Cleanliness:

The automatic transmission operates at a higher temperature than a manual gearbox and cooling is by radiation from the casing and air flow around the torque converter. Make sure that the casing is kept clean and that air intakes and exhausts are free.

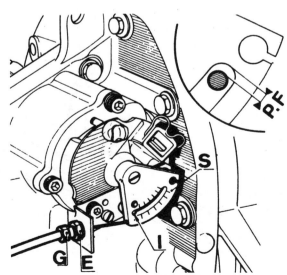

FIG 7:8 The governor and its cable attachments

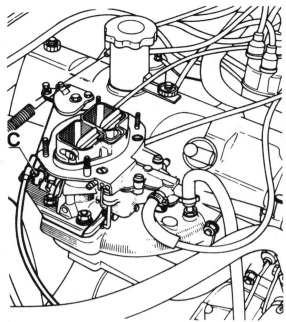

FIG 7:9 The governor cable attachments at the carburetter

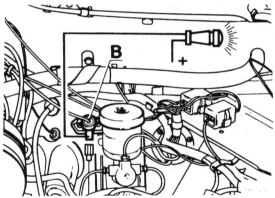

FIG 7:10 Checking the kick-down switch

If the unit is allowed to become covered in mud or road dirt this can act as an insulation and make the unit overheat, particularly in areas of high ambient temperatures.

Great care must also be taken not to allow dirt into the unit when checking the oil level or refilling.

7:4 Adjustments

The adjustments of the selector mechanism will be dealt with separately in the next section. The checking and adjustment of oil pressures will not be dealt with as they require special test equipment which is only held by agents.

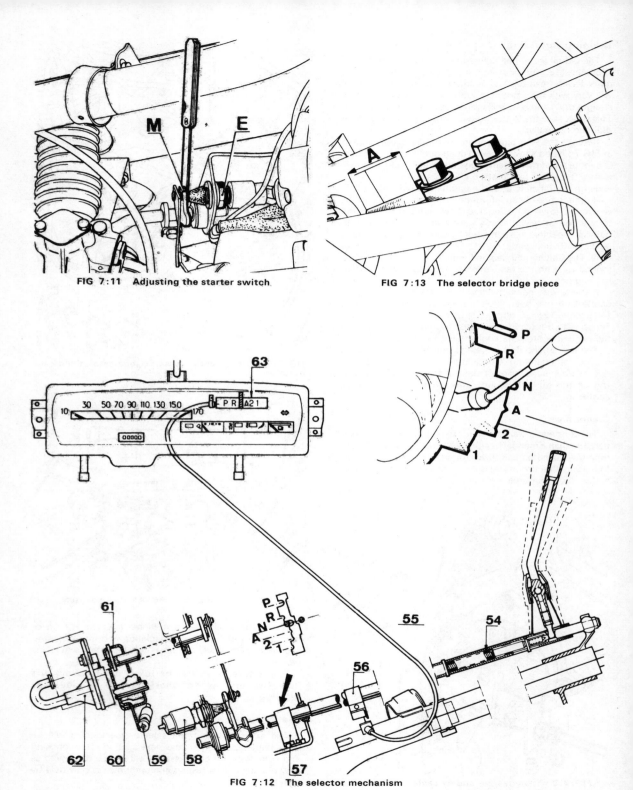

FIG 7:11   Adjusting the starter switch

FIG 7:13   The selector bridge piece

FIG 7:12   The selector mechanism

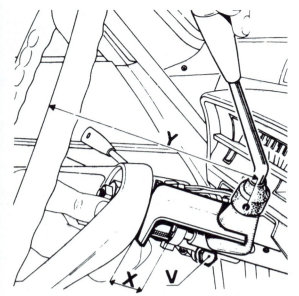

FIG 7:14 Setting the upper selector linkage

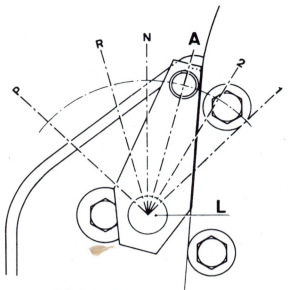

FIG 7:15 Setting the control lever

Governor control cable:

This adjustment must be carried out after the cylinder head has been removed and refitted, the cable changed, or the governor changed.

The attachment at the governor is shown in **FIG 7:8**. Set the adjuster **G** to its midway position and refit the cable to the sector at **S**. Refit the inner cable to the cam on the side of the carburetter, shown in **FIG 7:9**, and press the accelerator pedal right down so that the throttles are fully open. Move the outer cable in its clamp **C** until the cable is taut with no play and tighten the clamp **C** that holds the outer cable. Release the throttle and tighten the adjuster **G** in by one turn. Again press the accelerator pedal right down and check that there is a clearance of .3 to .5 mm (.012 to .020 inch) between the sector **S** and the stop **I**. When the adjustment is satisfactory tighten the locknut **E**.

Kick-down switch:

The adjustment of the kick-down switch is checked using a test lamp between the kick-down switch and positive (+ve) terminal of the battery, as shown in **FIG 7:10**. The lamp should light when the pedal is pressed fully and firmly down. The adjustment is carried out on the accelerator cable and when the pedal is pressed down as far as the detent there should be a small amount of slack in order to allow for movement, 3 to 4 mm ($\frac{1}{8}$ to $\frac{5}{32}$ inch) of the compensating spring pad in the switch. It should be noted that altering the accelerator cable may also alter the governor cable so all adjustments should be checked.

Starter safety switch:

The starter motor must not operate when the selector is in a drive position because of the danger of the car moving off as soon as the engine starts. If the switch requires adjustment put the selector mechanism into the

A position. Slacken the locknut **E**, shown in **FIG 7:11**, and screw the switch in its mounting until the gap between the switch and lever **M** is correct at .3 mm (.012 inch). Retighten the locknut and check that the adjustment has not altered.

7:5 The selector mechanism

A general view of the selector linkage is shown in **FIG 7:12**. The six lever positions have their exact corresponding positions in the electronic computer 62 and the manual valve on the hydraulic distributor 59. The positions on the manual valve are set by means of two toothed arms 60 and 61. A cam 56 and cable 55 operates the indicator on the instrument panel 63.

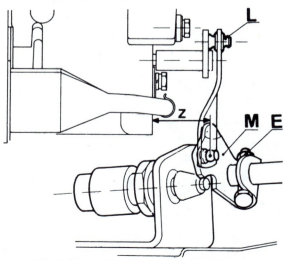

FIG 7:16 Setting the lower control linkage

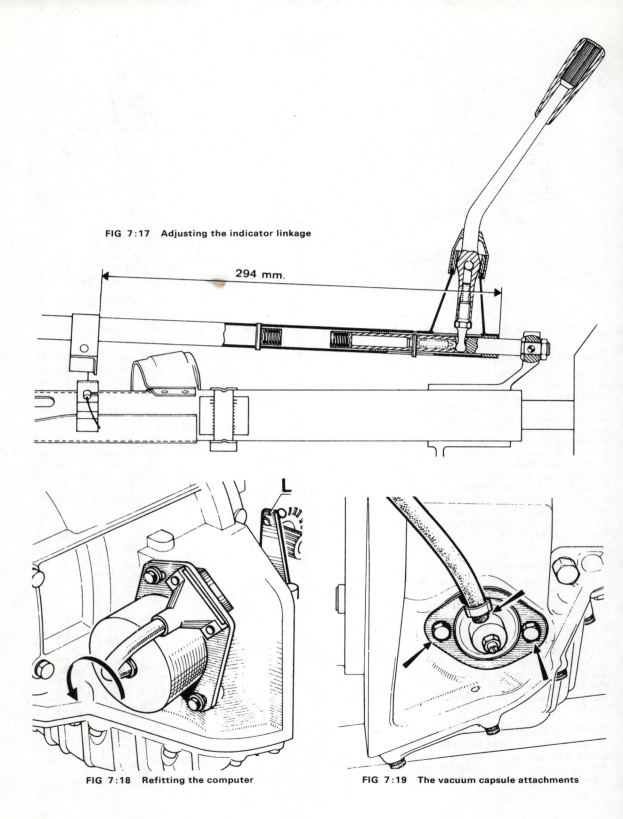

FIG 7:17 Adjusting the indicator linkage

294 mm.

L

FIG 7:18 Refitting the computer

FIG 7:19 The vacuum capsule attachments

Adjusting upper portion:

Before carrying out adjustments remove the covers from the lighting switch, disconnect the link to the computer and unscrew the starter switch.

Slacken the bolts on the bridgepiece, shown in **FIG 7:13**. Engage the selector quadrant into the first notch (**P** position) and press it down onto the bottom peg.

Unscrew the locknut **V**, shown in **FIG 7:14**, and remove the locknut from the selector ball joint. The easiest method of setting is to use the special tool B.Vi.464 as shown in the figure as this tool automatically sets the dimensions **X** and **Y**. If the tool is not available the dimension **Y** should be set to 208 mm ($8\frac{3}{16}$ inch) and **X** to 25 mm ($\frac{63}{64}$ inch). The angular setting of the gearlever from the horizontal should be 55 deg. from the horizontal for lefthand drive models and 33 deg. for righthand drive models. *Note:* On models from February 1975 dimension **Y** is amended to 203 mm (8 inch).

Set the dimension **A** shown in **FIG 7:13** to 20 mm ($\frac{25}{32}$ inch) and tighten the bolts to a torque of 2 kg m (15 lb ft).

Check that the linkage moves freely and that the selector lever moves towards the instrument panel on its own.

Adjusting lower portion:

Place the control lever in the automatic position **A** and line up the engagement shaft, as shown in **FIG 7:15**.

Refer to **FIG 7:16** and unscrew the nut **E**. Press the link arm back onto the ball joints of the shaft **L** and lever **M** so that the parts are not strained. Move the lever **M** until the centre of its ball joint is 38 mm ($1\frac{1}{2}$ inch) from the side of the housing as shown at **Z**. On righthand drive models the dimension **Z** is measured from the centre of the ball joint to the housing gasket face and the correct distance is 45.5 mm ($1\frac{25}{32}$ inch). Tighten the nut **E** and make sure that the adjustment has not altered.

Adjusting indicator:

The parts are shown in **FIG 7:17**. Slacken the screw that secures the selector cam to the shaft and move it until the distance shown is correct. Keep the cam at the correct distance and rotate it about the shaft until the indicator agrees with the selector lever position. Retighten the securing screw and check that the cam does not foul anywhere as the selector is moved.

7:6 Renewing components

The only components that may be renewed are the torque converter, vacuum capsule, governor, computer and speedometer drive.

Gaskets and seals may be renewed, as may wiring also, but any other faults require a new complete unit to be fitted.

The parts given in this section may be renewed without removing the transmission unit from the car.

Governor:

The unit is shown in **FIG 7:8**. Disconnect the cable and take out the Allen screws that secure the unit in place. Disconnect the leads and withdraw the unit from the transmission.

The governor is refitted in the reverse order of removal. Use a new gasket and smear it with Lowac Perfect Seal

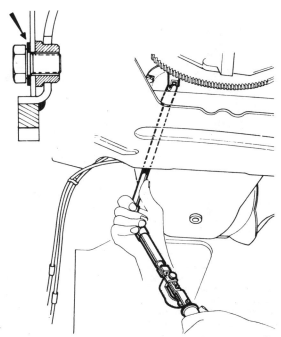

FIG 7:20 The torque converter attachments to the drive plate

No. 00.80.546.500. If difficulty is found in sliding the unit into place, gently turn the speedometer gear while sliding the unit in. When the unit has been refitted adjust its cable as described in **Section 7:4**.

Computer:

Disconnect the leads, unscrew the attachment screws and remove the unit.

When refitting the unit turn the centre shaft clockwise as far as it will go and place the selector mechanism into the 1 position (1st gear hold). Refit the computer, using

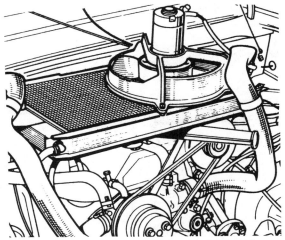

FIG 7:21 The radiator laid on top of the engine

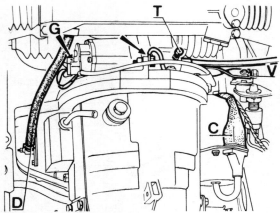

FIG 7:22 The connections for the controls on the transmission

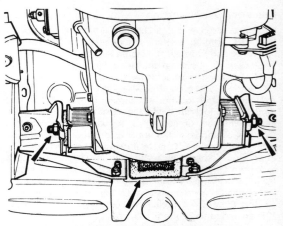

FIG 7:23 The transmission mountings

new plastic spacers, but do not yet tighten the screws. Turn the lever **L** and computer unit in the direction of the arrow in **FIG 7:18**. **Force must not be used when turning the parts but it is essential that they are turned in order to line up the manual valve.** Tighten the screw sufficiently to hold the unit in place without deforming the plastic spacers.

Vacuum capsule:

The attachments are shown in **FIG 7:19**. When refitting the capsule use a new gasket smeared with Lowac Perfect Seal.

7:7 Removing the transmission unit

1 Drain the oil out of the unit and remove the cover from below the torque converter. Unscrew the three bolts that secure the torque converter to the engine drive plate, using a 14mm socket and universal joint as shown in **FIG 7:20**.
2 Disconnect the battery and open the bonnet to its widest extent after removing the restraining cable. Remove the tie bar connecting the wheel arches. Take out the centre bolt and remove the camshaft pulley.

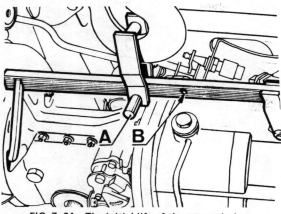

FIG 7:24 The initial lift of the transmission

3 Disconnect the leads to the radiator cooling fan and temperature switch and take out the two bolts that secure the radiator in place. Lift up the radiator and swivel it about the hoses so that it is laid on top of the engine as shown in **FIG 7:21**.
4 Refer to **FIG 7:22** and disconnect the speedometer cable **T**, control arm **V**, governor leads **G**, the cable loom from between the computer **C** and watertight junction on the bulkhead, the vacuum pipe at the capsule **D**, and the earth strap. Free the looms from their clips and lift them out.
5 Remove the steering rack as described in **Chapter 10**.
6 Drive out the rollpins that secure the drive shaft joints to the sunwheel on the transmission and hold the joints together with a length of soft wire to prevent them from falling apart. Remove the brake calipers and then disconnect the upper suspension ball joints (see **Chapter 9**). The suspension can then be pivotted outwards so that the drive shafts come free from the transmission. Protect the ends of the joints with caps to prevent dirt from entering them.
7 Support the transmission from underneath with a jack and free the front mountings, shown in **FIG 7:23**. Attach the tool No. B.Vi.455 to the transmission, using the hole **A** as shown in **FIG 7:24**. Raise the transmission using a suitable hoist and ease it away from the front support. Lower the transmission again so that it rests on the crossmember and transfer the hook to the hole **B**. **Immediately that it is accessible fit a plate, as shown in FIG 7:25, to prevent the torque converter from falling out and then raise the transmission out of the car.**

The transmission is refitted in the reverse order of removal. The driving plate has one flange machined and marked with white paint. The white paint mark on the torque converter must be fitted so that the two spots are face to face in order to preserve the balance, shown in **FIG 7:25**.

If the drive plate needs to be removed from the engine, make up a metal strap that bolts onto the crankcase and onto one of the torque converter attachment holes in the drive plate, as this will prevent the engine from turning when slackening or tightening the drive plate attachment bolts.

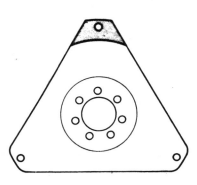

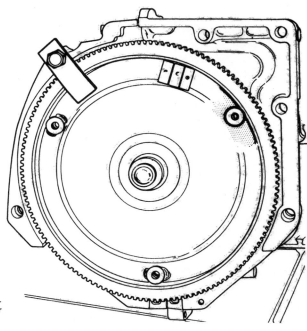

FIG 7:25 The torque converter and drive plate markings. Note the plate that prevents the torque converter from falling out

The torque converter can be lifted directly out of the transmission once the retaining strap has been removed. **Take care not to damage the joint face on the cover of the torque converter when handling the unit.** It will be found easier to refit the torque converter if the transmission is stood up vertically on end.

7:8 Fault diagnosis

(a) Creep in neutral

1 Incorrectly adjusted computer
2 Incorrectly adjusted selector linkage
3 Indicator incorrectly adjusted giving wrong reading

(b) Excessive creep in drive selection

1 Idling speed incorrectly adjusted
2 Accelerator linkage incorrectly adjusted

(c) Starter fails to operate

1 Check 2 and 3 in (a)
2 Defective leads, terminals or switch
3 Incorrectly adjusted switch

(d) Overheating

1 Incorrect oil level
2 Excess dirt on casing
3 Defective torque converter

(e) Slip

1 Check 1 and 3 in (d)
2 Defective torque converter
3 Have pressures checked and adjusted
4 Internal defects

(f) Uneven slow-running

1 Check 2 in (b)
2 Defective vacuum capsule

(g) Snatch

1 Check (b); 3 in (e) and 2 in (f)
2 Governor control cable incorrectly adjusted

(h) Incorrect shifts at kick-down

1 Check 2 in (a) and 2 in (c)
2 Defective or incorrectly adjusted kick-down switch
3 Defective computer

NOTES

CHAPTER 8

THE HUBS AND REAR SUSPENSION

8:1 Description

A general view of the suspension for the car is shown in **FIG 8:1**. The front suspension will be dealt with in the next chapter and this chapter is only concerned with the rear suspension.

Each rear wheel is independently mounted using a hub on a trailing arm. Each trailing arm is supported by a transverse torsion bar running nearly the full width of the car. The end of the torsion bar opposite to the trailing arm is anchored in the frame so that vertical movement of the road wheel is counteracted by the torsion of the bar.

A more detailed view of the rear suspension alone is shown in **FIG 8:2**. Sealed telescopic dampers are mounted between the trailing arms and frame to damp out oscillations and control the movement of each suspension. An anti-roll bar interconnects the two trailing arms to improve road holding and reduce body roll on corners.

A part sectioned view of one rear suspension is shown in **FIG 8:3**. The earlier type with rubber bushes has been superseded by the type with needle roller bearings, shown at **A**. If the trailing arms with rubber bushes are worn they must be renewed using the later type of arm with needle roller bearing sleeves; an external bearing for needle rollers must not be fitted onto an arm with rubber bushes.

Before carrying out any work on the rear suspension, jack up the rear of the car and place it securely onto chassis stands. The jack supplied with the car is only suitable for raising it and must not be used as the sole means of support. **Except for changing a road wheel the phrase 'jack up' means jacking up and using chassis stands so that the car is safely and securely supported, with the front wheels chocked.**

8:2 The hub assembly

The components are shown in **FIG 8:4**. It should be noted that the dimensions **A** and **B** vary. On R.1150 models from car No. 160.881 onwards as well as all R.1151, R.1152, R.1153 and R.1156 models the wheel location diameter **A** is 118 mm ($4\frac{5}{8}$ inch) while on earlier R.1150 models the dimension is 126 mm ($4\frac{15}{16}$ inch). On R.1150 models before No. 221.331 the internal diameter of the bearing **B** is 17 mm (.670 inch), but on all later models the diameter is increased to 20 mm (.788 inch). Note also that two different road wheels are made and the later type can only be fitted to drums with 118 mm wheel location diameter.

Removal:

Jack up the car and remove the road wheel. Remove the grease cap. Special pliers (Rou.08 or Rou.441) are made for removing the cap but if care is taken the cap can be gently levered and tapped off.

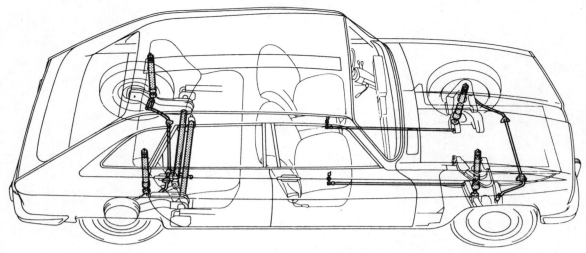

FIG 8:1 The car suspension system

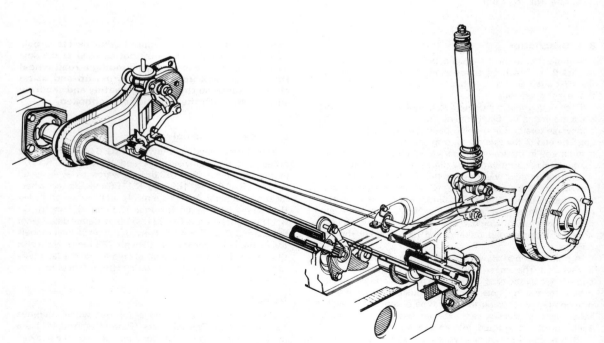

FIG 8:2 General view of the rear suspension

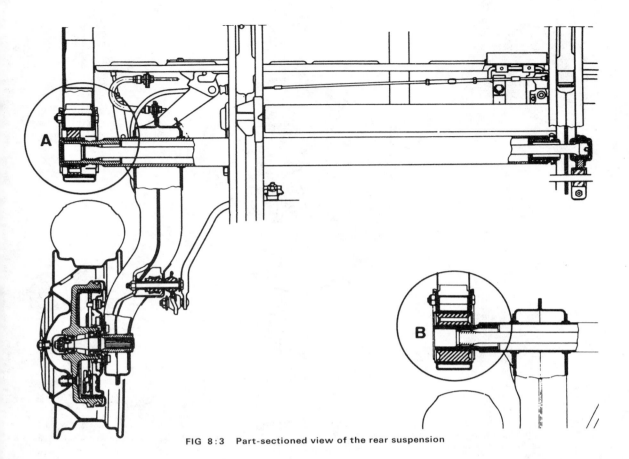

FIG 8:3 Part-sectioned view of the rear suspension

Take out the splitpin and unscrew the locknut and nut so that the thrust washer can be drawn off. In some cases it is possible to remove the hub by tapping evenly around the brake drum with a copper hammer but if the hub is too stiff to remove in this manner the extractor No. T.Av.235 must be used as shown in **FIG 8:5**. Collect the inner race of the outer bearing as it comes free.

Bearings:

If the bearings are worn they must be renewed. The outer races can be driven out of the brake drum using a suitable drift.

The inner race of the inner bearing is a very tight fit on the axle and an extractor must be used to remove it, or the bearing complete with thrust washer. The special tools Rou.370 (Rou.370.01 for the later models with the 20 mm axle) are shown fitted for removing the bearing alone in **FIG 8:6**. The centralizing sleeve 3 is fitted first, followed by the half sleeves 1, and the half sleeves are then locked using the sleeve 2. If the thrust washer also is to be removed the half sleeves 1 are turned round so that the square end fits over bearing and thrust washer so that they are both pulled off together. Special tool Mot.49 is then clamped over the assembly and used to draw the bearing off the shaft.

The best method of fitting the bearing is to heat the thrust washer and fit it back into place using no tools. If this method is not used press the bearing and washer back into position using the sleeve 3 and a nut on the threads of the shaft to pull the parts back into position.

Reassembly:

Wipe out the old grease with newspapers or rags and then wash the parts with clean fuel. **Avoid getting grease onto the brake linings, and wipe the inside of the drum to make sure that it is free from grease or finger marks.**

Smear the inner races of the bearings with grease and pack some grease inside the hub of the brake drum. Make sure that the seal is in place and press the brake drum back into place by hand. Refit the inner race of the outer bearing followed by the thrust washer and nut.

Use a medium length spanner and tighten the nut while spinning the hub. Moderate hand pressure will be required and the nut should be tightened until there is drag felt on the hub as it spins. Mount a DTI (Dial Test Indicator) onto the brake drum so that its stylus rests vertically on the end of the axle and slacken back the nut until the end float of the hub is correct at .06 to .09 mm or .01 to .05 mm on 16TX models. Rotate the hub at each adjustment to settle the bearings.

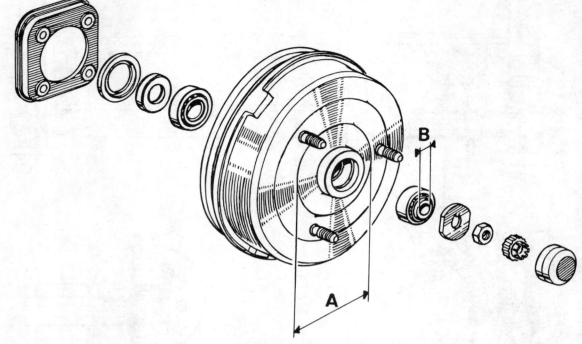

FIG 8:4 The rear hub assembly components

When the end float is correct refit the locknut and splitpin it, making sure that the main nut does not rotate. Three-quarters fill the grease cap with grease and fit it back into position.

8:3 The dampers

Four different types of damper can be fitted. They are either De Carbon normal, 'poor roads', special version, or else Allinquant normal. There are slight differences in the design of the upper mounting rubbers and cups and the correct arrangement for each type is shown in **FIGS 8:7** and **8:8**.

Removal:

Jack up the car and remove the road wheel. Support the trailing arm with a jack underneath it, as the damper acts as a limit stop for the travel. From inside the car take off the two nuts, cup washers and rubber bushes for the top attachment. Make sure that the opposite trailing arm is at the same height to ensure that the anti-roll bar is not under torsion. Remove the nut and take out the bolt that secures the lower attachment and remove the damper from the car.

The damper is refitted in the reverse order of removal. Make sure that all the rubber bushes are in good condition and renew them if they are defective or perished. Pass the bolt through the distance piece 1, washer 2, damper eye 3, anti-roll bar link 4 and washer 5 as shown in **FIG 8:9**. The bolt should be lubricated with HATMO grease No. 00.80.666.100.

Testing:

As a rough check bounce the suspension by leaning on the car and suddenly releasing it. The oscillations should damp out rapidly. Faulty dampers may also be suspected if the car keeps pitching after going over a hump in the road. The only effective check is to have the dampers tested on a special machine but their average life is usually 50,000 kilometres (30,000 miles). It is most advisable to renew all four dampers at the same time and unless one damper has suffered physical damage (such as a bent ram or dented case) they should always be renewed in axle pairs.

8:4 The anti-roll bar

Refer to **FIG 8:10** and remove the nut and bolt 2 that secures the bearing clip, then take out the nuts and bolts 1 that secure the bearing clip to the frame. If the Silent-bloc bush is worn or defective the old one can now be removed and a new one fitted, making sure that the slit aligns with the joint in the clip.

Disconnect the brake limiter by undoing the nut 3, shown in **FIG 8:11**.

Disconnect the ends of the anti-roll bar from the bottom damper attachments or at the ends of the links, shown in **FIG 8:9**, and remove the anti-roll bar from the car.

The anti-roll bar is refitted in the reverse order of removal. Once it is in place connect and adjust the brake limiter, using the calibration setting given on the plate.

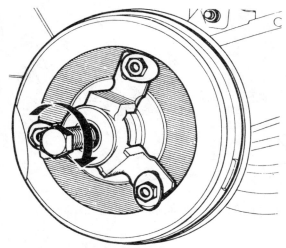

FIG 8:5   Removing the rear hub assembly

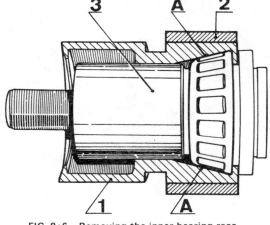

FIG 8:6   Removing the inner bearing race

FIG 8:7   The Allinquant damper upper attachment

FIG 8:8   The De Carbon damper upper attachment

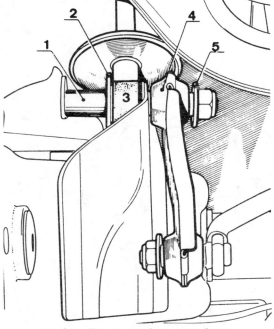

FIG 8:9   The damper lower attachment

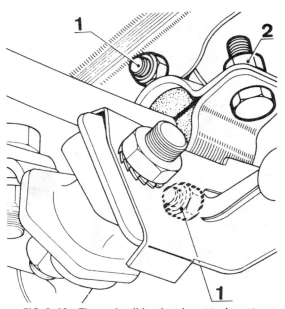

FIG 8:10   The anti-roll bar bearing attachments

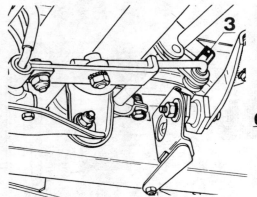

FIG 8:11 The brake limiter attachment

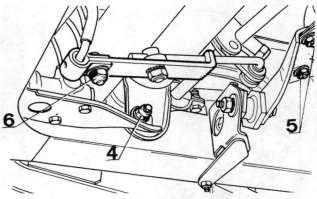

FIG 8:12 The inner bearing attachments

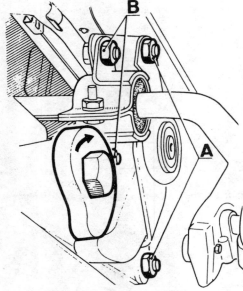

FIG 8:13 The anchor housing attachments

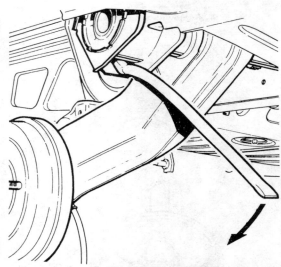

FIG 8:14 Easing out the outer bearing bolts

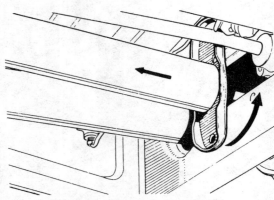

FIG 8:15 Freeing the inner bearing

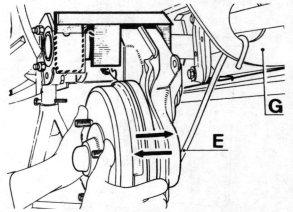

FIG 8:16 Refitting the suspension assembly

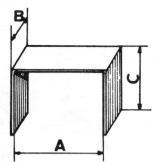

FIG 8:17 Additional clip for use with special tool on earlier models

Key to Fig 8:17
B=40 mm (1 $\frac{9}{16}$ inch)
Metal thickness 6/10 mm (.024 inch)
A=100 mm ±.2 mm (3 $\frac{15}{16}$ inch)
C=70 mm (2 $\frac{3}{4}$ inch)

8:5 The trailing arm assembly

The righthand side arm cannot be removed until the lefthand side arm has been taken off because of the layout of the parts.

Removing lefthand assembly:

1 Jack up the car and remove the rear road wheels. Disconnect the handbrake cable and the hydraulic brake line from the frame (see **Chapter 11**). Disconnect the lower damper attachment (see **Section 8:3**).
2 Refer to **FIG 8:12** and remove the two bolts 4 which secure the inner bearing. Also remove the two bolts 5 that secure the silencer (muffler) and the brake limiter adjusting nut and bolt 6.
3 Refer to **FIG 8:13**. Slacken off the bolt that secures the height adjusting cam and turn the cam to its zero position. Remove the nuts and bolts **A** that secure the anchor casing and the bolts **B** that secure the anti-roll bar bearing. Pull the assembly as far rearwards as possible.
4 Remove the nuts that secure the outer bearing and then apply pressure with a lever, as shown in **FIG 8:14**, so that the bolts can be withdrawn.
5 Free the inner bearing by pulling it towards the rear and then turn it through 90 degrees, as shown in **FIG 8:15**.

Removing righthand assembly:

This is removed in a similar manner after the lefthand assembly has been freed and pulled out of the way without actually removing it.

Reassembly:

If both sides have been removed then the righthand side assembly must be refitted first.

Pass the assembly, with the torsion bar attached, through the aperture in the sidemember, and fit the outer bearing using a lever to help align the bolt holes. Refit the anchor casing to the torsion bar, making sure that the punch marks on the end of the torsion bar and anchor housing are in line. Attach the outer bearing to the sidemember and fit the special tool No. T.Ar.386.01 to locate the parts. Hang the trailing arm on a hook **E**, made from strong wire or rod, so that it makes an angle of 45 degrees.

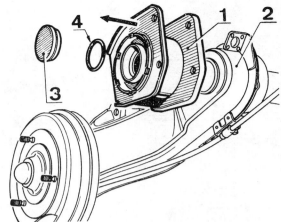

FIG 8:18 Outer needle roller bearing

Pull or push the arm so that it fits freely into the fork of the special tool, as shown in **FIG 8:16**. On pre-September 1966 models (arms 100 mm thick) a clip made up to the dimensions shown in **FIG 8:17** must be fitted between the gauge and arm. The clip is made of material .6 m (.024 inch) thick.

The rest of the parts are then refitted in the reverse order of removal. Do not forget to bleed the braking system and adjust the handbrake (see **Chapter 11**).

Once the parts have been refitted the brake limiter must be adjusted and the underbody height correctly set.

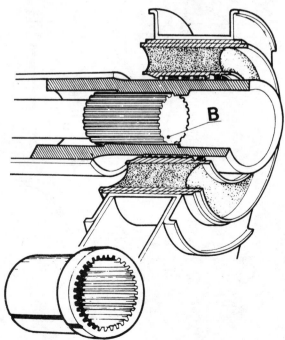

FIG 8:19 The special sleeve for checking the position of the torsion bar in the suspension

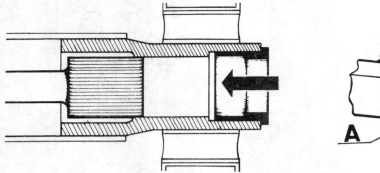
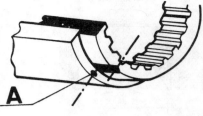

FIG 8:20   The special sleeve aligned with the suspension

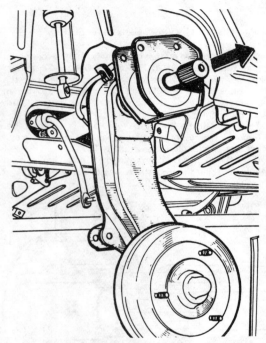

FIG 8:21   Removing the torsion bar

Outer bearing:

If the rubber bush fitted to earlier models is worn or damaged then the parts must be replaced using the later type fitted with needle roller bearings, as no repairs are possible to the rubber bush type.

The attachments of the later needle roller type bearing are shown in **FIG 8:18**. With the parts removed from the car prise out the plastic plug 3, remove the O-ring 4, and pull the bearing 1 off the arm 2.

Fit a new bearing back into place after smearing the sleeve with Elf Multi grease.

Inner bearing:

If the Fluidblock bearing is worn it should be renewed by fitting a complete new inner bearing. The outer sleeve remains in the tube and if it is worn it should be carefully sawn through, without damaging the tube, and then bent inwards and withdrawn using a pair of pliers. A new sleeve must then be refitted using a press and it should protrude 2 to 4mm ($\frac{5}{64}$ to $\frac{5}{32}$ inch) from the tube. Grease the Fluidblock with SI.33 grease before fitting it into the sleeve.

Checking:

The rear suspension geometry should be checked by an agent using specialist equipment. The location of the trailing arms can be checked using a special gauge T.Ar.393 but again this should be left to an agent.

Incorrect geometry or settings will cause excessive tyre wear and may also make the handling of the car difficult or unsafe.

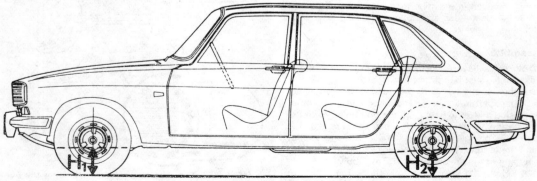

FIG 8:22   Checking the suspension height

8:6 The torsion bars

The larger diameter of the torsion bar fits into the trailing arm and it should be noted that 28 splines are fitted to one end and 30 to the other so that differential adjustments are possible.

The torsion bars are not interchangeable from side to side. On early models the lefthand bar is identified by a spot of yellow paint or the letter **G** on the end of the bar, and the righthand side by a spot of red paint or the letter **D**. On later models the lefthand bar is identified by two punch marks on the chamfer in the centre of the end face of the bar, while the righthand side is identified by three punch marks. A single punch mark just inside the teeth on the end face is used for aligning the bar with its attachment.

Removal:

The torsion bars cannot be removed until the attachments of the suspension arms have released from the chassis (see **Section 8:5**).

Before removing the anchor housing, mark the torsion bar and the housing with grease crayon or suitable marker, making the marks align at a convenient point. Remove the anchor housing. Count the number of splines between the made mark and the centre dot on both the housing and the bar. If the number of splines is the same in each case then the punch marks on housing and bar are refitted in line. If the number of splines is not the same between the two sets of made marks and centre dots, the difference represents the amount of offset required to set the suspension to the correct height. Note and remember this offset for reassembly.

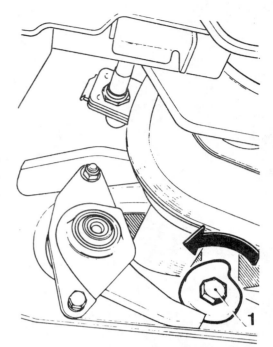

FIG 8:23 The cams for adjusting the rear suspension height

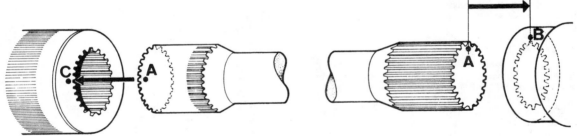

FIG 8:24 The torsion bars at their normal settings

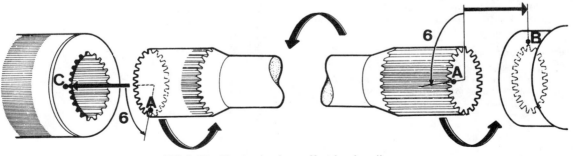

FIG 8:25 The torsion bars offset by six splines

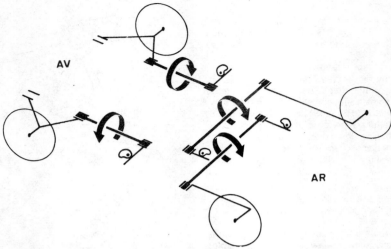

FIG 8:26 Turning the torsion bars to raise the suspension height

The marks on the suspension arm side are difficult to check as the bar is recessed by approximately 4 cm. To ensure the accuracy of the marks use the sleeve Sus.439, shown in **FIG 8:19**. Slide the sleeve into place so that its mark is in line with the mark **A** on the suspension, as shown in **FIG 8:20**. Push the torsion bar outwards until its end is flush with the end of the sleeve. The alignment of the mark **A** with **B** on the torsion bar can then be checked using the mark of the sleeve as a guide. If there is any offset note the number of splines and remember it for reassembly.

Disconnect the suspension so that it hangs down freely and withdraw the torsion bar as shown in **FIG 8:21**.

Reassembly:

Slide the torsion bar back in, making sure that the correct torsion bar is fitted and with the larger diameter at the suspension end. Fit the special sleeve to the outer end of the bar so that the difference between the marks on the sleeve and bar is the correct number of splines offset. Turn the bar and sleeve assembly until the mark on the sleeve is in line with the mark on the suspension and press the bar in so that it fits into the splines of the suspension. Remove the special sleeve and fit a plug in the arm to prevent the torsion bar from being pushed out when the anchor housing is being refitted.

Refit the anchor housing, allowing for any offset found on dismantling. Reattach the suspension in the reverse order of dismantling.

Height setting:

The suspension height for both front and rear suspension is measured between the sidemembers and the ground, with tyre pressures correct, the tank full, and the car on level ground, at the points **H1** and **H2** shown in **FIG 8:22**. The settings for all the different models covered by this manual are given in Technical Data.

The rear suspension height is altered by setting the cam shown in **FIG 8:23**. Turning the cam clockwise as shown will increase the clearance to the ground. The

brake limiter must be readjusted if the suspension height is altered.

If the correct settings cannot be set by altering the cams then a differential setting must be made on both torsion bars to bring the height within limits. It is advisable that this is done by an agent who will have all the tools and gauges necessary. The method is briefly shown in **FIGS 8:24, 8:25 and 8:26**.

FIG 8:24 shows the normal settings of the torsion bars with the marks in alignment. **FIG 8:25** shows the torsion bar being offset by 6 splines, noting that 1 spline offset will alter the rear suspension height by 6 mm ($\frac{1}{4}$ inch). **FIG 8:26** shows the directions in which the torsion bars must be rotated to raise the vehicle. Note that the adjusting cams must be unloaded before setting the torsion bars.

8:7 Fault diagnosis

(a) Wheel tramp or wobble

1 Worn hub bearings
2 Worn suspension bearings
3 Unbalanced wheels and tyres
4 Defective suspension geometry

(b) Car wanders or pulls to one side

1 Check (a)
2 Damaged frame or components

(c) Settling or car low

1 Incorrectly adjusted cams
2 Incorrectly refitted torsion bars
3 Weak or damaged torsion bars

(d) Suspension bottoms

1 Check (c)
2 Defective dampers

(e) Rattles or noisy operation

1 Check 1 and 2 in (a) and 2 in (d)
2 Damper mountings loose or worn
3 Anti-roll bar broken
4 Anti-roll bar attachments loose or worn

CHAPTER 9

DRIVE SHAFTS, FRONT SUSPENSION AND HUBS

9:1 Description

A general view of the front suspension is shown in **FIG 9:1**. Unequal length wishbones support a stub axle assembly, using special ball joints at the outer ends. The inner ends of the wishbones are pivotted so that they can move vertically and the lower wishbone pivots on the torsion bar. The motion of the suspension is controlled by a sealed telescopic damper mounted between the lower wishbone and frame of the car. An anti-roll bar interconnects the two lower wishbones to improve the road holding and reduce body roll on corners.

The wheels are attached to hubs which revolve about the stub axle on ballbearings. The brake disc is attached to the hub and the components are shown in **FIG 9:2**. The curvi-linear type of hub **B** is only fitted to R.1150 models before No. 160.852. All other models are fitted with the circular hub **A**.

Drive is transmitted from the transmission sunwheels to the hubs by drive shafts. The drive shafts are fitted with a joint at either end which allows them to transmit drive while allowing the suspension and steering to move freely.

It is essential that the car is supported on chassis stands when carrying out work on the front suspension parts and the jack supplied with the car must not be used as a sole support for the car. Whenever the expression jacking up' is used in this chapter it infers that the car is raised and then supported on stands, with the rear wheels chocked and the handbrake applied.

9:2 Hub assembly

Removal:

Jack up the car and remove the appropriate road wheel and then remove the brake caliper (see **Chapter 11**).

Prevent the hub from rotating and unscrew the hub nut. A special tool is made for holding the hub but it can just as easily be held by laying a suitable bar across two studs. Attach the special tool T.Av.235, without its central screw, to the wheel studs and then fit the special tool Rou.378.01 as shown in **FIG 9:3**. Turn the screw so that it does not press on the stub axle, but on the tool attached to the wheel hub, and draw the hub assembly off, collecting the bearing spacer.

The bearings:

The outer bearing will stay in the hub and it can be withdrawn using a suitable two-legged extractor. Check the condition of the baffle washer and refit the bearing

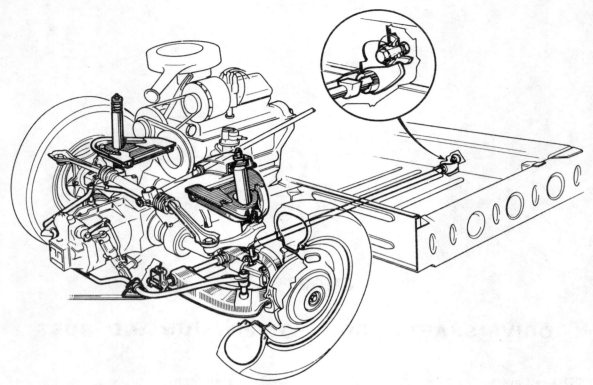

FIG 9:1   General view of the front suspension

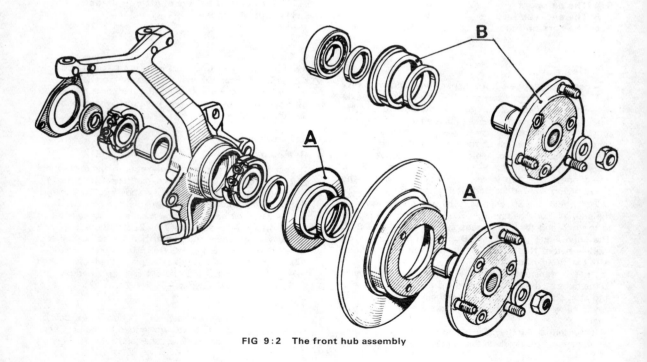

FIG 9:2   The front hub assembly

using a press as shown in **FIG 9:4**, with a tube 36mm ($1\frac{7}{16}$ inch) in diameter as drift. The bearing is fitted with its sealed face towards the hub.

The stub axle assembly must be taken off in order to remove the inner bearing. Remove the nuts that secure the suspension ball joints and the steering ball joints, shown in **FIG 9:5**, and then separate the ball joints from the stub axle using T.Av.54.01 for the upper ball joint and T.Av.237.01 for the lower ball joint, as shown in **FIG 9:6**. The stub axle assembly can now be removed. Remove the inner bearing closure plate and deflector washer. Support the stub axle on a suitable tube (88 mm in diameter) and press the bearing out of the stub axle. The new bearing is pressed back into place using a 68 mm ($2\frac{11}{16}$ inch) diameter tube. The closure plate should be sealed with a fillet of sealing compound No. 08.566.47.00 and secured in position.

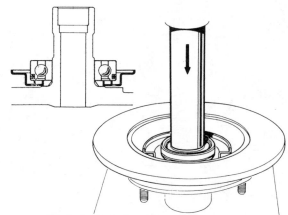

FIG 9:4   Refitting the outer hub bearing

Reassembly:

Refit the stub axle in place to the three ball joints and secure them with their nuts. Pack the bearings with grease and line the inside of the stub axle with a coating of grease as a reservoir. Slide on the hub complete with bearing and distance piece.

Attach special tool No. T.Av.236 to the stub axle and T.Av.436 to the hub. Line up the parts and tighten the nut E, shown in **FIG 9:7**, to draw the hub back onto the splines. Remove the special tools and tighten the hub nut to a torque load of 16 kgm (115 lb ft). Refit the brake caliper in the reverse order of removal.

Automatic transmission:

When removing the automatic transmission it is necessary to disconnect the drive shafts from the unit. The mountings prevent the transmission unit from being moved (as for manual transmissions). Remove the brake caliper and disconnect the upper suspension ball joint and steering ball joint from the stub axle. Drive out the rollpins that secure the drive shafts to the transmission sunwheels and, by pivoting both suspensions outwards about the bottom ball joints, the drive shafts can be drawn out of the transmission.

9:3 The suspension ball joints

These should be examined at regular intervals for damage to the rubber dust cover. If the dust cover is worn or split then the ball joint must be disconnected from the stub axle and a new dust cover fitted. A damaged dust cover will allow dust and dirt to enter the ball joint, causing rapid and excessive wear, and once dirt has entered it cannot be removed. **Dirt in the ball joint therefore necessitates renewal of the ball joint.**

The make of ball joints has been changed so make sure that correct spares are obtained. Before 1969 Gemmer or Bendix ball joints were used but from 1969 onwards the make was changed to Ehrenreich.

When fitting a new dust cover to a ball joint half fill it with Molykote BR.2 grease. The retaining ring is lifted into place using a piece of cord passed through it to pull on.

A sectioned view of the suspension unit is shown in **FIG 9:8**.

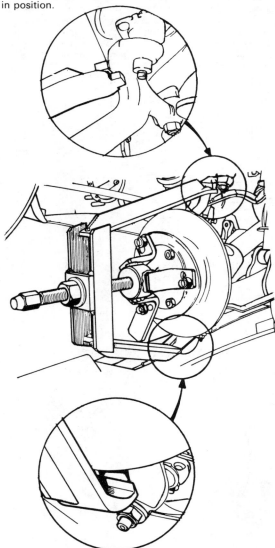

FIG 9:3   Removing the hub assembly

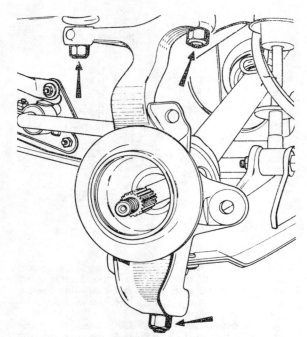

FIG 9:5 The nuts that secure the ball joints to the stub axle

9:4 The dampers

The dampers can be roughly checked by bouncing the car on its suspension and checking that the oscillations are rapidly damped out, though special equipment is required for checking them accurately. The dampers should be suspect if the car keeps pitching after going over a hump in the road. Dampers which show physical damage such as bent ram, dented body, or oil leaks should be renewed.

To remove the damper jack up the car and remove the road wheel. **Support the suspension from underneath as the damper acts as a limit stop.** The upper attachment is shown in **FIG 9:10**. Slacken the locknut and then unscrew both nuts so that the cup washers and rubber bush can be removed. The lower attachment to the wishbone is shown in **FIG 9:11**. Remove the attachment bolt and withdraw the damper from the car.

The damper is refitted in the reverse order of removal after lubricating the bottom attachment bolt with Hatmo grease. Make sure that all the rubber bushes are in good condition before refitting the damper and renew them if they are defective.

Renewal:

To renew the upper ball joint it is only necessary to jack up the car and remove the road wheel and then disconnect the ball joint from the stub axle. When renewing the lower ball joint it is best to disconnect all three of the ball joints at the stub axle and then drive out the rollpin that secures the drive shaft to the transmission. Remove the disc brake caliper and withdraw the stub axle, hub and drive shaft assembly from the car.

When disconnecting the ball joints it is always best to use the special extractors, as shown in **FIG 9:6. Never hammer on the threaded portion of the ball joint as even if a slave nut is fitted internal damage can be caused to the joint.** If an extractor is not available slacken off the nut to the last few threads and lay a block of metal on the tapered eye of the stub axle. Pull the wishbone or tie rod firmly away from the stub axle and give blows with a copper hammer on the tapered eye opposite to the block. The nut will prevent the parts from flying apart suddenly when the tapers free.

File a flat on the heads of the securing rivets and then centre punch them on the flat. Use a drill slightly smaller than the head of the rivet and drill down until the head comes off. **Do not attempt to drill out the rivet itself,** as if the wrong sized drill is used or the drill set at an angle damage will be caused to the wishbone. When the head has been removed drive out the stem using a suitable punch and remove the old ball joint.

Refit the new ball joint, using the nuts and bolts supplied in the kit. The bolt or screw heads must face towards the dust cover and on the upper ball joint the thrust washer is fitted as shown in **FIG 9:9**.

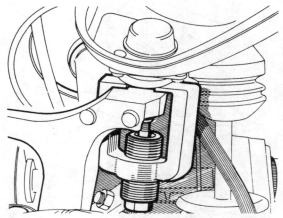

FIG 9:6 Freeing a ball joint

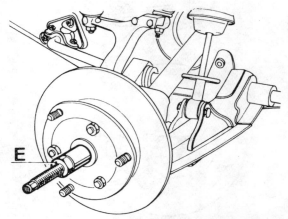

FIG 9:7 Refitting the hub assembly

104

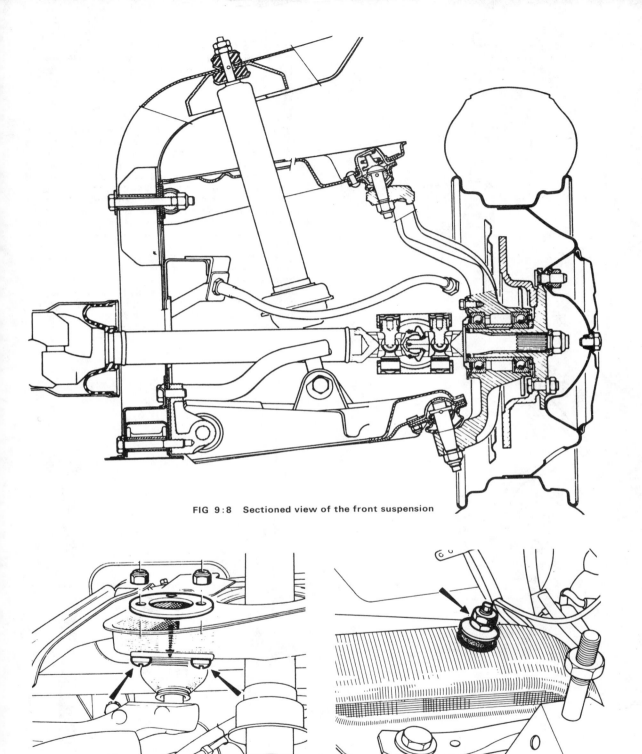

FIG 9:8 Sectioned view of the front suspension

FIG 9:9 Refitting upper ball joint

FIG 9:10 The damper upper attachment

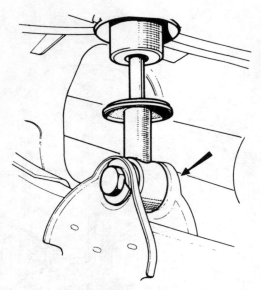

FIG 9:11   The damper lower attachment

9:5 The anti-roll bar

The anti-roll bar components are shown in **FIG 9:12** and the bearing attachments to the frame in **FIG 9:13**.

Removal:

Jack up the car and remove the righthand front road wheel. Disconnect the links from the lower wishbones. Split the bearing by taking off the nuts 1 and then free the bearing from the frame by taking out the nuts and bolts 2 to free the bearing assembly. Support the transmission with a jack underneath it and then remove the nuts and washers that secure the transmission to its front mounting. Raise the transmission slightly until it touches the steering rack unit. Push the anti-roll bar outwards towards the righthand side and remove it over the drive shaft, as shown in **FIG 9:14**. Before removing the anti-roll bar it is advisable to mark one end with paint to ensure that it is refitted the right way round.

The anti-roll bar is refitted in the reverse order of removal. Make sure that all the bushes are in good condition and renew them if they are defective. The bearing bush must be refitted so that its slit is in line with the joint of the bearing metal parts, and it should be noted that as they are split they can be renewed without removing the anti-roll bar from the car.

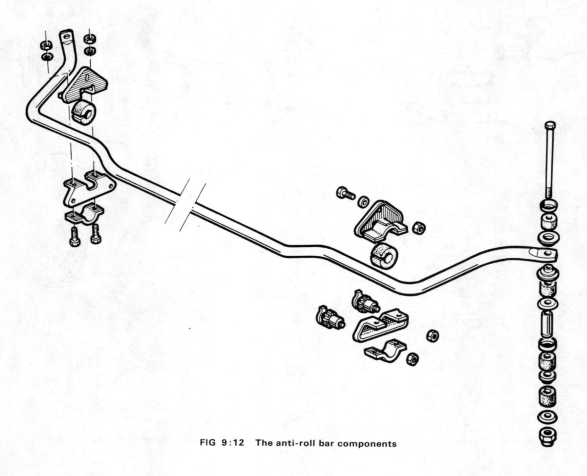

FIG 9:12   The anti-roll bar components

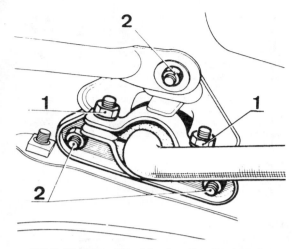

FIG 9:13 The anti-roll bar bearing attachments

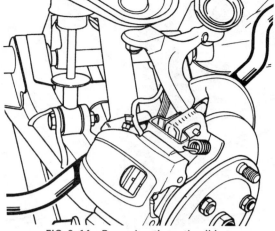

FIG 9:14 Removing the anti-roll bar

9:6 The torsion bars

Removal of the torsion bars is best carried out over a pit or using a hydraulic hoist. Remove the road wheel after supporting the car on chassis stands.

Removal:

1 From inside the car remove the coverplate and then slacken the locknut 2, shown in **FIG 9:15**, so that the cam 1 can be turned to its zero position (towards the outside of the car). Fit the special tool No. Sus.234 into the anchor housing and use the tool as a lever to take the pressure of the torsion bar. The tool has splines that fit into the anchor housing and is shown fitted in **FIG 9:16**. From inside the car take out the two

bolts on either side of the cam, shown in **FIG 9:15**. From underneath the car remove the bolt 5 and nut 6 shown in **FIG 9:16**.

2 Allow the torsion bar to release and the anchor housing to hang down. Make a mark on the torsion bar splines in line with the mark on the edge of the anchor housing and then remove the anchor housing. Normally the mark made should be in line with the punch mark on the end of the torsion bar, but if it is not then note the direction and amount of offset for reassembly.

3 Pull the torsion bar back without allowing it to come free from the lower wishbone, and make a mark on the splines in line with the mark on the edge of the wishbone. Fully withdraw the torsion bar and check the amount of offset, noting it for reassembly.

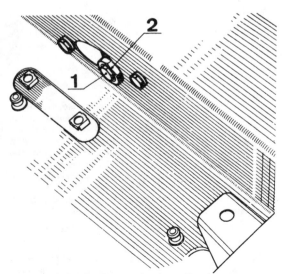

FIG 9:15 The torsion bar adjusting cam

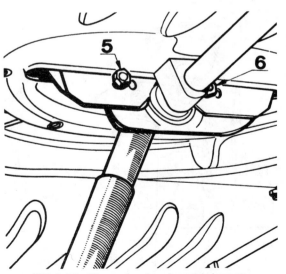

FIG 9:16 The anchor housing attachments

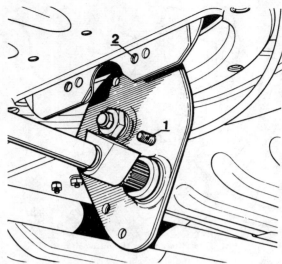

FIG 9:17   Refitting the anchor housing

Reassembly:

The parts are reassembled in the reverse order of dismantling. Lubricate the torsion bar splines with Hatmo grease and fit them back into the suspension and anchor housing so that the marks align or the correct amount of offset found on dismantling is set. Note that the suspension end of the arm has 24 splines while the anchor housing end has only 23 splines. **The torsion bars must not be interchanged from side to side.** On early models the lefthand bar is marked with a spot of yellow paint or letter **G** on the end while the righthand bar is marked with red paint or the letter **D**. On later models

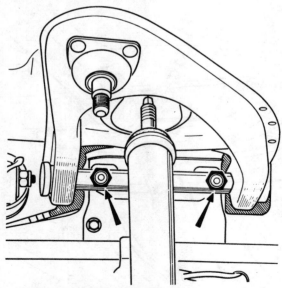

FIG 9:18   Removing the upper wishbone assembly

the lefthand bar has two punch marks on the chamfer in the centre of the bar while the righthand bar has three punch marks.

Pass the stud 1 on the anchor housing through the mounting hole 2, shown in **FIG 9:17**, and loosely attach the nut and washer. Use the special tool Sus.234 in the anchor housing to twist the torsion bar until the bolt can be fitted. Refit the two bolts inside the car. Check and set the height of the suspension using the cams shown in **FIG 9:15**. Fuller details of measuring and setting the suspension heights are given in **Chapter 8, Section 8:6**.

9:7 The wishbones

In either case if the inner pivot bearings for the wishbones are worn a complete new wishbone must be fitted, as the wishbones cannot be separated from the pivots.

Upper wishbone:

Jack up the car, remove the road wheel, and support the suspension with a jack underneath it. Disconnect the damper upper attachment and free the upper suspension ball joint from the stub axle. Undo the bolts shown in **FIG 9:18** and remove the upper wishbone.

If it is suspected that the wishbone is damaged or distorted, it should be checked by an agent using special jigs and gauges.

The wishbone is refitted in the reverse order of removal but the attachment bolts should be lightly smeared with Molykote BR.2 grease.

Lower wishbone:

Remove the torsion bar as described in the previous section and remove the brake caliper. Disconnect the drive shaft from the sunwheel on the transmission and also disconnect the damper and anti-roll bar from the lower wishbone. Disconnect the lower ball joint from the stub axle and then take out the bolts that secure the pivot to the frame, collecting any shims fitted and noting their positions for reassembly. Lift out the lower wishbone assembly.

The wishbone is refitted in the reverse order of removal, after having it checked by an agent if it is suspected to be damaged. Lubricate the bolts that secure the inner pivot with Molykote grease.

9:8 Suspension geometry

Incorrect suspension geometry will cause the car to handle badly as well as causing excessive wear on the tyres. The geometry is set by shims and if there is any doubt about its accuracy the car should be taken to an agent who will use special gauges and tools to check the settings accurately and adjust them if required.

It is advisable to have the geometry checked after major work has been carried out on a suspension, or if the car has been involved in an accident such as the wheel hitting a solid obstruction.

9:9 The drive shafts

The different couplings that can be fitted are shown in **FIG 9:19**. The shafts can be used in any combination except that spider GE 86 couplings must not be used on

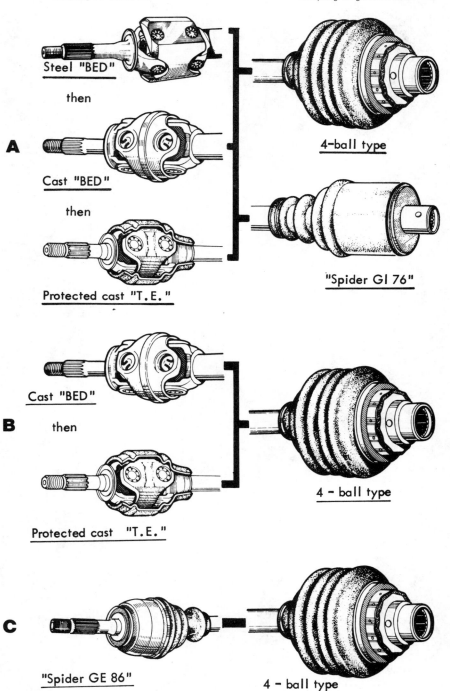

Coupling on wheel end   *Coupling on gearbox end*

A

Steel "BED"

then

Cast "BED"

then

Protected cast "T.E."

4-ball type

"Spider GI 76"

B

Cast "BED"

then

Protected cast "T.E."

4 - ball type

C

"Spider GE 86"   4 - ball type

FIG 9:19   The different drive shaft couplings

Key to Fig 9:19   **A** Vehicle type 1150   **B** Vehicle types 1151, 1152, 1153, 1155   **C** All models (see text)

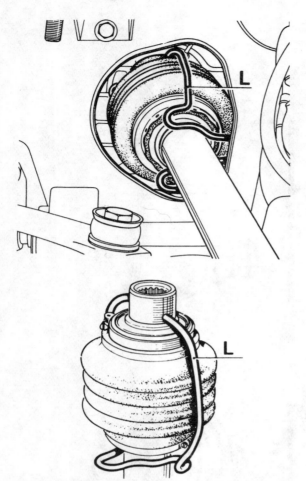

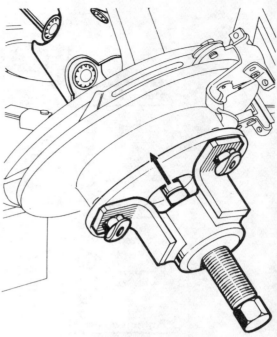

FIG 9:21   Pressing the drive shaft out of the hub

FIG 9:20   The special clip for holding the 4-ball type couplings

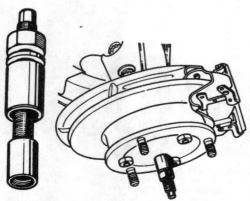

FIG 9:22   Refitting the drive shaft to the hub

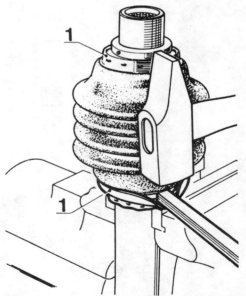

FIG 9:23   Removing the crimped clamps on 4-ball type couplings

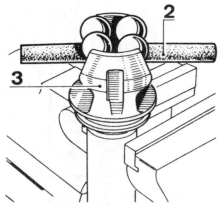

FIG 9:24   Refitting the balls to a coupling

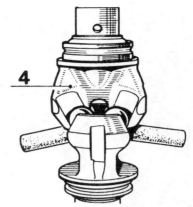

FIG 9:25   Refitting the yoke to a drive coupling

vehicles prior to the following chassis numbers unless the lower suspension arms are modified. All types R.1154, and R.1156 are modified.

> R.1150 NR and PR 502653
> R.1150 Special versions 550209
> R.1151 NR and PR 129839
> R.1151 Special versions 153128
> R.1152 8858
> R.1153 NR and PR 4240

Cars for use in extreme cold have a stainless steel protective sleeve and rubber cover fitted over the outer couplings.

The repair to the inboard couplings are dealt with in the next section but **it should be noted that the outboard coupling, except spider GE 86, cannot be repaired and if it is worn or defective a new drive shaft must be fitted.**

Removal:

1 Jack-up the car and remove the road wheel. On models fitted with 4-ball type couplings next to the transmission a retaining clip **L** must be fitted to the coupling to prevent it falling apart as shown in **FIG 9:20**. The special clip is supplied with new drive shafts but if one is not available use soft wire wrapped around the coupling instead. Drive out the rollpin that secures the coupling to the transmission sunwheel.
2 Disconnect the upper suspension ball joint and the steering ball joint from the stub axle after removing the brake caliper. Pivot the stub axle outwards about the lower suspension ball joint so that the coupling frees from the transmission, and protect the bearing seal with the special protective cap or a length of rubber hose or masking tape.
3 Fit the special tool T.Av.235 to the hub and use the central bolt of the tool to press the drive shaft out of the hub, as shown in **FIG 9:21**.

Reassembly:

The stub axle splines should be smeared with Molykote grease and the shaft then passed through the sidemember. Pull it into place using the special tool T.Av.236, as shown in **FIG 9:22**, taking care to ensure that the deflector plate in the stub axle is correctly positioned.

Remove the protective cover and refit the drive coupling to the transmission using new rollpins and sealing their ends with Rhodorsil.

Reconnect the ball joints, tighten the hub nut to a torque of 16 kgm (115 lb ft) and refit the brake caliper. Check the level of the transmission oil.

9:10 Servicing the drive shaft couplings
Bed and TE couplings:

These are fitted to the outboard end of the drive shaft nearest the road wheels, and they can either be machined out of steel or made out of castings. In either case if the coupling is worn a new drive shaft must be fitted so check these couplings before servicing the inboard couplings.

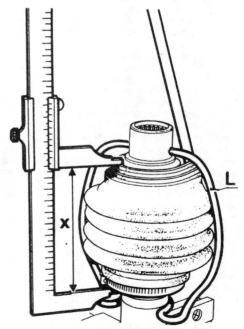

FIG 9:26   Setting a 4-ball type coupling

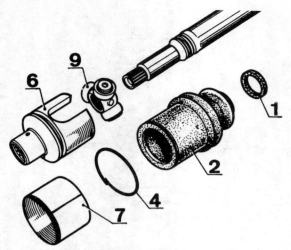

FIG 9:27 The Spider GI 76 coupling components

Key to Fig 9:27 1 Ring 2 Bellows 4 Circlip 6 Yoke
7 Cover 9 Spider

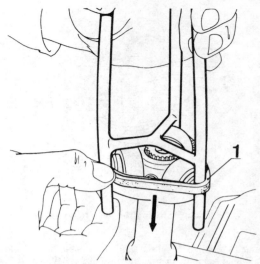

FIG 9:28 Refitting the ring with the aid of the special
tool

4-ball type couplings:

A kit is available for servicing these couplings and it
consists of a new bellows, two worm-driven clips and a
measure of special oil.

Mount the shaft vertically with the coupling upwards
in the padded jaws of a vice. Remove the two crimped
clips as shown in **FIG 9:23**. Mark the position of the yokes
relative to one another using light scribe marks and split
bellows with a sharp knife so that they can be removed.

If possible the four balls should be refitted into their
original positions, though they are of exactly the same
diameter on each coupling and it will not matter unduly
if their positions are interchanged. Pull the coupling apart
and collect the balls.

Wash all the parts in clean fuel and then examine them
for wear or damage. Check the ramps for pin holes, signs
of seizing, excessive blueing marks, or cracks. Use a
finger to check that there are no depressions in the ramps.
Also check the rollpin holes, splines, and bearing sealing
surface. If any of the parts are worn or damaged then a
complete new drive shaft must be fitted.

Mount the drive shaft vertically in the padded jaws of a
vice and place a piece of rubber tube 2, 10 mm (.4 inch)
in diameter, across the coupling as shown in **FIG 9:24**
and then lay the balls back into place. Press the yoke 4
back into place to locate the balls, as shown in **FIG
9:25**, and withdraw the rubber tube.

Place the special tool No. T.Av.51 over the coupling
so that its legs rest on the vice and then lightly oil the legs.
Slide the new bellows down the special tool into position
and then withdraw the special tool. Fit the bellows into
the grooves on the yokes and secure them with the bottom
clip only. Pull the upper end of the bellows away from
the upper yoke and pour in all the oil from the measure.
Use a rod to pull the bellows away from the yoke and
leave the rod in position so that air can escape when the
coupling is set.

Fit the special clip **L** to the coupling and slide it
along until the dimension **X** between the machined faces

on the yokes is correct at 113 ± 1 mm ($4.45 \pm .04$ inch),
as shown in **FIG 9:26**. Fit the new upper clip after removing the rod, and leave the special clip **L** in place until the
drive shaft has been refitted.

Spider GI 76 coupling:

The components of a Spider GI 76 coupling are shown
in **FIG 9:27**. Kits are available for servicing the coupling.
The first kit consists of a new set of bellows 2 with ring 1
and circlips 4, as well as three sachets of grease. The
second kit is a new yoke 6 and cover 7, while the third
kit is a new spider 9.

Normally only the first kit is required for servicing but if
parts are found to be worn after dismantling further kits
should be obtained as required.

Cut or prise off the ring 1 and prise off the circlip 4
with the drive shaft mounted horizontally in the padded
jaws of a vice. Split the bellows with a knife and remove
them. Carefully slide the yoke 6 and cover 7 off the
spider **taking great care not to allow the roller
cages to come free from the trunnions of the
spider.** Once the yoke is off, wrap the spider with
masking tape or a strong elastic band to keep the roller
cages in place. **The yoke and cover can be washed
in fuel but the spider assembly must only be
wiped and never washed in solvent.**

Check the parts for wear and renew them as required.
If the spider is worn or damaged press it off using a
hydraulic press. The three locking points on the shaft will
free themselves. Drive the new spider back onto the shaft
using a copper hammer, with the chamfer towards the
shaft, until the chamfer touches the shoulder, and then
use a pin punch to spread the metal of the splines over
the spider so as to lock it in place. The locking points
should be made at three places spread evenly around the
hub.

Tool No. T.Av.410 should be used for reassembling the
coupling as it holds the rollers in place while allowing the
ring and bellows to be slid into place. Fit the ring 1 to the

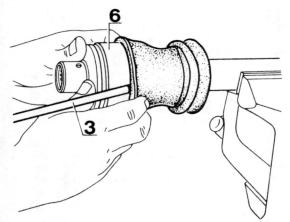

FIG 9:29   Refitting the yoke to a Spider GI 76 coupling

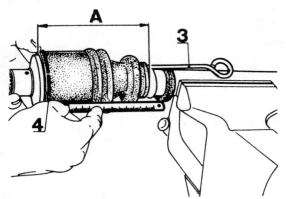

FIG 9:30   Setting a Spider GI 76 coupling

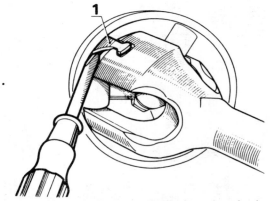

FIG 9:31   Lifting the starplate clips from the yoke slots

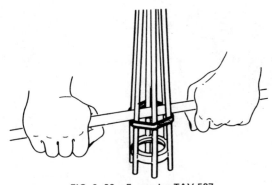

FIG 9:32   Expander TAV 537

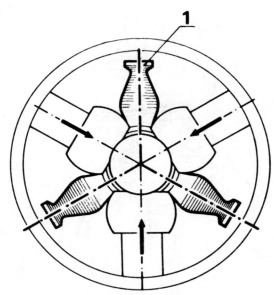

FIG 9:33 Positioning the starplate

shaft as shown in **FIG 9:28**. Fit the new bellows to the tool and slide the bellows into place along the tool so that they fit into the drive shaft groove. Pour the contents of one grease sachet into the bellows and the contents of the other two sachets into the yoke. Remove the elastic band or masking tape that is holding the rollers in place, **taking great care not to allow the rollers to fall off,** and smear the ends of the trunnions with a little of the grease.

Position the yoke and its cover opposite to the shaft and slide the assembly into position, using a rod 3 to guide the bellows into place as shown in **FIG 9:29**, and then fit the bellows into the groove on the yoke. Refit the circlip 4.

Make sure that the bellows are correctly in their grooves and slide a rod into the bellows to allow air to escape. Adjust the coupling until the dimension **A** between the ends of the bellows is correct at 156 mm ($6\frac{1}{8}$ inch), as shown in **FIG 9:30**, and then remove the rod 3 and secure the bellows by fitting the ring 1 back into place.

Spider GE 86 coupling:

The spider GE 86 has a stub axle with a bell shaped housing for the spider and rollers and the drive shaft yoke is retained by a starplate.

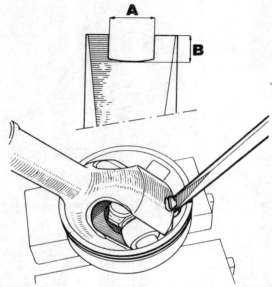

FIG 9:34 Reassembling the starplate clips to the yoke slots

Key to Fig 9:34 **A** = 5 mm ($\frac{13}{64}$ inch) **B** = 3 mm ($\frac{1}{8}$ inch)

FIG 9:35 Fitting clip to bellows

Cut off the bellows and remove as much grease as possible. Free the drive shaft yoke from the starplate by lifting each of the clips in turn (see **FIG 9:31**). **Do not bend the starplate.**

Remove the thrust ball and spring. The clip and bellows expander T.AV 537 will be required to fit the new parts. Lubricate the expander rods and slide the clip onto the expander, as far as the former (see **FIG 9:32**).

Locate the expander over the drive shaft yoke and slide the clip onto the shaft. Position the bellows in a similar manner.

Hold the stub axle in a padded vice and refit the spring and thrust ball. Move the rollers towards the centre and position the starplate as shown in **FIG 9:33**. Insert the drive shaft yoke, tilting it to engage one of the starplate clips into the yoke slot. Engage the other starplate clips similarly using a modified screwdriver as shown in **FIG 9:34**.

Ensure that the starplate is correctly located and check that the coupling operates without tight spots. Pack the 270 g ($9\frac{1}{2}$ oz) measure of grease evenly round the coupling.

Fit the new bellows correctly into the grooves, lift the large end of the bellows with a smooth rod to relieve any air pressure, fit the clip and retaining collar over the bellows with a piece of soft iron wire as shown in **FIG 9:35**.

9:11 Fault diagnosis

(a) Wheel wobble

1 Unbalanced wheels and tyres
2 Worn hub bearings
3 Uneven tyre wear
4 Worn suspension pivots
5 Worn suspension ball joints
6 Loose wheel attachments

(b) Bottoming of suspension

1 Weak or distorted torsion bars
2 Dampers defective

(c) Judder or vibration

1 Check 2, 4 and 5 in (a)
2 Incorrect suspension geometry
3 Defective drive shafts

(d) Heavy steering

1 Check 2 in (c)
2 Defective suspension ball joints

(e) Excessive tyre wear

1 Check 1, 2, 4 and 5 in (a); 2 in (b) and 2 in (c)

(f) Rattles

1 Check 2 in (b) and 3 in (c)
2 Defective damper bushes or loose attachments
3 Defective anti-roll bar bushes or loose attachments
4 Broken anti-roll bar
5 General wear throughout the suspension

(g) Knocks

1 Defective drive shaft couplings

CHAPTER 10

THE STEERING SYSTEM

10:1 Description

All models are fitted with a rack-and-pinion steering unit which is mounted on a crossmember between the front wheel arches. Sectioned views of the steering unit are shown in **FIG 10:1** but it should be noted that the unit cannot be serviced and if it is defective a complete new steering unit must be fitted in its place.

The pinion shaft of the steering unit is connected to the inner column of the steering column by a coupling so that there is a direct connection between the steering wheel and pinion shaft. As the pinion rotates it moves the rack from side to side. Steering arms on the ends of the rack transmit the movement directly to stub axles of the front suspension and there is therefore a minimum of moving parts. This ensures that the steering is precise with little lost motion and that the 'feel' at the steering wheel is good. The simplicity of the layout can be seen in **Chapter 9, FIG 9:1**.

Pivot bolts attach the inner ends of the steering arms to the rack while sealed ball joints connect the outer ends of the steering arms to the stub axles. If the ball joints are worn then the complete steering arm must be renewed.

10:2 Removing the steering unit

Jack up the front of the car and place it securely on chassis stands. Remove the front road wheels and disconnect the battery. The procedure immediately following is for removing the steering unit only, leaving the crossmember still fitted.

1 Disconnect the ball joint from the stub axle on the opposite side to which the steering column is fitted. The best method of disconnecting the ball joint after removal of the securing nut is to use the special tool T.Av.54.01, which has a fork that fits between the steering arm and stub axle with a screw that then presses the tapered portion of the ball joint out of the stub axle. Disconnect the other steering arm from the steering unit by taking out the pivot pin shown in **FIG 10:2**. If the special extractor is not available it is best to disconnect both steering arms directly from the steering unit and leave them both attached to the stub axles.

2 Remove the two bolts that secure the Straflex coupling between the pinion shaft and steering column, shown in **FIG 10:3**. Take out the four bolts that

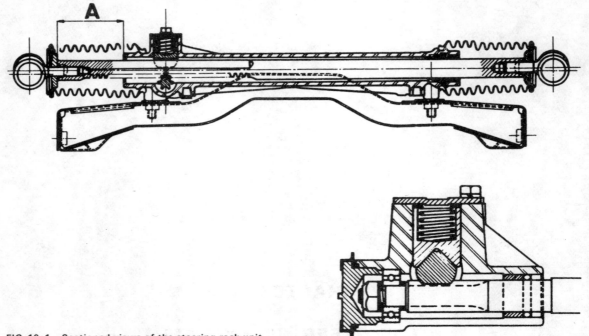

FIG 10:1   Sectioned views of the steering rack unit

secure the steering unit, shown in **FIG 10:4**, to the crossmember.

3 Turn the steering to full lock opposite the side on which the steering column is fitted, and pull the end of the steering unit nearest to the steering column forwards so that the pinion shaft frees from the steering column, then lift the unit out of the car. **Carefully collect the shims under the unit and keep them in order.**

The method of removing the steering unit complete with the crossmember is very similar and this should be done whenever the engine or transmission is to be removed. Disconnect the Straflex coupling and both steering arms from the steering unit. Remove the four bolts (two on each side as shown in **FIG 10:5**) that secure the crossmember, and then remove the assembly as for removing the unit alone.

Refitting:

The unit is refitted in the reverse order of removal. Make sure that the shims fitted between the steering unit and crossmember are refitted into their original positions, as they control the track. If a new steering unit is fitted then use shims to a thickness of 2 mm (.079 inch) under either end and have the shimming and tracking checked by an agent after reassembly. Lubricate the pivot pins that connect the steering arms to the unit with Hatmo grease and make sure that they are horizontal after reassembly.

Steering arms:

It should be noted that these are not interchangeable from side to side. The straight part of the arm must be fitted to the front of the car as shown in **FIG 10:2** (AV forwards).

The arm is removed by disconnecting it from the stub axle and steering unit as described earlier. If the dust cover on the ball joint is wearing or splitting it must be renewed before dirt enters the ball joint. Disconnect the ball joint and prise off the old cover with a screwdriver. Fill the new cover with 6 to 7 grammes ($\frac{1}{4}$ ounce) of Elf No. 962 grease before refitting it with the aid of a 32 mm ($1\frac{1}{4}$ inch) diameter tube.

10:3 The steering wheel

To remove the steering wheel first remove the embellisher by taking out its two securing screws from underneath the steering wheel. Undo the nut that secures the steering wheel to the column and lightly mark across the hub and column so that the wheel will be refitted back in its original position.

Remove the steering wheel, preferably using a special extractor, Dir.372 for models before 1968 and Dir.21A for later models. It may be possible to remove the steering wheel without the special extractor. Try rocking gently on the rim of the wheel while applying a steady pull, or else try to remove the wheel with firm blows at the base of the spokes by the hub, using the flat of the hand.

The steering wheel is refitted in the reverse order of removal. If a new wheel is being fitted or the parts were not marked on dismantling set the steering unit to the straight-ahead position (see next section) and refit the steering wheel so that the spokes make equal angles with the horizontal. If the spokes are not level when driving straight-ahead, the wheel should be removed and correctly refitted as described in this section.

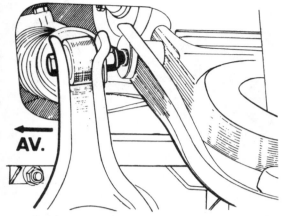

FIG 10:2 The attachment of the steering arm to the rack

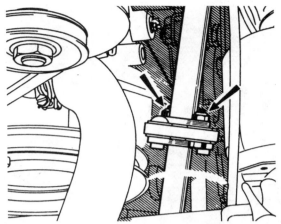

FIG 10:3 The Straflex coupling attachment bolts

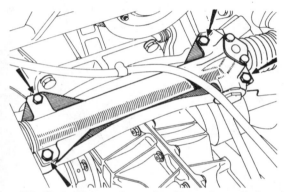

FIG 10:4 The steering rack unit attachment bolts

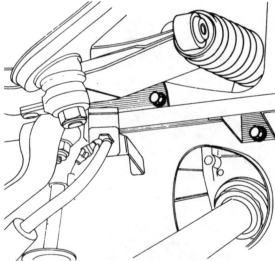

FIG 10:5 The bolts attaching the crossmember to the frame

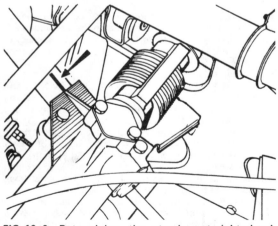

FIG 10:6 Determining the steering straight-ahead position

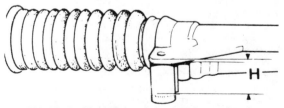

FIG 10:7 The height of the steering rack unit

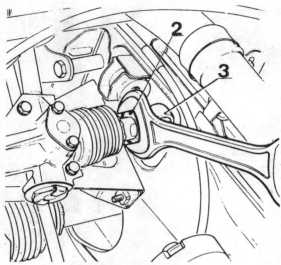

FIG 10:8   Adjusting the track

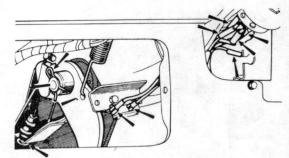

FIG 10:10   The pedal and electrical connections

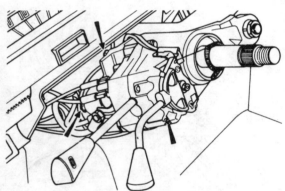

FIG 10:9   The switch attachments

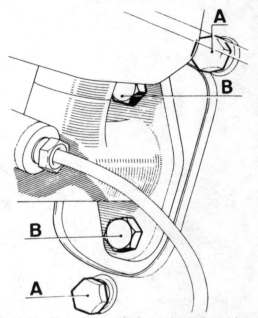

FIG 10:11   The master cylinder and steering column attachments

10:4 The steering geometry

Finding straight-ahead position:

There are three methods available. The most accurate method is to use the special tool Dir.229 which is fitted between the end of the rack housing and the locknut on the end of the rack, as shown in **FIG 10:6**. Another method is to turn the steering until the mark on the pinion shaft aligns with the web on the housing, as shown by the arrow in **FIG 10:6**. The third method is to turn the steering until the dimension A, shown in **FIG 10:1**, is correct at 78 mm ($3\frac{1}{16}$ inch).

Once the straight-ahead position has been found the steering can be locked by fitting the special clamp T.Av.34 to the steering column just above the Straflex coupling.

Track and steering box shimming:

The shims fitted between the steering rack unit and its crossmember control the track and steering geometry. There is no easy way of checking the shimming without

the use of special equipment and for this reason the car must be taken to an agent if adjustments are required. If a new steering box is fitted then shims of a thickness of 2 mm should be fitted under either end as a starting reference but these will probably not be the correct final ones required.

On all R.1150 models made before January 1968 and fitted with original steering units the correct track setting is 0 to 3 mm (0 to $\frac{1}{8}$ inch) **toe-in.** On all other models the correct setting is 0 to 3 mm (0 to $\frac{1}{8}$ inch) **toe-out.** On the earlier models the height **H** of the steering unit (shown in **FIG 10:7**) was 42 mm ($1\frac{21}{32}$ inch), but on the later models the height is reduced to 37 mm ($1\frac{15}{32}$ inch). The earlier steering units are no longer available as spares and therefore if a new steering rack unit is fitted the track should be set to the later setting of toe-out.

When measuring the actual tracking it is most advisable to have this done on accurate gauges though it can be checked by the owner if a trammel is made up. Set and lock the wheels in the straight-ahead position and then push the car forwards for a few yards on level ground to settle the suspensions and bearings. Measure the gap between trammel and rim, with the trammel touching the inner rim of the other wheel, at wheel centre height and at the front of the wheel. Mark the positions on the rims with chalk and roll the car forwards so that the wheels turn exactly half a revolution. Again measure the gap between trammel and rim at wheel centre height but at the rear of the rim and the difference between the two dimensions represents the tracking of the wheels.

Provided that the shimming under the steering rack unit is known to be correct and the track requires adjustment, shown by the tyres wearing with a characteristic feathered edge to one side of the tread, the track can be adjusted at the inner attachments of the steering arms. Disconnect the steering arm from the rack and slacken the locknut 2, shown in **FIG 10:8**. Screw the end fitting 3 inwards to give toe-in and outwards to give toe-out. Each half turn of the end fitting will alter the track by 1.5 mm ($\frac{1}{16}$ inch). Reconnect the steering arm and make sure that the pivot pin is horizontal before retightening the locknut 2.

10:5 Removing the steering column:

1 Disconnect the battery and put the steering column lock into the 'Garage' position. Remove the steering wheel as described in **Section 10:3**.

2 Take off the cover from the steering column switches. Disconnect the indicator switch return spring and remove the bolts (shown in **FIG 10:9**) which secure the lighting switch, so that it can be freed. Mark the clamp position in relation to the steering tube. Remove the bolt that secures the gear selector clamp and unscrew the gearlever ball joint, see **Chapter 6, Section 6:3**.

3 Remove the glove compartment and disconnect the clutch and brake pedal springs. Remove the clip and take off the pedals and also free the outer cable' from its stop on the pedals. Label the electrical leads and disconnect them from the brake light switch and the steering lock. All the attachments in this operation are shown in **FIG 10:10**.

4 Disconnect the steering column from the steering unit. This can be done by removing the pin at the pedal assembly end from the universal joint. It can also be done by taking out the two bolts that secure the Straflex coupling but in this case great care must be taken not to damage the grommet on the scuttle as the flange is drawn through it.

FIG 10:12   The column universal joint

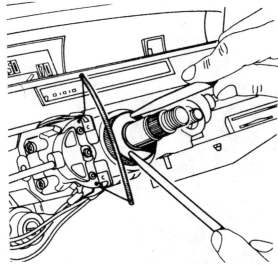

FIG 10:13   Removing the steering column upper bush

5 Remove the steering column top fixing, noting that it will be necessary to disconnect the speedometer cable in order to free the pin.

6 On cars not fitted with a Master-Vac unit remove the bolts **B** that secure the steering column and master cylinder. On cars fitted with a Master-Vac also remove the additional bolts **A** shown in **FIG 10:11**. Withdraw the steering column out of the car.

Refitting:

The steering column is refitted in the reverse order of removal. The upper clamp must not be tightened until the unit is fully back in place and all other operations completed.

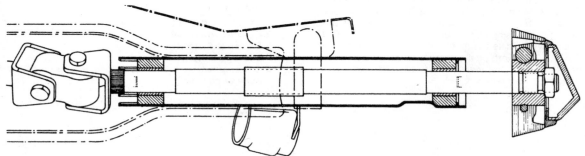

FIG 10:14   Sectioned view of the steering shaft assembly

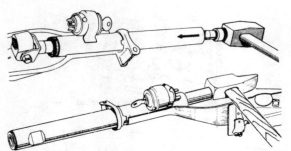

FIG 10:15   Removing the bushes

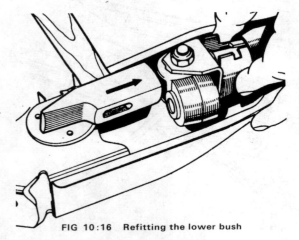

FIG 10:16   Refitting the lower bush

The universal joint pins should both be tightened to a torque of 3.5 ± .5 kg m (25 ± 4 lb ft) but they must be tightened with the steering correctly positioned. Jack-up the front of the vehicle. The lower pin **A**, shown in **FIG 10:12**, should be tightened with the steering in the straight-ahead position and the steering should then be turned $\frac{1}{4}$ turn to the right for tightening the upper pin **B**.

Once the unit has been refitted all the controls and services which have been disturbed should be checked and adjusted as required.

10:6 Servicing the steering column

Upper bush:

Disconnect the battery and remove the steering wheel. Take off the switch cover and disconnect the direction indicator return spring. Unscrew the gearchange control clamp securing bolt and remove the snap rings. Remove the old bush, using two scribers as shown in **FIG 10:13**.

Lightly lubricate the new bush with Spargraph grease and fit it back into position using a tube of 20 mm (.79 inch) internal diameter. Reassemble the parts in the reverse order of removal.

Shaft bushes:

To renew these it will be necessary to remove the steering column as described in the previous section. Remove the brake pedal pin. A sectioned view of the assembly is shown in **FIG 10:14**.

Fit a protective drift over the end of the shaft and drive both it, and the bush nearest to the universal joint, out by tapping lightly on the end as shown in **FIG 10:15**.

Remove the circlip that secures the bush nearest the steering wheel and pass a long tube of 26 mm (1$\frac{1}{32}$ inch) external diameter up inside the tube so that it can be used to drive the bush out through the open end, as shown in the lower portion of **FIG 10:15**.

Lightly lubricate the new bushes with Spargraph grease. Drive the upper bush back into position using a drift of 20 mm (.79 inch) external diameter and secure it with the circlip, making sure that the bush is correctly fitted between the dishings. Slide the inner column back into place.

Fit the new split lower bush back onto the steering column shaft and then fit the two halves of the special tool Dir.321 around the shaft between the fork and bush. Drive the bush back into position, while holding the special tool in place, as shown in **FIG 10:16** and then remove the tool when the bush is correctly positioned.

Refit the steering column in the reverse order of removal.

10:7 Fault diagnosis

(a) Wheel wobble

1 Defective or worn suspension
2 Worn hub bearings
3 Unbalanced wheels and tyres
4 Slack or worn steering connections
5 Incorrect geometry

(b) Wander

1 Check 1, 4 and 5 in (a)
2 Front and rear suspensions not in line (damaged frame)
3 Uneven tyre pressures or wear

(c) Heavy steering

1 Check 5 in (a)
2 Defective ball joints
3 Defective steering rack unit
4 Very low tyre pressures
5 Bent or distorted steering column
6 Defective bushes in steering column

(d) Lost motion

1 Check 1 and 4 in (a) and 2 and 3 in (c)
2 Defective universal joint
3 Defective Starflex coupling
4 Loose steering wheel
5 Steering wheel hub or column splines excessively worn or damaged

CHAPTER 11

THE BRAKING SYSTEM

11:1 Description

All the models are fitted with disc brakes at the front wheels and drum brakes at the rear wheels as standard, and all four brakes are operated by hydraulic pressure when the footbrake is operated. The brake pedal is connected by a pushrod to a master cylinder and hydraulic pressure is generated in this master cylinder and then led to the individual brakes through a system of flexible hoses and metal pipes, shown in **FIG 11:1**. The rear drum brakes are operated by cables from the handbrake lever for parking the car, and on certain later cars include a device for automatic compensation for wear of the friction linings.

Different types of front disc brakes have been fitted at different times to the various models and the three types of disc brake are shown in **FIG 11:2**. The Bendix type 11 disc brakes are fitted to all R.1150 models made before 1969 while later R.1150 models and R.1152 and R.1153 can be fitted with either Bendix type 111AS or Girling brakes. All the other models are fitted with Bendix type 111AS brakes as standard from the first, except R.1156 which is fitted with Bendix type 111AC. Some very early models of the R.1150 may be fitted with Bendix type 1 brakes but these are very similar to the type 11 brakes.

The design and make of the rear drum brakes has also been altered throughout the range and the different types of brake fitted are shown in **FIG 11:3**.

All models, except the R.1150, are fitted with a Master-Vac brake servo. This is a unit that fits between the brake pedal pushrod and the hydraulic master cylinder and it is supplied with vacuum from the inlet manifold of the engine. When the brakes are applied the piston in the unit assists the brake pedal and doubles the pressure applied to the master cylinder piston so that for the same retardation the brake pedal load is reduced.

On later cars and those for the North American market a tandem master cylinder is fitted in place of the conventional master cylinder. The unit contains two pistons in series and the front and rear brakes are hydraulically isolated from one another, so that failure in one system will leave fluid in the other system and some retardation will still be possible, though a longer pedal travel will be required. A pressure drop indicator is fitted to the side of the master cylinder and if there is a pressure differential between the two systems, such as when one system has failed or run out of fluid, the indicator operates a warning lamp on the dashboard.

Later pressure drop indicators incorporate a by-pass

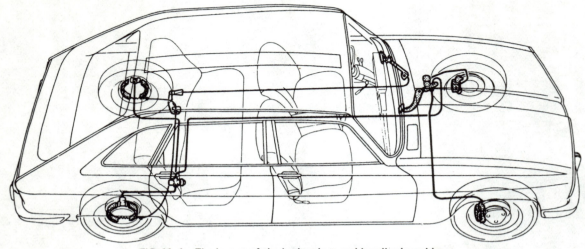

FIG 11:1   The layout of the brake pipes and handbrake cables

IDENTIFICATION OF FRONT BRAKES

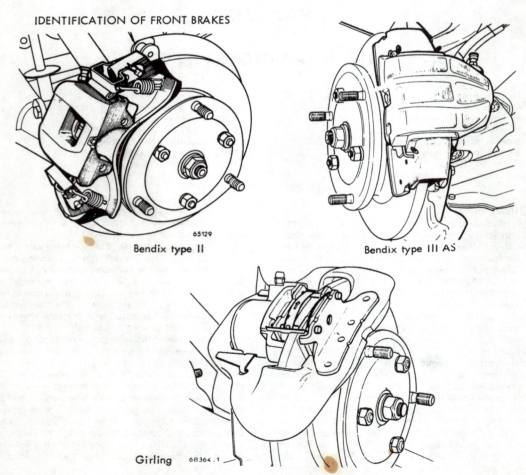

Bendix type II

Bendix type III AS

Girling

FIG 11:2   Identification of the front disc brakes

to the rear brakes downstream of the limiter giving full pressure to the rear brakes in case of a failure of the front brakes.

A pressure limiter switch is fitted into the pipe line to the rear brakes. The unit is connected by a link to the rear suspension and it limits the maximum pressure obtainable in the rear brakes. This ensures that the rear brakes do not lock under heavy braking.

11 : 2 Adjustments

The front disc brakes are self-adjusting though the thickness of lining material on the pads should be checked at regular intervals and the pads renewed when the linings are thin.

Rear brakes :

The rear drum brakes should be adjusted when the brake pedal travel becomes excessive. The adjustment of Bendix brakes, using special tool Fre.279, is shown in **FIG 11 : 4**. With the rear of the car jacked up, turn both adjusters **C** and **T** in the directions shown by the arrows until the brake shoes are in contact with the drum and then slacken them off until the wheel rotates freely. Adjust the other rear brake in a similar manner and then lower the car back to the ground.

The adjustment on Girling brakes, using special tool No. Fre.458, is shown in **FIG 11 : 5**. Jack up the rear of the car and turn the adjuster clockwise until the brake shoes contact the brake drum, then slacken off the adjuster until the wheel revolves freely. Adjust the other brake in a similar manner and lower the car back to the ground.

Certain later cars are fitted with a mechanism by means of which the clearance between the brake shoes and the drum is kept at a constant figure and so compensates for wear on the friction linings.

This is achieved by the use of a spreader bar of adjustable length between the webs of the two shoes, the threaded adjusting screw of which is operated by a spring loaded lever each time the brakes are applied.

Handbrake :

Normally adjustment of the brakes should reset the handbrake as well. If after the brakes have been adjusted the handbrake travel is still excessive, jack up the rear of the car and support it securely on chassis stands. Slacken both locknuts 3, shown in **FIG 11 : 6**, and turn the sleeve 1 until the cables are shortened sufficiently for the brake shoes to make contact with the drums. Slacken off the sleeve 1 until the rear wheels rotate freely and then lock it with the nuts 3.

If adjustment of the sleeve 1 is not sufficient to reduce the handbrake travel then, and only then, should adjustments be made at the clevis 2, shown in **FIG 11 : 7**.

On those cars fitted with automatic adjustment for the rear drum brakes handbrake adjustment is carried out in the same way as for those with manual adjustment. In order to maintain correct operating conditions for the automatic mechanism, it is important to ensure a minimum travel of 12 notches for the handlever.

Master cylinder clearance :

There must always be a small amount of free play on the brake pedal to ensure that the master cylinder piston returns fully to its rest position. The attachment of the standard master cylinder is shown in **FIG 11 : 8** and **K** is the clearance to be set correctly. Slacken the locknut **E** and turn the pushrod 1 until the clearance is correct at .5 mm ($\frac{1}{64}$ inch). The clearance cannot be measured and it must be set by feel. When correct tighten the locknut **E**.

On models fitted with a Master-Vac the clearance is set at the Master-Vac pushrod, see **Section 11 :11**.

Brake limiter :

This device, which is mounted beneath the rear end of the car, is designed to ensure that the rear wheels do not lock up under heavy braking and is connected in such a way as to react to the loading on the rear wheels of the car from a spring connected to the anti-roll bar.

It does not limit the pressure to the rear brake units to any specific figure, but, from a certain pressure value, ensures that for any pressure applied to the front wheels a correspondingly lower pressure is applied to the rear units.

The method of checking the limiter is shown in **FIG 11 : 9**. Fit the special pressure gauge Fre.214.02 to a rear brake in place of the bleed screw. Bleed the system through the bleed screw **P** so as to remove the air from the gauge. Make sure that the car is on level ground with an operator in the driver's seat and the fuel tank full. Have the assistant apply heavy pressure to the brake pedal and check that the rear brake pressure is between 29 and 34 kg/sq cm (415 to 485 lb/sq inch).

If the pressure is incorrect refer to the top of **FIG 11 :10**. Make sure that the rod 1 is securely attached to the anti-roll bar and then slacken the nut 2. Adjust the cut-off pressure by sliding the rod 1 through the clamping bolt as necessary. Tighten the nut 2 and check the pressure on several brake applications.

If the valve is defective it cannot be repaired and a new valve must be fitted in its place. If the valve is removed, label the pipes to avoid confusion on refitting.

Remove the gauge and refit the bleed screw so that the braking system can be bled.

Brake compensator :

This unit is only fitted to the R.1156 model. It is controlled by a spring hooked onto a clamp on the anti-roll bar as shown in the middle diagram of **FIG 11 :10**. It is checked under the same conditions as the limiter.

Before checking pressures a positional check must be made on the operating units.

The clamp on the anti-roll bar must be 93 mm ($3\frac{21}{32}$ inch) from the sidemember as shown at **a** and the centre of the smaller hole in the clamp for the operating spring must lie 3.5 mm ($\frac{9}{64}$ inch) behind the vertical centre line of the anti-roll bar as shown at **b**.

The spring adjusting sleeve 1 must be set with a clearance of .5 mm (.020 inch) between it and the operating lever 2 as shown at **A**.

Connect a pressure gauge to a front brake bleed screw, and a pressure gauge to a rear brake bleed screw, and bleed the brakes and the pressure gauges.

Press down on the brake pedal until a pressure of 50 kg/sq cm (710 lb/sq inch) is shown on the front gauge, the corresponding pressure at the rear should be 30 ± 2 kg/sq cm (400 to 455 lb/sq inch), apply more pressure to the brake pedal until the front pressure is 80 kg/sq cm

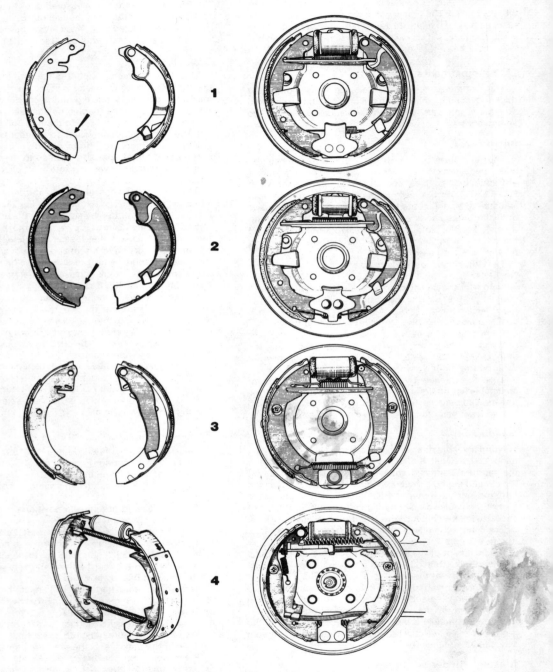

FIG 11:3 Identification of the rear drum brakes

Key to Fig 11:3 1 Bendix, normal fulcrum point 2 Bendix, lowered fulcrum point 3 Girling, manual adjustment 4 Girling, automatic adjustment

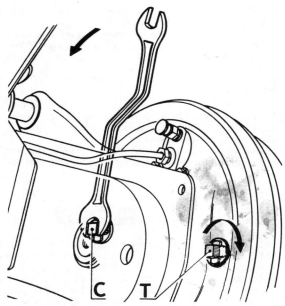

FIG 11:4   Adjusting a Bendix rear brake

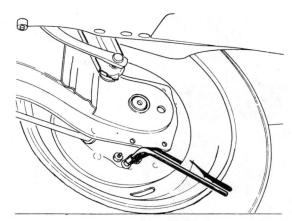

FIG 11:5   Adjusting a Girling rear brake

(1140 lb/sq inch); the rear pressure should be 37 ± 2 kg/sq cm (500 to 555 lb/sq inch).

If there is a variation from these values, renew the brake compensator.

11:3 Preventive maintenance

At regular intervals check the fluid level in the master cylinder reservoir. If the reservoir is made of translucent plastic it is not necessary to remove the filler cap as the level can be seen through the reservoir. On models fitted with metal reservoirs the cap must be removed. **Before removing the filler cap wipe it and the top of the reservoir clean to prevent any dirt from falling into the reservoir.** The level will fall slowly as the disc brake pads wear but this is normal. A rapid rate of fall or sudden drop indicates a leak in the system and this must be found and repaired as soon as possible. **It is essential to use the correct type of hydraulic fluid as the wrong type will damage seals and cause the system to fail.** On all models a fluid meeting specification SAE.70.R3 should be used but on pre 1969 models a fluid to specification SAE.70.R1 can be used instead.

At longer intervals the brake drums should be removed from the rear brakes and the lining thickness checked. Blow and brush out all loose dirt before refitting the brake drum. At the same time the disc brake pads should also be checked for wear.

At approximately 2 year intervals the hydraulic fluid should be drained out of the system. The pipes should be flushed through with methylated spirits to clean out any sediment or dirt and the components can then be dismantled for examination. Renew defective parts and reassemble the system using all new seals and then fill and bleed with fresh hydraulic fluid.

The flexible hoses should be renewed at intervals of 5 years as this is normally their safe maximum life.

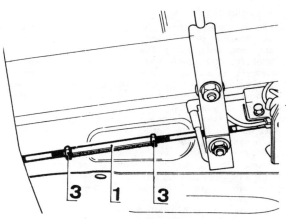

FIG 11:6   Adjusting handbrake secondary cables

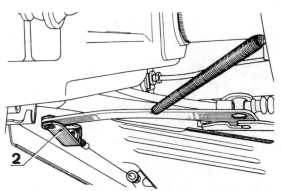

FIG 11:7   Adjusting handbrake primary cable

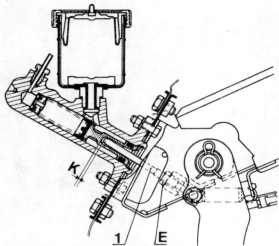

FIG 11:8 The standard master cylinder, without Master-Vac, attachments

11:4 Flexible hoses

Great care must be taken not to twist or strain the flexible portion of the hose either when removing or refitting. The union nut that secures the metal pipeline to the flexible hose should be unscrewed first and then any clips that secure the hose to the bracket removed. Disconnect the hose from the bracket and then unscrew the other end of the hose, allowing the flexible portion to rotate freely.

Refit the hose in the reverse order of removal, making sure that the flexible portion is not under strain when the hose is in position.

If a hose is blocked and cannot be cleared by blowing through it then it must be renewed. **Do not attempt to clear a hose by poking wire through it.** Renew hoses which show signs of softening or chafing.

11:5 Removing a brake caliper

If care is taken it is possible to remove the caliper and its bracket without disconnecting the flexible hose. This is particularly useful when carrying out work on the

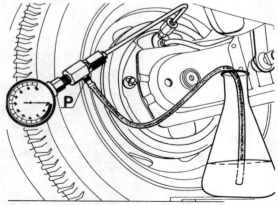

FIG 11:9 Checking the brake limiter

suspension or hub as there will then be no need to bleed the hydraulic system after reassembly.

When disconnecting the hydraulic flexible hoses, blank off the fluid reservoir outlets or fit a filler cap which has had the vent filled in, as this will prevent the hydraulic fluid from flowing out.

Bendix type 11:

Refer to **FIG 11:11**. Remove the spring clips and pins 13 and then tilt the swing clamps 14. Remove the caliper by pulling it out towards the rear and then, if need be, disconnect the flexible hose.

The caliper is refitted in the reverse order of removal. Use a new copper sealing washer if the flexible hose has been disconnected.

Bendix type 111AS:

Remove the pins **A** shown in **FIG 11:12** and then slide out the keys **B** shown in **FIG 11:13** so as to free the caliper.

The method of refitting the caliper is shown in **FIG 1:14**. Fit one end of the caliper into place as shown and then compress both springs so that the other end can be fitted. Refit one key **B** and then use a screwdriver to lever the caliper so that the second key can be slid back into place. Lock the keys in place with the pins **A** fitted so that their flat section faces the caliper bracket.

Girling:

The attachments of the Girling caliper are shown in **FIG 11:15**.

Caliper bracket:

The attachments of the caliper bracket to the stub axle are shown in **FIG 11:16**. Remove the deflector by taking out the two smaller bolts arrowed and then remove the bracket by taking out the two large bolts. Carefully collect any shims **A** fitted. The shims **A** are shaped like an open-ended spanner so that they can be removed or fitted without having to remove fully the two bolts that secure the bracket.

Refit the bracket in the reverse order of removal and then check the shims. Measure, with feeler gauges, the clearances between the disc and bracket at the points **a** and **b** shown in **FIG 11:17**. For Bendix 11 brakes both clearances should be the same at 2.5 ± .5 mm (.098 ± .020 inch) while for Bendix 111AS they should be 3 ± .5 mm (.118 ± .020 inch). The clearance is set by removing or fitting shims **A**, which are available in thicknesses from .5 to 2.5 mm (.020 to .098 inch) in increments of .5 mm (.020 inch).

11:6 Renewing friction pads

The friction pads must be renewed when they are worn otherwise damage will be caused to both the brake disc and the brake caliper. **Only approved pads should be fitted and all four pads should be renewed at the same time, making sure that they are all of the same grade.** New pads must be fitted as new linings cannot be bonded to the olds pads effectively or safely.

Bendix brakes:

On the very early models of the R.1150 a Bendix type 1 brake may be fitted. This is identified by measuring the

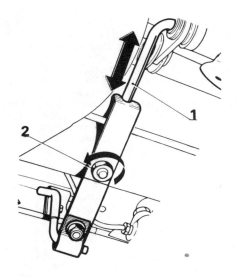

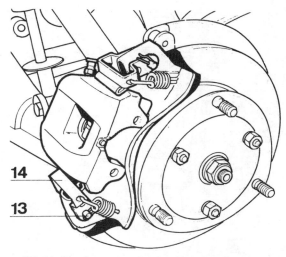

FIG 11:11 Removing the Bendix type 11 caliper

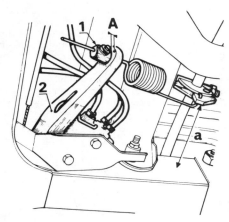

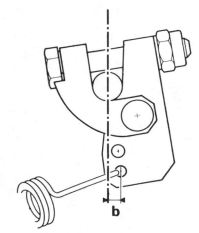

FIG 11:10 Adjusting the brake limiter or compensator

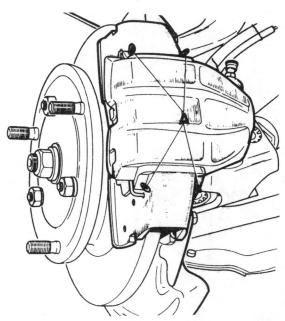

FIG 11:12 The lockpins on the Bendix type 111.AS caliper

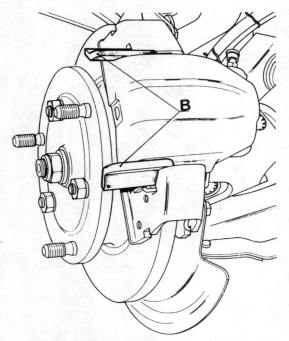

FIG 11:13 The keys on the Bendix type 111.AS caliper

dimension **A** shown in **FIG 11:18** and on the type 1 models it is 34.5 mm ($1\frac{3}{8}$ inch) but on the Type 11 model it is 37 mm ($1\frac{7}{16}$ inch). Different brake pads are fitted on the two types so make sure of obtaining the correct replacement parts. If a Type 11 brake is fitted in place of the earlier brake then both brakes must be renewed and a larger reservoir fitted to the master cylinder.

Some models are fitted with a warning device on the brake pads which operates a lamp on the dash when the friction linings are worn to the minimum thickness.

The wear on the shoes is checked on Type 11 brakes with a suitable depth gauge, such as Fre.363 shown in **FIG 11:19**, by measuring the recess between the caliper 2 and pad 1. The pads must be renewed when the depth of the recess exceeds 5 mm ($\frac{13}{64}$ inch). On Type 111 brakes, the pad thickness including backplate can be checked with a rule and the minimum thickness is 7 mm ($\frac{9}{32}$ inch).

Free the caliper from its bracket and then pull out the brake pads (upwards on Type 11 and outwards on Type 111) and if necessary disconnect the wear warning lead. Remove the thrust springs and check them for weakness or damage.

Remove the rubber dust cover from around the piston and wash the end of the piston with methylated spirits. Fit the special tool No. Fre.447 into the caliper as shown in **FIG 11:20** and use the tool to prevent the piston from coming fully free when the brake pedal is pressed to move the piston outwards.

Wash the skirt of the piston with methylated spirits and then use a paint brush to apply Spargraph grease around it. Push the piston fully back into the caliper by tightening

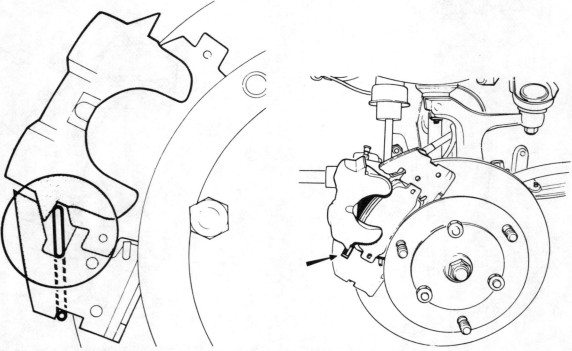

FIG 11:14 Refitting the Bendix type 111.AS caliper

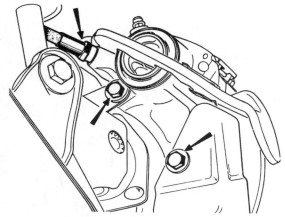

FIG 11:15 The Girling caliper attachments

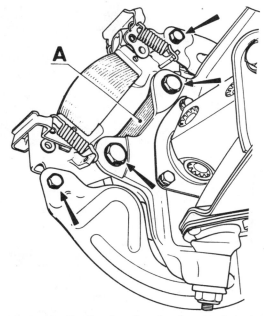

FIG 11:16 The Bendix caliper bracket attachments

FIG 11:17 Setting the Bendix caliper bracket

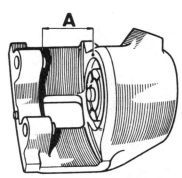

FIG 11:18 Check dimension for early Bendix calipers

the special tool. **During this operation check the level in the reservoir and syphon off surplus fluid to prevent it from overflowing.**

Refit the pads and caliper in the reverse order of removal. On Type 111 brakes the springs are fitted as shown in **FIG 11:21**. On the Type 11 brakes the spring 1 is fitted to the inside and the spring 2 to the outside, see **FIG 11:22**.

Girling brakes:

The minimum pad thickness, including backplate, is 6 mm ($\frac{1}{4}$ inch).

Remove the clip **A** shown in **FIG 11:23** and then remove the clips **B** that secure the two pins in place.

Withdraw the retaining pins and then pull out the pads. A piece of cord may be needed through the holes in the lugs so as to get a firm pull on them.

Clean the area with methylated spirits and push the piston back in, **taking care not to allow fluid to overflow from the master cylinder reservoir.**

Refit the pads in the reverse order of removal, tapping them into place if need be with the wooden handle of a screwdriver.

11:7 Servicing brake discs

The brake disc can be removed from the hub after the hub has been taken off as described in **Chapter 9, Section 9:2.**

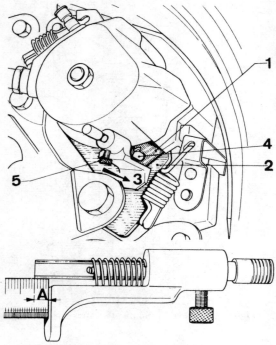

FIG 11:19   Checking the wear on Bendix pads

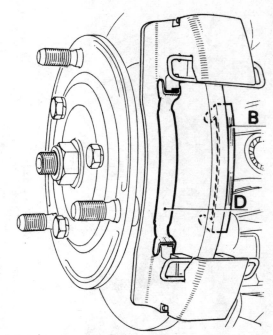

FIG 11:21   The springs correctly fitted on Bendix 111.AS caliper

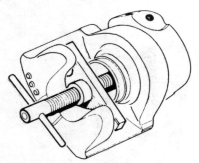

FIG 11:20   The tool Fre.447

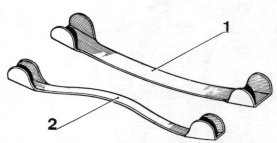

FIG 11:22   The springs for Bendix 11 caliper

When refitting the disc to the hub make sure that the mating surfaces are scrupulously clean otherwise dirt may cause the disc to run out excessively.

When the hub has been refitted correctly use the DTI (Dial Test Indicator) to check the runout of the disc. If the runout is greater than .2 mm (.008 inch) for Bendix 11 and Girling, .1 mm (.004 inch) for Bendix 111AS, or .05 mm (.002 inch) for Bendix 111AC, measured on a diameter of 218 mm ($8\frac{9}{16}$ inch) try rotating the disc in relation to the hub but if this does not cure the fault then a new disc must be fitted.

Light concentric scoring on the disc is perfectly normal but if the scores are deep or radial then a new disc must be fitted.

The brake caliper can be dismantled and new seals fitted but it is advisable to have this carried out by an agent who will have the special tools necessary both for dismantling and checking the parts after reassembly.

11:8 The rear drum brakes

The method of removing the rear brake drum is dealt with in **Chapter 8, Section 8:2**.

Relining brakes:

New shoes must be fitted when the old linings are worn down nearly to the shoes or rivet heads. Do not attempt to reline the old shoes as the result is never satisfactory and always fit approved factory-reconditioned

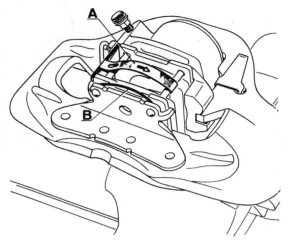

FIG 11:23 Renewing the pads on a Girling disc brake

shoes. All four brake shoes should be renewed at the same time.

Brake shoes must also be renewed if the linings are contaminated with oil grease or paint, so take care when handling the shoes and use clean hands.

The best method of removing the shoes on manually adjusted models is shown in **FIG 11:24**. The clamp Fre.05A prevents the pistons in the wheel cylinder from coming out and the tool Fre.06 protects the linings from damage by the leg of the spring removal pliers Fre.03. If the tools are not available the springs can be removed and refitted using a length of cord through the eye and a wooden handle to pull them in or out of the shoes.

When the return springs have been freed remove the clips **A** and pull back the shoes to free the plate **B**. Disconnect the handbrake cable and remove the old shoes.

The new shoes are fitted in the reverse order of removal. On Girling brakes the brake shoe retaining clips and rods must be renewed at the same time as the shoes. Cover the clips **A** on the backplate side with sealing compound. Refit the brake drum and adjust the brakes before refitting the road wheel.

On self-adjusting brake drums remove the brake drum and unhook the handbrake cable. Unhook and remove spring 5. Remove the adjusting lever C. Remove the top shoe spring in a similar manner to the manually adjusted brakes. Remove the shoe retainers. Unscrew the ratchet wheel adjuster B to shorten the link and remove it. Cross the brake shoes over each other to release the bottom spring tension and pull them upwards.

Refit in the reverse order, but before fitting the top spring adjust the thrust link to suit the lining diameter, approximately 228 mm (9 inch).

Position the adjusting lever parallel to the wheel cylinder so that the ratchet finger is 7 mm (.276 inch) below the centre line of the adjusting lever. Push the handbrake lever back against the shoe. Check that the pull-back springs are hooked on correctly.

After assembly is complete, apply the brakes several times to correct the shoe adjustment.

Ensure on these brakes, as the brake shoes are not identical, that the shoe is fitted with the arrow pointing in

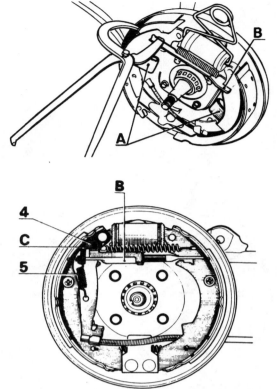

FIG 11:24 Changing the rear brake shoes. Manually adjusted models, top; self-adjusting models, bottom

FIG 11:25 The rear wheel cylinder attachments

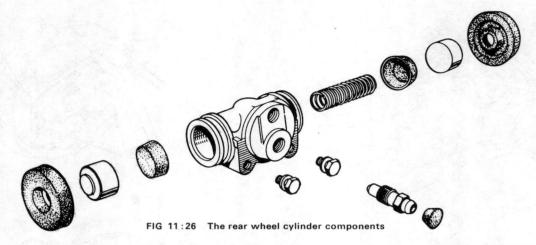

FIG 11:26   The rear wheel cylinder components

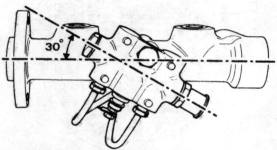

FIG 11:27   The pressure drop indicator position

the direction of drum forward rotation. The thrust links are also handed and must not be interchanged. The lefthand brake threaded pushrod has a lefthand thread with the adjusting thimble marked by a flange. The right-hand brake has a threaded pushrod with a righthand thread and the adjusting thimble is marked by a chamfer.

Wheel cylinder:

The attachments of the wheel cylinder are shown in **FIG 11:25** and the wheel cylinder can be removed after the brake shoes have been taken off.

The components of the wheel cylinder are shown in **FIG 11:26**. Remove the dust covers and gently pull or push out the pistons and seals. Check that the pistons slide freely in the cylinder bore and that the cylinder bore

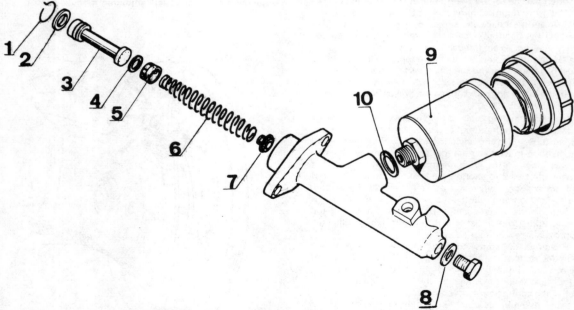

FIG 11:28   The components of the standard master cylinder

Key to Fig 11:28   1 Snap ring   2 Stop washer   3 Piston   4 Copper washer   5 Seal   6 Return spring
7 Check valve   8 Washer   9 Reservoir   10 Seal

132

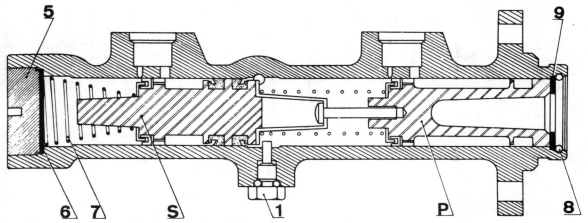

FIG 11:29 Sectioned view of the tandem master cylinder

Key to Fig 11:29   **P** Primary piston   **S** Secondary piston   1 Stop bolt   5 End plug   6 Seal   7 Return spring
8 Snap ring   9 Stop washer

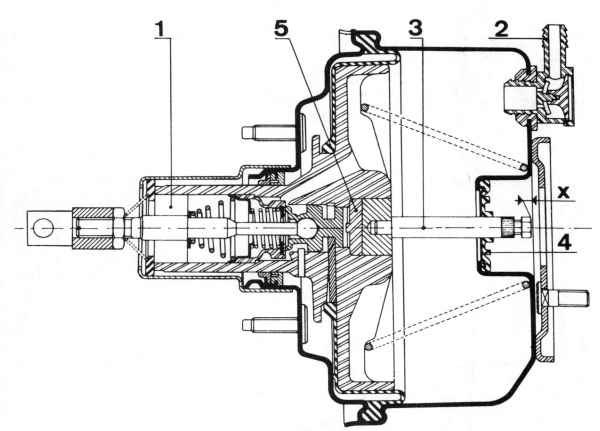

FIG 11:30 Sectioned view of the Master-Vac single master cylinder

Key to Fig 11:30   1 Air filter   2 Non-return valve   3 Pushrod   4 Diaphragm seal   5 Reaction disc

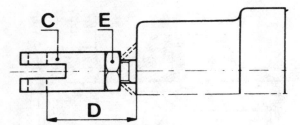

FIG 11:31   Setting the Master-Vac pushrod

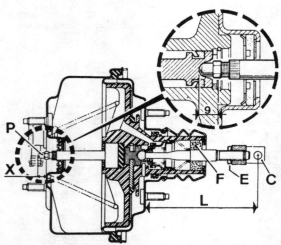

FIG 11:32   Section through Master-Vac on later models

Key to Fig 11:32   C Clevis   **E** Locknut   **F** Filter
L 97 mm   **P** Servo pushrod   **X** 9 mm

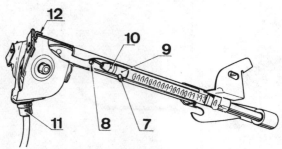

FIG 11:33   The handbrake lever early type

is not worn or scored. Renew the assembly complete if the bore is damaged.

Wet the seals in hydraulic fluid and press them back into the cylinder bore, **taking great care not to bend back or damage the lips of the seal.** Refit the pistons and dust covers and then replace the unit onto the brake backplate. Once the remainder of the parts have been refitted the brakes must be bled and adjusted.

Brake drum:

When the brake drum has been removed check it for cracks or scoring. A cracked brake drum must be renewed though light scoring can be turned out by a specialist firm. If one drum has to be ground oversize then the other drum should also be ground to preserve the braking balance.

Make sure that the braking surface of the drum is free from grease or finger marks before refitting the drum.

11:9 The pressure drop indicator

This is only fitted on models with a tandem braking system and it is mounted onto the master cylinder as shown in **FIG 11:27.** To remove the unit disconnect all four hydraulic pipelines as well as the electrical lead to the switch. Remove the bolt that secures the unit to the master cylinder and take off the unit.

The unit is refitted in the reverse order of removal, setting it at the angle shown in the figure. When the pipes have been reconnected both halves of the hydraulic system must be bled.

The flow for both halves of the brake system passes directly through the unit and the two systems are connected by a metal plunger with seals to make the unit fluid-proof. If the pressure in one half of the system is greater than in the other half, as can be caused by a leak in the system, air in the system, or a defective master cylinder, then the plunger is forced over to the low-pressure side and as it moves it actuates a switch.

If the warning light does come on first find and rectify the fault. Bleed the system through to remove any air. The plunger will have moved to the side with the fault in it so make sure that this side is correctly bled and filled. Open a bleed screw on one of the brakes of the other axle system and apply gradually increasing pressure to the brake pedal until a faint click is heard from the pressure drop indicator and the warning light goes out. Do not apply too much pressure otherwise the plunger will move right over to the other side. Close the bleed screw.

If the unit is defective it cannot be repaired and a new unit must be fitted in its place.

11:10 The master cylinder

The components of the standard master cylinder are shown in **FIG 11:28** and its attachments on models without a Master-Vac are shown in **FIG 11:8.**

The sectioned view of a tandem master cylinder is shown in **FIG 11:29.** The tandem master cylinder is always fitted in conjunction with a Master-Vac.

Removal:

Syphon the fluid out of the reservoir(s) and partially empty the system by pumping the brakes with a bleed screw open on a front and rear brake. Disconnect the pipelines from the master cylinder outlets. There are three pipes connected to a standard master cylinder and two to a tandem master cylinder. **Use rags to catch any drips as hydraulic fluid is a rapid-action paint remover.** On the tandem master cylinder remove the bolt that secures the pressure drop indicator and move the indicator to one side. Take out the two nuts or bolts that secure the master cylinder flange and remove the unit from the car.

The master cylinder is refitted in the reverse order of removal. Fill the system and bleed the brakes. If necessary adjust the brake pedal free play.

Dismantling:

Remove the reservoir, noting that on some models it is screwed into place and on others it is a push fit into a sealing ring. It is not necessary to remove the end plug from either type of unit. If the plug 5 is removed from the tandem master cylinder then a wide well-fitting blade must be used, and because of the torque the handle must be at right angles for leverage and not as a normal screwdriver.

Lightly press the piston down the bore of the tube against the pressure of the return springs, using a tool like a pencil. Remove the snap ring and stopwasher. On the tandem master cylinders still keep the pressure on the primary piston and remove the stop screw 1 that holds the secondary piston in place. Remove the interior parts. This can be done by applying gentle air pressure at a port or by tapping the open end of the cylinder firmly against the palm of the hand so as to dislodge the parts.

Dismantle the internal parts and remove all the old seals using the fingers only.

Reassembly:

Discard all the old seals unless they are in excellent condition. Do not turn the seals inside out as this will damage them. New seals and parts required are available in a service kit.

Wash all the parts in methylated spirits. **No other solvents should be used as they will rot the seals if traces are left.** Check the bore of the cylinder for wear or corrosion and renew the complete unit if the bore is the slightest bit defective.

Wet the new seals and refit them into their respective positions, making sure that the lips are facing in the correct direction. Use only the fingers when refitting the seals and work them around until they seat squarely and fully in their recesses.

Reassemble the internal parts and dip them into hydraulic fluid. Press the internal parts back into the bore of the cylinder, **taking great care not to bend back or damage the lips of the seals as they enter.** Press the piston lightly into the bore and refit the stopwasher and snap ring. Still applying pressure, refit the stop screw 1 and new seal on the tandem master cylinders. Check that the piston returns freely under the action of the return spring and refit the reservoir(s).

11:11 The Master-Vac

This component, which is bolted to the engine compartment bulkhead and coupled directly to the brake pedal, uses the depression in the inlet manifold to augment the pressure exerted by the driver on the brake pedal. It does not improve the braking, but enables a certain braking effort to be achieved with less pressure on the pedal. In the event of failure the Master-Vac should be

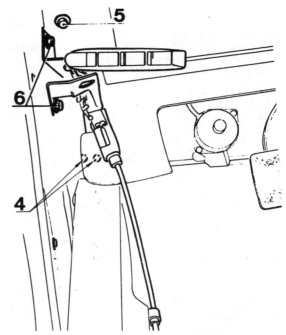

FIG 11:34 The handbrake lever attachments, early type

renewed as unqualified repair is not possible. A sectioned view of a unit as fitted to early cars is given in **FIG 11:30**.

Removal:

Syphon out the fluid from the master cylinder reservoir(s) and disconnect the lines to the master cylinder. On tandem units free the pressure drop indicator from the master cylinder. Disconnect the vacuum hose from the non-return valve 2. Take out the two bolts, on either side of the pedal assembly, that secure the Master-Vac and remove it from the car complete with the master cylinder. Free the master cylinder from the Master-Vac.

The unit is refitted in the reverse order of removal and the brakes must be bled after the unit has been refitted.

Maintenance:

At approximately 20,000 kilometre (12,000 mile) intervals the filter should be renewed. In very dusty conditions the interval should be reduced. The filter can be renewed without removing the Master-Vac from the car. From inside the car remove the clevis pin that secures the pushrod to the brake pedal. Slacken the locknut **E** and remove it and the fork **C**, shown in **FIG 11:31**. Remove the spring holding the filter in place and withdraw the filter. Fit a new filter in the reverse order of removal and adjust the dimension **D** to 42 mm ($1\frac{21}{32}$ inch) before tightening the locknut. This dimension **D** sets the brake pedal movement.

Repairs:

If the non-return valve 2 fails it can be renewed without removing the Master-Vac from the car. Disconnect the vacuum hose and then pull and twist the non-return valve out of its rubber sealing washer. Press a new valve back into position and reconnect the hose.

The diaphragm seal 4 can also be renewed, after the flange that secures the master cylinder has been taken off. **Do not pull on the pushrod 3** as if this is done it is possible for the reaction disc 5 to fall out into the reservoir. Carefully prise out the old seal 4. Lightly grease the push-rod 3 and wrap masking tape around the grooved portion to protect the new seal. Press the new seal back into place using a piece of 40mm (1½ inch) diameter tube.

The dimension **X** should be checked, and adjusted if required, to 6 +0, −.2mm (.228 to .236 inch). This dimension **X** controls the full return of the master cylinder piston.

Later cars:

The Master-Vac installation on later cars, including the 16TX, is slightly different from that shown in **FIG 11 : 30** and is illustrated in **FIG 11 : 32**. This necessitates different dimensions to be observed when refitting the unit after renewing the air filter or removal for any other reason.

Firstly, the clearance between the servo pushrod and the master cylinder. This is correct when the dimension **X** between the end of the pushrod **P** and the mounting face of the master cylinder is 9 mm. This may be obtained by screwing the threaded tip of the pushrod **P** in or out as necessary.

The other dimension which must be set before assembly is **L**, between the centre of the hole in the clevis **C** and the rear mounting face of the servo unit. This must be 97 mm and is obtained by releasing the locknut **E** and screwing the clevis in or out as required.

Renewal of the air filter on these models requires the removal of the servo unit. Then screw off the clevis and locknut and withdraw the filter retaining spring. The filter element can be prised out with a small screwdriver and a new element fitted. Check the dimension **L** before finally securing the clevis.

11 : 12 Bleeding the brakes

This is not routine maintenance but it must be carried out whenever air has entered the braking system. Air can enter either because there is a leak, the fluid level in the reservoir has been allowed to fall too far, or the system has been dismantled and reassembled.

On the models fitted with tandem brakes only the system that has air in it needs to be bled, as the two sets of brakes are hydraulically independent.

Before starting to bleed the system fill the reservoir right up without it actually spilling and then keep a constant check on the level as bleeding progresses. **Use only an approved fluid which meets specification SAE.70.R3.**

Fluid that has been bled through the system should be discarded, and only kept if it is absolutely and perfectly clean. If the fluid is kept it must be stored in a sealed clean container for at least 24 hours to allow all air to disperse. **Fluid from bleeding must never be returned directly to the reservoir.**

The brakes are bled with the car standing on its wheels and in the order of decreasing pipe runs, starting with the brake that has the longest pipe run. On the models fitted with tandem brakes try bleeding by letting the fluid flow through the opened bleed screw until it comes out free of air, and if this does not succeed then bleed the brakes by pumping the pedal. **Take care not to apply excess pressure to the brake pedal when bleeding tandem brakes otherwise the pressure drop indicator will operate and have to be reset.**

Fit a length of plastic or rubber tube to the bleed screw on the brake to be bled and dip the free end of the tube in a little clean hydraulic fluid in a glass container. Open the bleed screw ½ to ¾ turn and have an assistant in the driver's seat. The assistant presses down the brake pedal through its full range of travel and the bleed screw is then tightened before the pedal is released and allowed to return. Carry on with this sequence until the fluid coming out of the tube is perfectly free from air bubbles. Close the bleed screw fully and bleed the remainder of the brakes in a similar manner.

Where a system incorporates a pressure drop indicator with a bypass valve, the bypass circuit should be bled through the bleed screw on the pressure drop indicator after all wheel cylinders have been bled.

Top up the reservoir to the correct level and refit the filler cap. Have the assistant apply heavy pressure to the brake pedal, with the engine running if a Master-Vac is fitted, and check the system for leaks. Note that bleeding is carried out with the engine off and the Master-Vac pumped several times so that it does not operate.

11 : 13 The handbrake

The early lever mechanism is shown in **FIG 11 : 33** and its attachments in **FIG 11 : 34**. The later type has been simplified both in fitting and operation, but servicing procedures are similar.

The primary cable can only be removed after the lever assembly has been freed from inside the car and it can then be disconnected from the lever at the clevis fork, shown in **FIG 11 : 7**.

The two secondary cables are connected by a sleeve, shown in **FIG 11 : 6**. Unscrew the sleeve completely and free the cables from the bracket and cable cover clamp. Remove the brake drums and disconnect the cables from the levers on the brakes.

New cables are refitted in the reverse order of removal and the adjustment is dealt with in **Section 11 : 3**.

11 : 14 Fault diagnosis

(a) Spongy pedal

1 Air in the hydraulic system
2 Fluid leak in the hydraulic system
3 Excessive disc runout
4 Gap between lining and shoes on rear brakes

(b) Excessive pedal movement

1 Check 1 and 2 in (a)
2 Rear brakes require adjusting
3 Excessively worn linings or pads
4 Very low fluid level in reservoir
5 Incorrectly set pedal or Master-Vac pushrod

(c) Brakes grab or pull to one side

1 Check 3 in (b)
2 Wet or oily friction pads or linings
3 Cracked or distorted brake drum
4 Cracked or distorted brake disc
5 Seized handbrake cable
6 Seized wheel cylinder or caliper
7 Uneven tyre pressures
8 Badly worn tyres
9 Mixed linings or pads of different grades
10 Broken shoe return spring
11 Defective suspension or steering

NOTES

CHAPTER 12

THE ELECTRICAL SYSTEM

12:1 Description

All the models are fitted with a 12-volt electrical system in which the Negative (—ve) terminal of the battery is earthed.

An alternator driven by a belt from the engine supplies the current for the system and for charging the battery when the engine is running. **It is essential that the correct polarity of the circuits is observed as reverse voltage can damage the alternator. The charging circuit must always be correctly connected when the engine is running and the regulator must be correctly earthed. When charging the battery or carrying out arc-welding repairs to any part of the car always disconnect both battery cables from the battery. If these precautions are not observed the alternator or its regulator may be damaged.**

A lead/acid battery supplies the power for starting the engine and operating the accessories when the engine is stopped. It also provides the initial excitation current for the alternator and to a degree controls the voltage of the electrical system.

A low-wattage 12-volt test bulb, or any 0 to 20 volt-meter, can be used for checking the continuity of circuits by connecting the tester between the suspect terminal and a good earth on the car. Cheap instruments must not be used when testing the performance or adjusting components as they are unreliable and will not be able to measure to the accuracy required. For such measurements use high-grade, preferably moving-coil, instruments.

Wiring diagrams are given in Technical Data at the end of the manual to enable those with electrical experience to trace and repair wiring faults.

Instructions for servicing electrical equipment are given in this chapter but it must be pointed out that it is a waste of time and money to try to repair items which are seriously defective, either electrically or mechanically.

12:2 The battery

The battery is the most vital part of the electrical system as if it is in poor condition it may be impossible to start the engine and even if the engine is started the performance of the remainder of the electrical system will still be poor. The battery is also the component of the electrical system that will suffer most rapidly from neglected maintenance.

Maintenance:

1 **Always keep the top of the battery clean and dry.** Dirt or moisture will allow the charge to leak slowly away and this in combination with any acid vented will cause corrosion to the battery surrounds. If corrosion does appear, remove the battery and wash the affected parts with dilute ammonia, or baking powder disolved in warm water, and when the acid has been neutralized flush the area with plenty of clean water. When the parts are dry paint them with anti-sulphuric paint.

2 **Keep the battery terminals clean and tight.** Poor contact here is one of the commonest causes of starting difficulties. Wash away any corrosion with dilute ammonia followed by clean water. Oxides can be cleaned off with special wire brushes or by careful scraping with a sharp knife. Smear the posts and connectors with petroleum jelly as a preventative against further corrosion before reconnecting them.

3 **At regular intervals check the level of the electrolyte in the battery cells.** The level should be a little above the separators and if it is low, top up using **pure distilled water. Never add acid directly to the battery.** Electrolyte should only be added at the correct specific gravity to replace spillage or leakage losses.

Charging:

The best rate of charging is using a current which is 10 per cent of the battery capacity. Boost chargers give a current of up to 100 amps and they should only be used in an emergency and on a battery known to be in good condition.

A small trickle charger running at $1\frac{1}{2}$ to 2 amps is quite sufficient for boosting the battery and even for recharging a battery. The charge can be checked with a hydrometer but the battery is normally fully charged when it is gassing freely. **Do not examine the battery with a naked light as the gases given off are explosive.**

A poor battery can often be reclaimed by giving it a series of dischargings and charges, and the life of a good battery can be prolonged by discharging it right down and then recharging it. Use a suitable bank of lights to discharge the battery at a rate of approximately 3 to 5 amps and then recharge the battery.

Electrolyte:

If electrolyte leaks or spills it is best to buy more ready-mixed. If the electrolyte has to be mixed up use distilled water and pure sulphuric acid and mix in an earthenware or glass bowl. Heat is given off, so allow the mixture to cool before taking specific gravity readings. **Always add the acid to the water.** Never add water to acid as the heat will turn the water into steam instantaneously and acid will spatter out. Acid or electrolyte on the skin or clothing should be neutralized immediately with baking powder and then washed with plenty of clean water. **If acid or electrolyte splashes into the eye hold the eye open under a running tap and obtain medical assistance immediately.**

Testing:

Provided that distilled water has not just been added, the state of charge of the battery can be checked with a hydrometer. Draw up enough electrolyte to allow the float to be free from the bottom and sides and then take the reading at eye level. Before returning the electrolyte to its cell examine its condition. If it appears dirty or full of specks then it is likely that this cell is defective and this will be confirmed if the specific gravity of the cell differs radically from that of the five other cells. The readings give the following indications:

For climates above 22°C (70°F):

1.270 to 1.290	Cell fully charged
1.190 to 1.210	Cell half-discharged
1.110 to 1.130	Cell discharged

Replace spillage with electrolyte of 1.270 specific gravity.

For climates below 22°C (70°F):

1.210 to 1.230	Cell fully charged
1.130 to 1.150	Cell half-charged
1.050 to 1.070	Cell discharged

Replace spillage with electrolyte of 1.210 specific gravity.

The figures are given assuming a standard electrolyte temperature of 16°C (60°F). If the actual temperature is different, convert the reading to standard by adding .002 for every 3°C (5°F) rise in temperature, and subtracting for every similar drop in temperature.

If the intercell connectors are accessible the battery can also be tested on a heavy-duty tester. Do not use this tester on a battery known to be low in charge or in poor condition.

Storage:

Short term storage provides no problems as long as the battery is well maintained. If the battery is to be stored for long periods make sure that it is fully charged, the top clean and dry, and any exposed metal portions well covered with petroleum jelly. Keep the battery in a cool dry place well away from any extremes in temperature.

At monthly intervals give the battery a freshening-up charge and at three-month intervals discharge it on a lamp bank and fully recharge it. If this is not done the battery will discharge itself and the plates will sulphate up, to the detriment of the battery.

12:3 Servicing electrical motors

All motors fitted to cars operate on basically the same principles and therefore have many constructional similarities. To avoid constant repetition general instructions for servicing all electrical motors are gathered into this one section.

It should be noted that on models fitted with electrically operated window winders and sunshine roofs the motors for these cannot and must not be dismantled. If a motor for one of these services fails then a new motor must be fitted in its place.

Dismantling and specific details of the various motors will be given in the relevant sections. Note that the cooling fan motor is in **Chapter 4** and that motors for body operation are in **Chapter 13.**

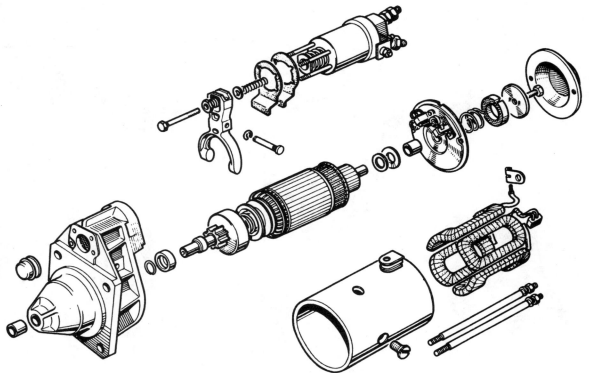

FIG 12:1   Ducellier starter motor components

Brushgear:

Dismantle the motor sufficiently for the brushgear to be accessible, taking great care not to damage the brushes if the commutator is withdrawn from under them. If possible the brushes should be partially lifted out of their brush holders and held in position with the springs resting on the brush sides as the parts are removed, as this will ensure that they clear any sharp edges on the commutator.

Renew the brushes if they are excessively worn. On some motors the connector is soldered into place so the connector should be gripped with a pair of pliers to prevent solder from creeping up it when resoldering the parts.

If the brushes stick in their holders they should be removed and the brush sides lightly polished on a smooth file. Clean the brush holder with a piece of cloth dipped in methylated spirits or fuel before refitting the brush. Make sure that the brushes are refitted into their original positions as this ensures that the bedding-in is not disturbed.

Check the brush springs and renew them if they are weak or broken.

New brushes are normally supplied with their ends ground to shape but if further bedding-in is required wrap the commutator with a piece of glasspaper and rotate the commutator with the brushes lightly pressed against the abrasive.

Before reassembling the motor wipe the commutator with a piece of cloth dipped in methylated spirits or fuel and blow out all loose dust and dirt.

Armature and commutator:

If the commutator is scored or worn then the armature assembly must be removed from the motor. Light score marks on the commutator can be polished off using a fine-grade of glasspaper. **Never use emerycloth as this leaves particles embedded in the copper.** If the wear marks are deep the damage can be skimmed off in a lathe, using a high-speed and a very sharp tool. On some starter motors it will be found that the insulation between the segments is undercut. Grind a hacksaw to the exact width of the insulation and use it to squarely undercut to a depth of .8mm ($\frac{1}{32}$ inch) if need be. Take a light final skim cut with a diamond- or carbide-tipped tool and if such a tool is not available then the commutator should be polished in the lathe using a very fine grade of glass-paper. If the damage is excessively deep then a new armature assembly must be fitted.

Apart from reconditioning the commutator very little can be done to the armature assembly apart from checking it for damage. A special tester is required for checking the condition of the armature windings though shortcircuits may be suspected if individual commutator segments are burnt. Check that there are no loose laminations, windings or segments. Check also for scoring on the laminations. Scoring all round indicates excessively worn bearings or loose polepieces, while scoring on one side only indicates a bent armature shaft. **A defective armature cannot be repaired and it must not be machined or straightened, so fit a new armature and discard the old one.**

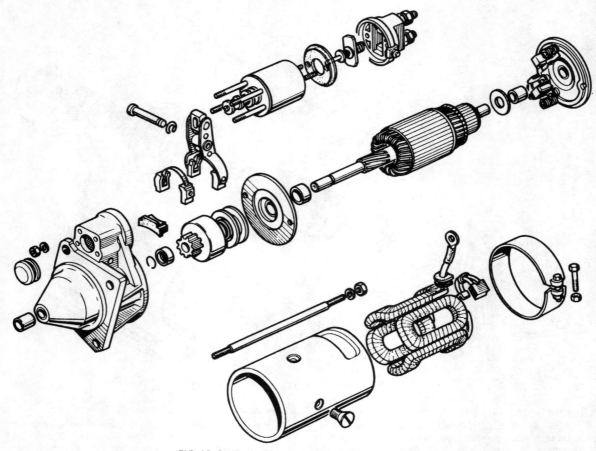

FIG 12:2   Paris-Rhone starter motor components

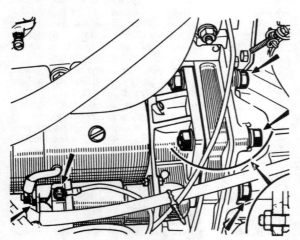

FIG 12:3   Removing the starter motor

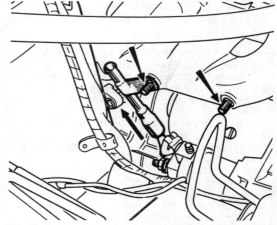

FIG 12:4   Removing the starter shield and dipstick tube

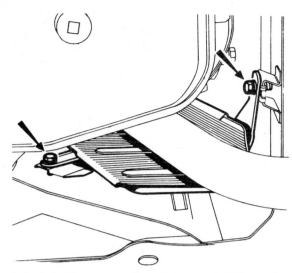

FIG 12:5   The exhaust clip and shield on R.1152 models

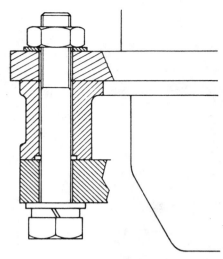

FIG 12:6   The correct method of locking the starter mounting bolts

Field coils:

On some smaller motors a permanent magnet is fitted in place of the field coils and on this type care must be taken in dismantling, as the magnet is attached inside the cover and will draw out the armature as the cover is removed.

The field coils can be tested using a 12-volt battery and lamp across their terminals and this check can also be used for the insulation. A better method is to connect an ohmmeter across the terminals and measure the resistance. If an ohmmeter is not available an ammeter and 12-volt battery can be used instead. By measuring the current and knowing the voltage the resistance can be calculated using Ohms law (Voltage ÷ Current = Resistance).

The field coils on the starter motor are held in place by the polepieces which are in turn secured by large screws. A special wheel screwdriver is required to slacken and tighten these screws and therefore the polepieces and field coils should not be removed by the owner.

Bearings:

All the motors covered by this manual use bushes for the armature shaft bearings. On smaller motors self-aligning bushes are used and these are secured to the end covers by riveted spring clips. This type of bush should be checked for freedom of movement in its mounting and lightly lubricated with oil on reassembly. If the bush is badly worn it may not be possible to obtain replacement parts (usually the complete cover) and the motor may have to be renewed.

On the starter motor pressed-in porous metal bushes are used and these are renewable. The old bushes can be driven out with a drift, or drawn out using an appropriate sized tap screwed into them. The new bushes should be soaked in oil for 24 hours and then pressed back, using a stepped mandrel whose spigot is just slightly longer than the bush, highly polished, and of the exact diameter of the armature shaft.

Insulation:

Clean away all carbon and metal dust as this can provide a leakage path. **Under no circumstances may the armature or field coils be dipped into any solvent to clean them.** Wiping with a piece of cloth moistened with fuel or methylated spirits, and blowing away loose dust with an airline or tyre pump, will be sufficient for most parts.

The insulation can be tested using a 12-volt battery and suitable test lamp but a better method is to use a 110-volt AC supply and neon test lamp. 220 to 240 volts can be used but this can be very dangerous in inexperienced hands, so use a lower voltage unless absolutely confident. In all cases the lamp should not light when the probes are connected across the insulation.

12:4 The starter motor

A total of six different models of starter motor is fitted to the range of cars covered by this manual. The different models and their locked performance are given in Technical Data. It will be noted that the majority are made by Paris-Rhone, with the exception of some left-hand drive later models which are fitted with a Ducellier starter motor. Luckily all the starter motors are very similar in construction and all operate on the same principles, so general instructions will apply to all the different models. The components of the Ducellier 6.183 starter motor are shown in **FIG 12:1** and those of a Paris-Rhone D.8.E71 or D.8.E84 in **FIG 12:2**.

When the starter switch is operated current flows through the solenoid windings and the solenoid armature is drawn in. The armature moves the drive pinion into mesh with the flywheel teeth, through the action of the lever. If the teeth abut edge to edge the springs allow the armature to move through its full range, and initial rotation of the starter motor then allows the teeth to slip into mesh. The final movement of the solenoid armature

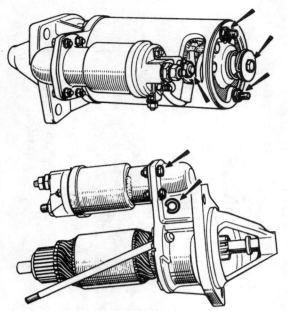

FIG 12:7 Dismantling the starter motor

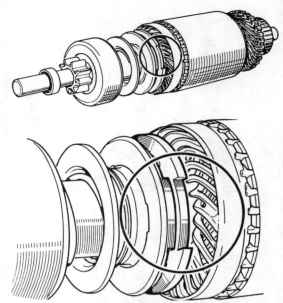

FIG 12:8 The correct relation of the drive to the armature on a Ducellier starter motor

closes heavy duty contacts and allows the current to flow through the starter motor. Lost motion springs are fitted which ensure that the current flow through the motor is cut off, by the contacts opening, just before the pinion disengages from the flywheel. An overrun clutch is fitted into the drive and this ensures that the engine does not drive and overspeed the starter motor when the engine starts. If loose segments or laminations are found on the starter motor armature then the overrun clutch should be checked with special care as it is likely that it is faulty. On

some models brake washers are fitted to slow the armature. These are not strong enough to slow the armature when current is flowing but they bring it to a rapid halt once the current is cut off and ensure that the starter motor armature is stationary if the engine stalls and has to be restarted within a short time after having used the starter.

Starter fails to operate:

1 Check the condition and charge of the battery, paying particular attention to the terminals and connectors, making sure that they are clean and tight.
2 Switch on some lights that can be seen from the driving seat and again operate the starter motor. If the lights go dim then the starter motor is taking current. Lack of rotation of the engine can be caused by a fault in the starter motor or it can be caused by the pinion jamming in mesh. Select a gear and rock the car backwards and forwards to free a jammed pinion. If this fails, or the pinion jams regularly, then the starter motor must be removed for further examination.
3 If the lights do not go dim then listen for the solenoid operation. If the solenoid does not click then use a test lamp or voltmeter to check if current is reaching the solenoid. If current is not reaching the solenoid trace back through the wiring and switches until the fault is found and can be repaired. If current is reaching the solenoid short across the heavy duty terminals with a thick piece of metal and if the solenoid is at fault then the starter motor will spin freely and at speed. A defective solenoid must be renewed.

Starter motor removal:

On righthand drive models it will be necessary to remove the manifold from the engine (see **Chapter 1**). Disconnect the battery and then disconnect the leads

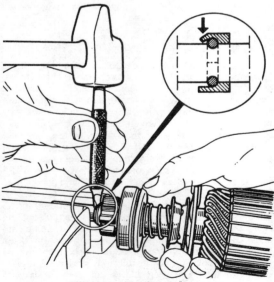

FIG 12:9 Peening the stop

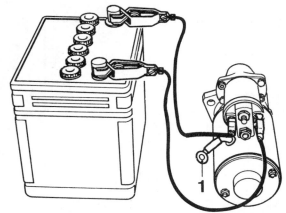

FIG 12:10   Energizing the starter solenoid only

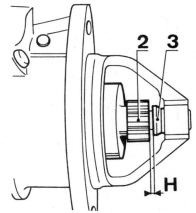

FIG 12:11   Checking the solenoid adjustment

from the starter motor solenoid. Take out the three bolts that secure the starter motor (shown in **FIG 12:3**) and then lift out the starter motor. On R.1151 models it will be necessary to remove the shield and dipstick tube, shown in **FIG 12:4**, while on R.1152 models it will also be necessary to remove the exhaust pipe clip and shield, shown in **FIG 12:5**.

The starter motor is refitted in the reverse order of removal. On models before 1969 the bolts were locked with locktabs but these washers should be discarded on reassembly and lockwashers fitted, as shown in **FIG 12:6**.

Dismantling the starter motor:

The method of dismantling the starter motor is shown in **FIG 12:7** and the figure is self-explanatory. **Care must be taken to observe the positions of all washers so that they can be correctly fitted on reassembly, and when removing the commutator end bracket make sure that the brush for the field coils is removed from its brush holder.**

The starter motor is reassembled in the reverse order of dismantling.

Pinion drive:

Dismantle the starter motor and then use a suitable length of tube to drive the stop from over the snap ring. Prise out the snap ring and withdraw the stop and pinion drive.

Light damage to the pinion teeth can be cleaned off with a smooth file or oilstone but if the damage is deep a new pinion assembly must be fitted. Check that the over-run clutch freewheels but immediately takes up drive in the opposite direction. Again if the clutch is defective a new pinion assembly must be fitted.

On the Ducellier starter motor the drive is matched to the armature and therefore if the drive is worn or damaged the complete armature and drive must be renewed as a unit. Refit the drive to the Ducellier motor, choice of three different positions, so that when the parts are assembled the grooves match as shown in **FIG 12:8**.

On the Paris-Rhone D8.E.49 and D.10.E.43 starter motors the stop is peened into place, as shown in **FIG 12:9**, and therefore a new stop must be fitted on reassembly and then peened into place.

Starter solenoid:

Removal of the starter solenoid is dealt with in dismantling. If a new starter solenoid is fitted, or the adjustment of the old one is suspect, connect the solenoid to a 12-volt battery as shown in **FIG 12:10**. Note that the lead from the starter motor 1 has been disconnected. The solenoid will operate and move the drive pinion into the engaged position. Lightly press the pinion towards the armature to take up any play and use feeler gauges to measure the clearance **H** between the pinion 2 and stop 3, shown in **FIG 12:11**. The correct clearance should be .5 to 2.5 mm (.020 to .099 inch). If the clearance is incorrect remove the solenoid and screw in or out the fork end 4, shown in **FIG 12:12**, until the clearance is correct with the solenoid energized.

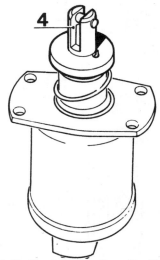

FIG 12:12   Adjusting the solenoid

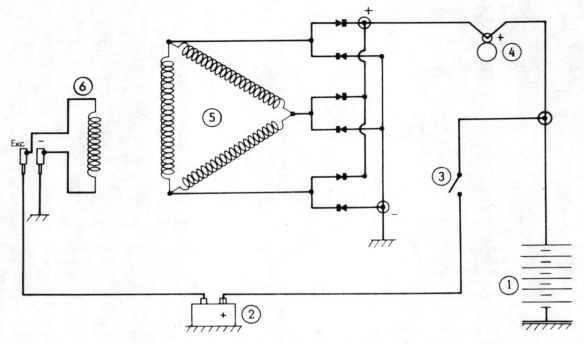

FIG 12:13   The charging circuit

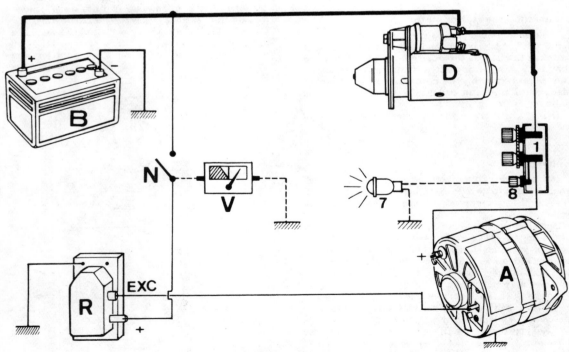

FIG 12:14   Checking the charging circuit

Starter motor testing:

For full checks a torque rig is required and the data is given in Technical Data. As a rough check mount the motor in a vice and connect it to a 12-volt battery, using heavy duty leads. The negative terminal of the battery should be connected to the yoke and the positive terminal to the lead 1, shown in **FIG 12:10**. The motor should then spin rapidly and freely in its normal direction of rotation.

12:5 The alternator

All the models covered by this manual are fitted with an alternator to supply the current for the system when the engine is running. An alternator has, by virtue of its operation, several advantages over a conventional generator. The main current is produced in the stator windings which can accordingly be made heavy without having to design for rotational forces. The light excitation current passes through the rotor windings and therefore the rotor is made much lighter than the armature on a generator and can be driven at higher speeds. The excitation current need not change polarity, so simple slip rings and light brushes are used instead of a complicated commutator.

The current produced in the stator is AC, not DC as produced by a generator, and a bank of diodes is required to rectify it to DC which is suitable for the battery. These diodes will not allow current to pass in a reverse direction, so no cut-out is needed in the system and the alternator automatically adjusts itself to the demand of the system.

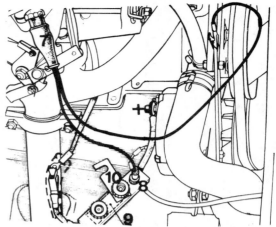

FIG 12:15 The special connector fitted for checking the charging circuit

Instead of the complex control box required with a generator a simple voltage regulator suffices for the alternator. The charging circuit is shown schematically in **FIG 12:13**.

A voltmeter is fitted into the system and this shows the state of charge of the battery. When the needle is in the orange zone the battery is at its normal correct charge and with the engine running the current in is balanced by the current out. The red zone shows that the battery is low

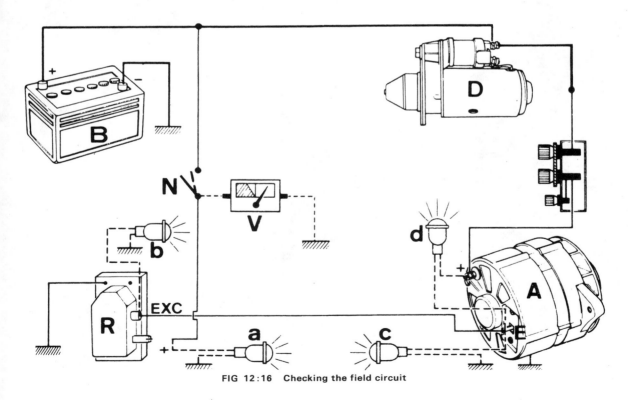

FIG 12:16 Checking the field circuit

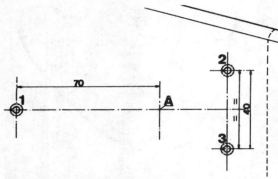

FIG 12:17 Additional mounting hole required when fitting a later type of regulator

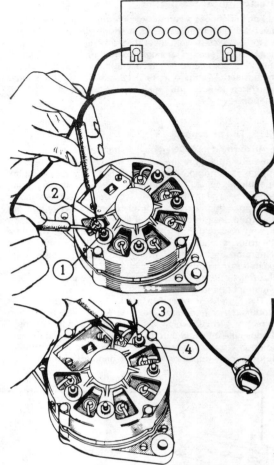

FIG 12:18 Checking the diodes with the alternator assembled

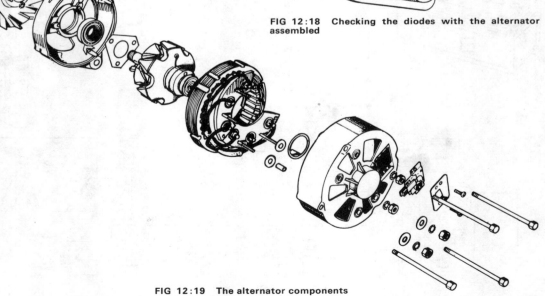

FIG 12:19 The alternator components

in charge or being discharged when the engine is running while the green zone shows that the battery is being charged with the engine running. The voltmeter works using a bi-metallic strip, so the reading will take a minute before it becomes stable and correct.

Alternator fails to charge or battery low:

With the ignition switched on but the engine not started the voltmeter needle should be in the orange section after a minute. If the needle is in the red section check the battery with a hydrometer, as described in **Section 12:2**. If the battery is charged then the voltmeter should be checked. Connect a 12-volt test lamp between a suitable live supply and the case of the voltmeter. If the lamp does not light then the earthing of the voltmeter is poor and causing a faulty reading. Also use the test lamp to check the supply from the Neuman ignition switch as a defective lead will also cause a faulty reading. If the instrument is defective then it should be renewed.

1 Check the tension of the drive belts, as described in **Chapter 4, Section 4:6**. If the belts are defective or slipping then the alternator output will be reduced.

2 Check all the connections and leads in the charging circuit, also making sure that the battery connections are clean and tight.

3 As a quick check disconnect the main lead from the +ve terminal of the alternator and connect a test lamp between the lead and a good earth. The lamp should light showing that current is flowing. A schematic layout of the circuit is shown in **FIG 12:14**. A special connector is made for this test and the circuit with this connector block fitted is shown in **FIG 12:15**. At the initial test the link 10 is left open so that the lead is isolated from the alternator but current can still pass through to the test lamp. Close the link and the test lamp should go out. Start the engine but keep it at idling speed. The test lamp should then come on if the alternator is producing current. If the lamp does come on but it is still suspected that the current is low then the output valve must be checked. If the lamp does not come on at all then the fault probably lies with the field circuit.

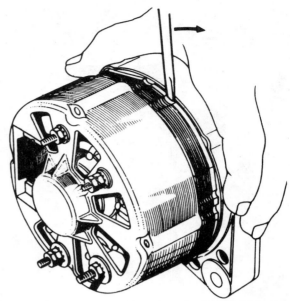

FIG 12:20 Levering off the front bearing assembly. The screwdriver must not be inserted to a depth of more than 2 mm

Checking output:

Remove the test lamp shown in **FIG 12:14** and fit into place an ammeter. If the special block is used, the swinging link should be left open. If the block is not used then the ammeter should be connected in series between the battery and alternator, in place of the block. Start the engine and run it at approximately 800 rev/min. The minimum current should be 6 amps though it may be higher if the battery is flat.

The output at speed can also be checked, though a special resistance is needed for this purpose and therefore it should be checked by an agent. A rough check can be carried out using the same method as for determining the slow speed output. It will be necessary to have a well charged battery. Switch on all the lights so that a drain is

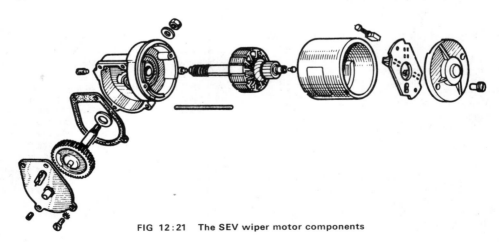

FIG 12:21   The SEV wiper motor components

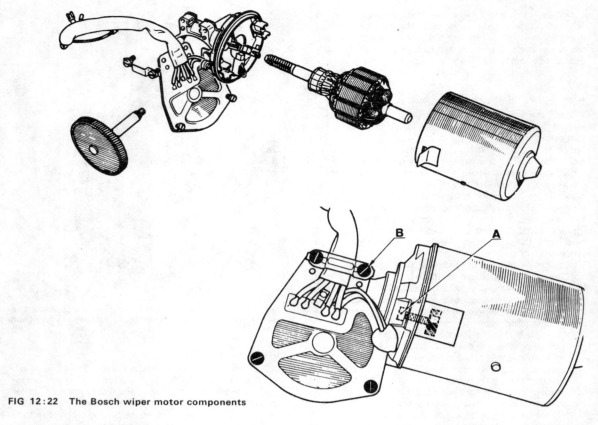

FIG 12:22 The Bosch wiper motor components

being put on the battery, and run the engine at a speed of approximately 3000 rev/min. Leave it to run for 2 or 3 minutes to allow the alternator to reach its operating temperature. The current produced by the alternator should be 30 to 35 amps.

Checking field circuit:

The four different positions of the test bulb for checking the field circuit are shown in **FIG 12:16**. Each position is checked in turn in alphabetical order and connections are restored to normal before proceeding to the next position. In each test the Neuman switch is switched on. If the lamp does not light in position **a** then the lead to the regulator is defective. If the lamp does not light in position **b** then the regulator itself is defective and must be renewed. The later type of reed regulator can be fitted in place of the earlier type, provided that an extra mounting hole is drilled at **A** shown in **FIG 12:17**. Position c checks the lead and position **d** checks the field coils. If the circuit is satisfactory then the fault is probably caused either by a defective diode or dirty slip rings and brushes.

Removal:

The attachment points of the alternator are shown in **Chapter 4, FIG 4:10**. On later models an extra lug is fitted to the bottom of the alternator to give extra rigidity. A later alternator can be fitted to an earlier model, provided that the new bolt No. 77.00.501.241 is also fitted,

but an earlier alternator must not be fitted to a later model of car.

When refitting the alternator make sure that the special turned washer is in place under the lug and then set the belt tension. The correct belt tension for the different models covered in this manual is given in **Section 4:6**.

Diode check:

The method of checking the diodes with the alternator assembled is shown in **FIG 12:18**. Once the alternator has been dismantled the individual diodes can be checked by the same method, using the test probes on the individual diode pins and a heat sink. An open circuit on a diode will limit the current to 5 amps, while a shortcircuited diode will limit the current between 7 and 8 amps as well as causing rumbling noises. Connect the probes to positions 1 and 2 for the positive diode carrier and between positions 3 and 4 for the negative diode carrier. Place the probes in position and note the test lamp. Remove the probes and fit them back into position so that they and the battery voltage are reversed, and again observe the test lamp. For both diode carriers the lamp should only light when the current is flowing one way but not when the polarity of the battery is reversed. If the lamp stays out, or comes on, in both directions, then one or more diodes in the carrier is defective.

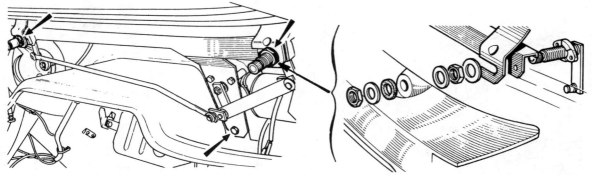

FIG 12:23   The wiper component attachments

Note that an earthed stator winding will give the same effect as though one of the diodes in the negative diode carrier is shortcircuited (lamp stays on in both directions) so check for this fault after dismantling the alternator.

Dismantling:

The components of the alternator are shown in **FIG 12:19**. In many ways the alternator can be treated as a special form of electrical motor (see **Section 12:3**). Ballbearings are fitted in place of bushes and under no circumstances may the slip rings be machined. The slip rings should never become excessively worn or burnt, and normal marks can be polished off using a fine-grade of glasspaper. **When soldering or unsoldering leads it is essential to use a hot iron and to grip the diode pins with a pair of long-nosed pliers, as a heat sink, as if the heat is allowed to soak into the diodes they will be damaged.**

1 Take out the two screws that secure the insulating cover and remove the cover and brush carrier.

2 Take out the four through-bolts that hold the alternator together. Insert the tip of a screwdriver into the slots shown in **FIG 12:20** and lever off the front cover. **The screwdriver must not be inserted to a depth greater than 2mm ($\frac{1}{16}$ inch) otherwise it will damage the windings of the stator.**

3 Remove the four nuts, shakeproof washers and two insulating washers so that the stator and diode carriers can be separated from the rear bearing housing.

4 If the rotor requires removal then wrap the pulley with a piece of rope or old drive belt and grip it in the jaws of a vice while undoing the securing nut. Remove the three screws that secure the front bearing cover and take off the cover. Free the housing by tapping the end of the shaft onto a piece of wood. If the bearings are worn draw them off the rotor using a suitable two-legged extractor.

Servicing and reassembly:

The general details of servicing the alternator follow quite closely those for servicing electrical motors (see **Section 12:3**) but **only a 12-volt .1 amp test bulb should be used for checking continuity or insulation.** Do not use 110 volts as this will damage the parts. The stator is checked between any two pairs of wires, while the rotor is checked between the slip rings and an ohmmeter may be used for the rotor. If a diode failure has been found before dismantling then the stator leads must be unsoldered (**using a hot iron and heat sink**) so that the individual diodes can be checked.

The alternator is reassembled in the reverse order of dismantling. Make sure that the bearings are well lubricated before refitting the housings.

12:6 The windscreen wipers

1966 models of the R.1150 are fitted with either a Bosch WS.1500.R1F motor or a SEV.116012 motor, whose components are shown in **FIG 12:21**. All later models are fitted with a Bosch motor WS.1500.R3F for single speed motors and WS.1500.R4F for two speed motors. The components of the later motor are shown in **FIG 12:22** and the later motor can be fitted to earlier models of car provided that the wiring is suitably modified.

Removal:

Remove the scuttle crossmember by undoing the attachment screws and nuts and carefully levering it out, noting that the cable to the vent must be disconnected. The complete linkage attachments are shown in **FIG 12:23** and once these have been freed and the leads disconnected the complete assembly can be removed. If only the motor requires removal its attachments to the linkage are shown in **FIG 12:24**.

The parts are refitted in the reverse order of removal but it is essential that the motor is run and then switched off so that it is in its park position before the link arms are refitted to the motor crank. The arms must be adjusted so that they fit freely back into place.

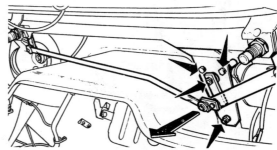

FIG 12:24   The wiper motor attachments

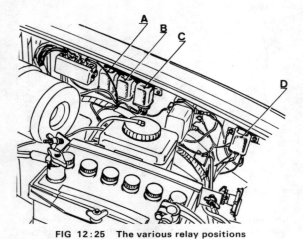

FIG 12:25 The various relay positions

Key to Fig 12:25
B Sunroof relay
D Cooling fan motor relay
A Windscreen wiper relay
C Quartz iodine headlight relay

If the wiper arm shaft bearing is worn it can be renewed. Take out the two screws that secure it to the assembly and free it from its operating link. Remove the dab of locking paint and then drive the shaft out of the splined end portion. New parts are then fitted in the reverse order of dismantling, making sure that the splined end piece is pushed down until it reaches the chamfer on the splined end of the shaft.

If should be noted that if the brushes are worn on the later types of motor the complete brush holder assembly must be renewed as neither the brushes or springs can be renewed individually.

12:7 Relays

The positions of the various relays are shown in **FIG 12:25**. A relay is fitted to allow the switch or control to operate at a low current and not take the full current of the component that it operates. The small current operates a solenoid which then closes the contacts for the heavy duty current. If relay failure is suspected, short across the terminals with a thick piece of wire and the component should then operate correctly.

12:8 Fuses and thermo switches

The standard models are fitted with fuse boxes containing two fuses while models with optional electrically operated equipment are fitted with six fuses. The fuse board is located on the lefthand side of the engine compartment adjacent to the air cleaner. **Never fit fuses of a higher rating than called for as the excess load will then be put onto the wiring system with possible danger of fire.**

If a fuse blows, briefly check the circuits that it protects and fit a new fuse. If the fuse blows again immediately then the circuits will have to be very carefully checked through until the fault is found and can be rectified. Intermittent but persistant blowing of fuses can be caused by defective insulation chafing under vibration, so shake the leads when examining them.

Thermal cut-out switches are fitted into the circuits for electrically operated windows and sunshine roofs. These contain a bi-metallic strip which heats and bends when there is excessive current. As the strip bends it opens the contacts and cuts off the current. The bi-metallic strip will then take approximately 10 seconds to cool and close the contacts again and if there is still an overload the strip will again bend and open the contacts.

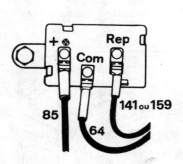

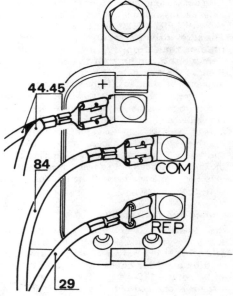

FIG 12:26 The flasher unit connections

12:9 The direction indicators

A flasher unit is fitted and its connections are shown in **FIG 12:26. The unit is a delicate piece of mechanism and will easily be damaged by mishandling, dropping, or incorrect connection, and once damaged it cannot be repaired.**

The direction indicator switch is mounted at the top of the steering column in conjunction with the lighting switch. The switch can be removed without taking off the steering wheel but it will be necessary to remove the glove box in order to have access to the connectors. Remove the covers from the combination switch and disconnect the return spring from the direction indicator portion. Disconnect the leads, carefully labelling them to ensure that they will be correctly reconnected, and then take out the three screws that secure the switch assembly to the bracket.

Flashers fail to operate:

Check all the bulbs as if one has blown the flash rate will be completely altered on that side.

If the flashers fail to operate at all then check the supply to the flasher unit. On R.1151 and R.1152 models operate the heater blower as this shares a common supply and failure in one will be shown in the other system. On all other models use a test lamp or voltmeter to check that the supply terminal is live. If the terminal is live disconnect all the leads from the flasher unit and connect them together. Operate the direction indicator switch and the appropriate lamps should then all come on continuously. If a single lamp does not light then check the wiring to the lamp and pay particular attention to the earth point, as corrosion on the body can cause a high resistance. If the lamps still do not operate correctly then the wiring will have to be traced and checked. If no lamps light then the fault lies between the flasher unit and switch or in the switch itself. If only one half does not operate then either the switch is defective or the wires for that half.

12:10 The headlamps

The standard headlamps are either rectangular or twin circular units on either side. Quartz iodine headlamps can be fitted to the front bumpers. The standard headlamps are sealed units where the filaments are sealed into the unit, the lens and reflector being integral, and once a filament blows or the glass cracks the complete unit must be renewed. Bulbs are fitted to the quartz iodine lamps and are accessible after the front lens has been removed. **The glass of these special bulbs must not be handled with the bare hands as the acids on the hand will damage the special glass at the high temperatures at which the bulb operates, so always use clean soft cloth to hold the bulb.**

Removal:

On the rectangular units remove the three parts of the grille panel by taking out the screws shown in **FIG 12:27**. **Do not alter the screws A and B.** Raise the catch and take out the four screws shown in **FIG 12:28** to remove the lamp unit.

On the twin-lamp installations remove the moulding by taking out the three screws arrowed in **FIG 12:29**.

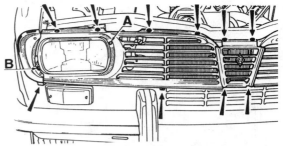
FIG 12:27   Removing the grille parts

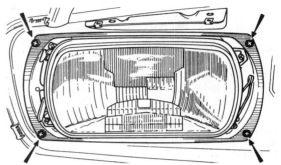
FIG 12:28   Removing a rectangular lamp unit

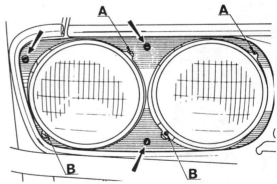
FIG 12:29   Removing the moulding

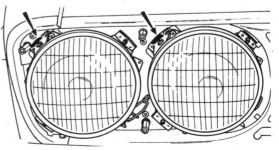
FIG 12:30   Removing a circular lamp unit

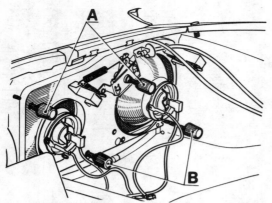

FIG 12:31 Beam setting screws on R.1156

Do not alter the screws A and B. Lift up the retaining clips arrowed in **FIG 12:30** and lean the lamp unit forwards to disengage it.

The unit is held in place by two retaining rings and these can be separated by taking out the three securing screws that hold them together.

The quartz iodine lamps can be removed by undoing their attachment nut under the bumper and disconnecting the lead from the wiring loom.

On R.1156 model, disconnect the wires, unhook the light unit retaining spring and withdraw the unit from the front.

All types of headlamp are refitted in the reverse order of removal. Once they are in place the beam setting should be checked.

Beam setting:

On the standard lamps the beam is adjusted vertically by the screws **B** and horizontally by the screws **A**, shown in **FIGS 12:27**, **12:29** and **12:31**. The quartz iodine lamps are adjusted by slackening their attachment nut and swivelling them into the desired position.

The beams can be checked by standing the car on level ground squarely to and about 5 metres (16 feet) from a plain blank wall. Blank off the other lamps with cardboard while adjusting one lamp. However, this method is not very accurate and as lighting regulations are nowadays very stringent in most countries it is best to take the car to an agent who will use special beam-setter equipment to set the light accurately.

In addition to these individual adjusters, certain later cars have also a control, situated under the instrument panel, by means of which the vertical setting of the headlamp beam can be regulated according to the loading and trim of the vehicle.

12:11 Fault diagnosis

(a) Battery discharged

1 Terminals loose or dirty
2 Insufficient charging current
3 Shortcircuit in wiring not protected by fuses
4 Accessories left on
5 Insufficient mileage to allow alternator to charge battery

(b) Battery will not hold charge

1 Low electrolyte level
2 Battery plates sulphated or distorted
3 Separators ineffective
4 Electrolyte leakage from defective case

(c) Alternator output low or nil

1 Drive belts broken or slipping
2 Defective regulator
3 Defective wiring or connectors in charging circuit
4 Diodes failed in rectifier pack
5 Brushes excessively worn or dirty slip rings
6 Weak or broken brush springs
7 Defective stator or rotor windings

(d) Starter motor lacks power or will not operate

1 Battery discharged or loose and dirty battery connections
2 Starter pinion jammed in mesh
3 Defective starter switch
4 Defective starter solenoid
5 Brushes excessively worn or sticking
6 Brush connectors detached or shorting
7 Weak or broken brush springs
8 Commutator excessively worn or dirty
9 Defective armature or field coil windings
10 Starter mechanically defective
11 Engine abnormally stiff

(e) Starter motor runs but does not turn engine

1 Defective overrun clutch
2 Incorrect adjustment of solenoid or broken springs
3 Broken teeth on flywheel or pinion

(f) Starter motor rough or noisy

1 Check 2 and 3 in (e)
2 Mounting bolts loose
3 Loose polepieces
4 Excessively worn bearings

CHAPTER 13

THE BODYWORK

13:1 Bodywork repairs

Large scale repairs to body panels are best left to experts and even small dents can be tricky, as too much or injudicious hammering will stretch the metal and make the dent worse instead of better.

The actual body is of monocoque construction and distortion to this must have specialist attention. However certain panels, shown in **FIG 13:1**, can be renewed and if one of these panels is damaged consideration should be given to fitting a new panel rather than having specialist repairs carried out to it.

The best method of repairing minor dents and damage available to the owner is filling and spraying, particularly as self-spraying cans of matching paint are readily available. It should be remembered that paint fades with age and therefore fresh paint may stand out on the old finish. The original lustre and colour can be partially restored by lightly using a mild cutting compound. Small dents and stone chips should be covered over using a retouching brush but when the damage is larger it is quite often best to spray the complete panel so that any difference in the paint is not so obvious.

Wash the surface to be sprayed with white spirits to remove all wax polish, noting that even more drastic treatment will be required if silicone-based polishes have been used. Scuff the area to give a good bond for the new finish and remove any corrosion down to bright bare metal. Use a primer surfacer or paste stopper as required and build up until the surface is just above the original finish, trying to make the surface as smooth as possible. When the surface is hard and dry rub it down with 400 grade 'Wet and Dry' paper using plenty of clean water. If required use further coats of stopper or filler to achieve a perfect result. Spend plenty of time and patience in obtaining the best possible result as it is on this that the final finish depends. When the surface is smooth wash it down with plenty of clean water. Allow the surface to dry and wash off any slurry that was missed the first time and check the finish.

Mask off surrounding areas using newspaper and masking tape. A better finish will be produced if handles and trim are removed from the panel rather than masked over. Spray the panel evenly all over. If only a patch is being sprayed then the paint should be applied more lightly at the edges so that it 'feathers' in. Apply two or more thin coats, lightly rubbing down between each coat, rather than one thick coat which will probably run.

Remove the surrounding masking and leave the paint to dry for as long as possible, at least overnight, and then use a cutting compound to lightly polish the surface and

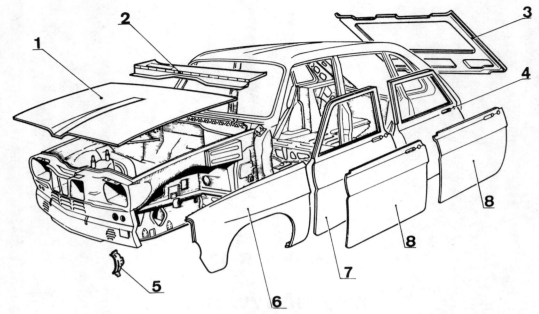

FIG 13:1   The body components that can be removed and renewed

Key to Fig 13:1   1 Bonnet (hood)   2 Scuttle grille   3 Tailgate   4 Rear door   5 Front wing flange*
6 Front wing (fender)   7 Front door   8 Door outer panels, front and rear*
*These components are provided specially as spare parts

remove any spray dust. Leave the paint to harden for a period of weeks before applying wax polish.

Do not use cellulose paint on a synthetic finish, and avoid using synthetic over cellulose.

13:2   Seat belts

Strong points for attaching seat belts are built into the frame. The strong points for the rear belt anchorages are shown in **FIG 13:2**. The strong points for the front seat belts are shown in **FIGS 13:3, 13:4** and **13:5**. On some models the strong point on the centre door pillars is concealed under a padding which is held in place by two screws.

Provided that the correct bolts are used and approved kits fitted then the owner should not have any difficulty fitting standard seat belts. **If reel or inertia belts are to be fitted it is most advisable to consult an agent.**

13:3   Special screws

Two new and special types of screw can be found on the models covered by this manual. A fairly new type of screw is the TACL, shown in **FIG 13:6**. This type of screw has the advantage of forming a waterproof seal, using its nylon washer **N**, without damaging paintwork. Using the special screwdriver it can be tightened to the torque where the shank will actually break off, though this much torque should obviously not be applied.

The other type of screw is shown in **FIG 13:7** and is used fairly generally on cars. The screw is called a Pozidrive and it strongly resembles the normal Phillips

head screw though it can be identified by the additional recess **C** which the Phillips screw does not posses.

For the most satisfactory results both types of screw require a special screwdriver for loosening or tightening them. An ordinary screwdriver can be used on the TACL and a Phillips screwdriver can be used on the Pozidrive screw but the advantages of having a firm connection will be lost and the special heads will most likely be damaged so that the screws cannot be fitted with any form of screwdriver.

13:4   Doors and door mechanism

The electrically operated window mechanism will be dealt with in the next section.

Door removal:

A special tool No. Car.281 is made for pushing out the hinge pins so that the door may be freed, but if this tool is not available the door may be removed by taking out the screws that secure the hinges to the frame posts.

When refitting the door make sure that the door runs in line with the body.

Door trim:

The method of removing the interior trim is shown in **FIG 13:8**. The winder handle should be removed using a suitable made up hook. Compress the spring **R** with the hook, pull the handle slightly downwards to free the catch and then slide the handle off in the direction **T**, still keeping pressure on the spring **R**. Remove the armrest by taking out its screws 3. The remote control handle is

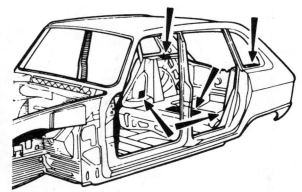

FIG 13:2   The rear seat belt attachment strong points

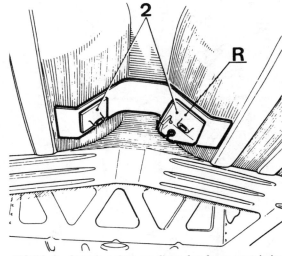

FIG 13:3   Strong points on floor for front seat belts

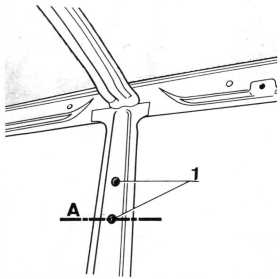

FIG 13:4   Strong points on pillars for front seat belts

FIG 13:5   Strong points on sidemembers for front seat belts

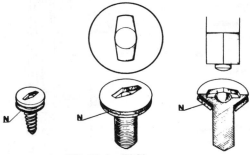

FIG 13:6   TACL screws

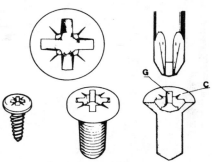

FIG 13:7   Pozidrive screws

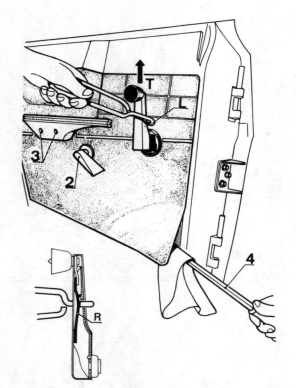

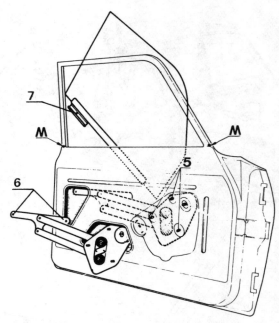

FIG 13:10 Removing the glass and regulator from a front door

FIG 13:8 Removing the door interior trim

FIG 13:9 Doors fitted with an upper embellisher

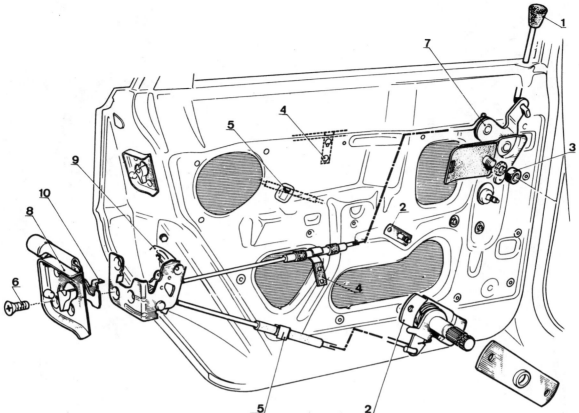

FIG 13:11 The latest door locking mechanism

secured either with a rollpin or with a screw. Unclip the trim panel by using a broad-bladed screwdriver or steel rule to lever out the fastening clips. Once the panel has been removed carefully peel off the plastic sealing panel from the door.

On some models an embellisher is fitted along the top of the door as shown in **FIG 13:9**, and secured by three plugs 3. Once the trim panel has been removed the three plugs can be levered out with a screwdriver and the embellisher removed by lifting it slightly.

The trim on the rear door is removed in a similar manner but the ashtray must also be removed. The ashtray is secured by two screws, accessible after the detachable portion of the ashtray has been removed. On later models also unscrew the lock button from its rod.

The trim is refitted in the reverse order of removal but the plastic sealing sheet must be stuck back to the door panel otherwise there is danger of water leaking into the car and spoiling the carpets.

Window glass and regulator:

The method of removal is shown in **FIG 13:10**. Raise the glass and remove the bolts 5 that secure the regulator. Free the bearing rollers 6 from the channel on the bottom of the glass by tilting the regulator and then remove it as shown. Support the glass by hand or with a wedge between it and the door. The glass can be removed by partially lowering it and then tilting it so that it can be withdrawn.

The parts on the rear doors are removed in a similar manner but it must be noted that the regulator arm is connected to the channel on the glass by clips and that the regulator sector also has an anti-rattle spring between it and the door.

Door locks:

The later locking mechanism is shown in **FIG 13:11**. Earlier models are similar but simpler.

Wind the window up, and take off the trim panel. Press the rod for the button 1 down and remove the nut 3 that secures the bellcrank mechanism 7. Similarly free the remote control 2 by taking out its securing screws. Free the anti-rattle clips 4 and 5 from their attachments in the inner door panel. Take out the three screws 6 that secure the lock 8. A little manoeuvering will now be required to remove the parts. Grip the lock and turn it a quarter turn away from the outside panel so that the pushbutton is drawn in through the outer panel. Turn the lock through a half turn so that the pushbutton hangs down inside the door and manoeuvre out the lock. The steps are shown in **FIG 13:12**. The inside portion of the lock can then be slid down and around the glass run channel.

The parts are refitted in the reverse order of removal.

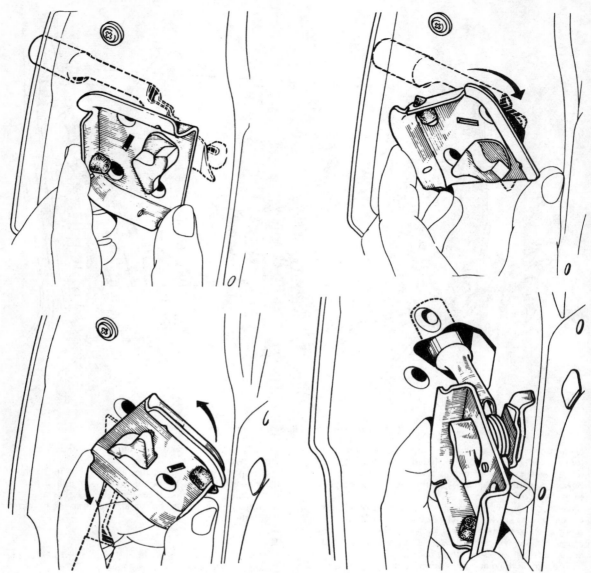

FIG 13:12 The sequence for removing a door lock

13:5 Electrically operated windows

The attachments of the mechanism are shown in **FIG 13:13**. After the door trim has been removed as for normal doors, and the motor set, disconnect the leads and remove the junction box. Operate the motor until the arms 23 and 24 are in line, as shown. With the arms in line the window top edge will be approximately 210mm ($8\frac{1}{4}$ inch) up as shown. Remove the three nuts 25 and push the assembly slightly into the door to free it. Support the window by hand and free the rollers 26 and 26Bis. Support the window in position using a wedge or strips of masking tape 27. Tilt the mechanism and remove it through the aperture as shown in the figure.

Motor and reduction gear:

Either of these can be removed from the mechanism leaving the remainder of the parts in place. Both are sealed units which cannot be repaired and must be renewed if they are defective. The motor is held in place by two nuts and once these have been removed the motor can be slid out from its mounting and the Silentbloc coupling.

The reduction gearing is secured by three bolts and once these have been removed the gearing can be removed.

Refit the parts in the reverse order of removal.

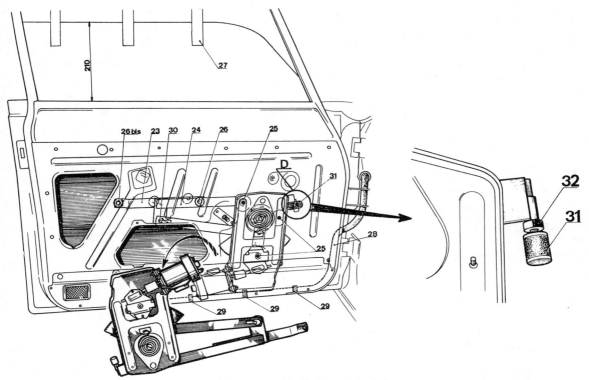

FIG 13:13 The electrically operated windows

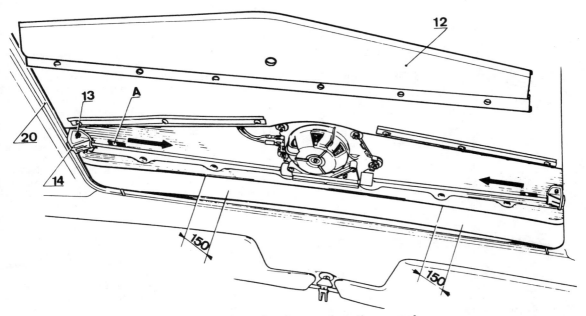

FIG 13:14 Removing the cover from the sun roof

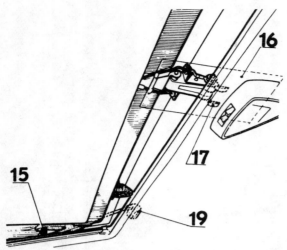

FIG 13:15   The packing pieces and electrical pickup

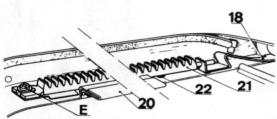

FIG 13:16   The sunroof track attachments

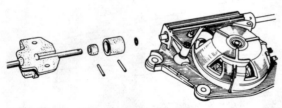

FIG 13:17   Freeing the drive shafts from the motor

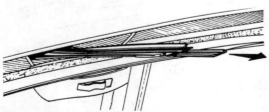

FIG 13:18   Removing the electrical track for the sun-roof

Reassembly and adjustment:

The mechanism is refitted in the reverse order of removal. If the arms 23 and 24 are not in line operate the motor directly from a battery to align them. If the motor turns in the wrong direction reverse the electrical connections and the motor will run in the opposite direction. Position the fixed roller 26 and then secure the mechanism with the nuts 25 finger tight. Position the removable roller 26Bis and reconnect the electrical leads. Release the glass and check the operation several times.

The window can be trued up by slackening the nut 30, through the inner door panel aperture, and moving the arm in its slotted adjustment hole before retightening the nut. The stop 31 positions the glass with reference to the upper edge of the door body and it should be adjusted, after slackening the locknut 32, until it is at the correct height. Tighten the nuts 25 and check that the window operates correctly.

The electrical cable 28 is secured along the door by the three welded clips 29.

13:6   The sun roof

On some models an electrically operated sun roof is fitted.

Removal:

Disconnect the battery after opening the sun roof just enough to enable access to the screws that secure the coverplate 12, shown in **FIG 13:14**. Remove the cover, slacken the bolts 13 and draw the guide bearings inwards by moving the lugs **A** in the direction shown by the arrows. From inside the car raise the front of the roof and lay it to one side. Remove the packing pieces 15, shown in **FIG 13:15**, otherwise the rubber seals may come unstuck.

Refitting and adjustment:

Open the feed tracks 16 by inserting a piece of cardboard between them so that the pads 17 will slip easily into place. Clean the lead-in ramps and grease them lightly, **but make sure that no grease goes onto the actual toothed tracks.** Position the sliding roof by tilting it slightly towards the rear and make sure that it is parallel to the frame. Hook the retaining springs 19 under the roof and insert the pick-up pads 17 into the track 16. Refit the packing pieces 15. Four different thicknesses of packing piece are available, in different colours for identification, and these are used to adjust the sun roof until it is in line with the body. Packing pieces need not necessarily be of the same thickness on either side. If necessary remove the slide fingers into which the packing pieces fit.

The rack attachments are shown in **FIG 13:16**. Position the roof so that there is a parallel gap of 150 mm at the front edge, as shown in **FIG 13:14**, by moving the racks as required. If the racks are removed do not forget to refit the anti-rattle spacers 22.

With the pinions in place on the racks push the bearings 14 outwards until they are in contact with the sides and then slacken each one back by 1.5 mm ($\frac{1}{16}$ inch) before tightening the nuts 13. Refit the coverplate 12.

Motor:

If the motor fails it cannot be serviced and a new unit must be fitted in its place.

Remove the cover 12 and slacken back the bearings 13 as described for removing the complete sunshine roof. Disconnect the feed wires and take out the screws that secure the motor in place. Lift the sunshine roof slightly and remove the motor and drive shafts. Check that the drive belt behind the motor has not failed. Disconnect the drive shafts by driving out the rollpins shown in **FIG 13:17** with a suitable drift or piece of rod.

The motor is refitted in the reverse order of removal and the adjustments are the same as for refitting the complete sunshine roof.

Track:

Remove the roof as described previously. Check that the pick-up pads are in good condition, that the two shoes are parallel and also make sure that the return springs work correctly.

The track itself can be drawn out using a pair of pliers, as shown in **FIG 13:18**. Make sure that the contact surfaces are clean and renew the tracks if they are defective.

13:7 The windscreen and backlight glass

The method of securing the glass in position is the same in both cases and the instructions apply equally.

On the windscreen it will be necessary to remove the wiper arms. On models fitted with heated backlight windows free the cable from its three clips on the frame and the contact assembly.

If the glass has broken it will be found easier to remove the pieces if sheets of paper are stuck on either side. Any pieces that fall into the car should be removed with a powerful vacuum cleaner. **Make sure that there are no particles left in the windscreen demisting system, even if it requires partially dismantling it,** otherwise particles may be blown into the faces of the front seat occupants. Slide the clips of the embellishers sideways to free the ends and then lever out the embellishers, taking care not to bend or distort them. Peel out the old rubber windscreen surround and discard it.

Check the flange in the aperture for damage or distortion. Dress out dents with a block and hammer and smooth down any protrusions. If this is not done stress points can be set up in the new glass, causing it to fail in use.

Fit the new surround to the windscreen and lay the windscreen on a padded bench. Lay a length of cord in the groove around the surround so that the cord completely encircles the surround and the two ends overlap and hang out, leaving enough to get a good grip on.

Into the bottom corners of the aperture lay strips of sealing plastic 25 x 200mm (1 x $7\frac{7}{8}$ inch). Have an assistant hold the glass assembly accurately in place and from inside the car pull on the ends of the cord so that as the cord comes out it lifts the lip of the surround over the body flange. Help the surround to seat by pressing it down and complete, after removal of the cord, by tapping it down lightly with a rubber mallet.

Inject sealant MPR.00.01.316.200 around the top **S** and sides **L** as shown in **FIG 13:19**. Press down the

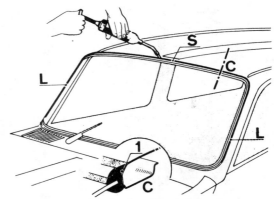

FIG 13:19 Sealing the windscreen

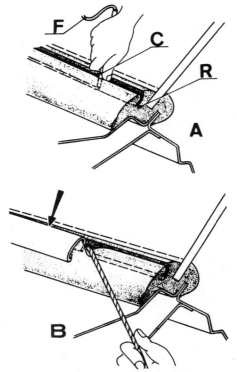

FIG 13:20 Fitting the embellisher

surround and wipe away surplus sealant with a piece of cloth moistened with fuel or white spirits. **Do not use excessive solvent otherwise it will creep under the surround and remove the sealer that should be there.**

Lay a length of cord **F** around the slit **R** for the embellisher using a short length of tube **C** to guide it into position, as shown at **A** in **FIG 13:20**. Pull out the cord as shown in **B** and press the embellisher into the slit as it opens. If lubricant is required use water, water and soap solution, or soft soap. When the embellisher parts are in place slide the clips along them to cover the joins.

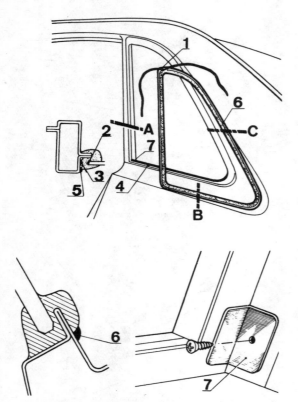

13:8 Quarterlight glass

The glass is held in place by a very similar method to that for the windscreen and backlight (see previous section).

When refitting the glass the cord 1 is fitted so that it overlaps at the top corner. Fit the glass from the inside and remove the cord from the outside taking great care not to split the rubber. The joints 2 and 3 between glass and surround, and surround and body should be sealed with 306 sealing compound. The outer parts 4, 5 and 6 should be protected with a fillet of 307 sealing compound. The small bracket 7 should be fitted as low down as possible to keep the glass in place. All the parts are shown in **FIG 13:21**.

13:9 The tailgate

The tailgate components are shown in **FIG 13:22**. The backlight glass is dealt with in **Section 13:7**.

The hinge arms 5 are secured by three screws each to the tailgate and by clip washers to the pivot posts on the body. When the tailgate is opened the weight is taken by the counterbalance arms 8.

To remove the tailgate open it and support it by hand in the open position. Take out the screws, two each, that secure the counterbalance arms to the tailgate, and disconnect the wiring for the wiper motor when fitted. Still supporting the tailgate take out the screws that secure the hinge arms to the tailgate and then remove it. The hinge arms can then be removed from the body by freeing the clip washers.

Refit the tailgate in the reverse order of removal. Do not attempt to remove the coil springs from the counterbalance arms as they will be extremely difficult to refit without special tools.

FIG 13:21 The quarter light attachments

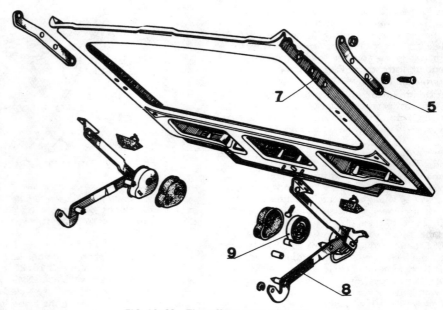

FIG 13:22 The tailgate components

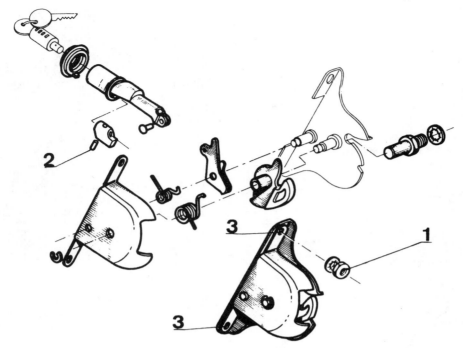

FIG 13:23   The tailgate lock components

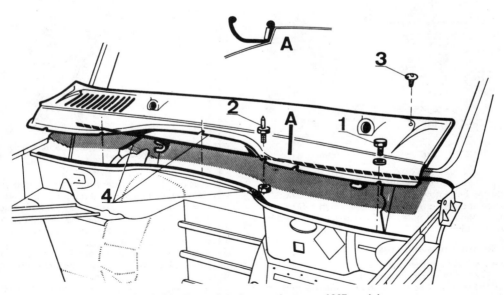

FIG 13:24   Removing the scuttle on pre 1967 models

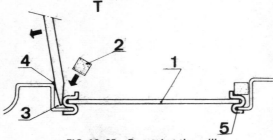

FIG 13:25   Removing the grille

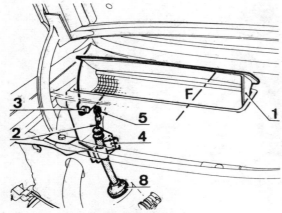

FIG 13:26   Freeing the vent control cable

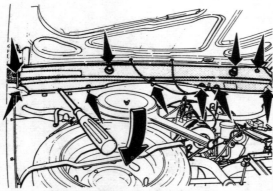

FIG 13:27   The later scuttle attachments

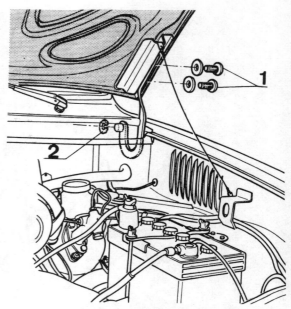

FIG 13:28   The bonnet attachments

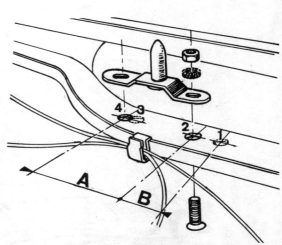

FIG 13:29 Modifying the guide when fitting a new bonnet to a pre 1967 model. A = 63 mm, B = 16 mm

The lock mechanism is shown in **FIG 13:23**. The assembly can be removed after taking out the two nuts 1 from inside the frame and adjustment when refitting is provided by the slotted holes 3. The lock barrel is held in place by the rollpin 2.

13:10 Scuttle grille and crossmember

On pre 1967 models the scuttle attachments are shown in **FIG 13:24**. The wiper arms must be removed before taking off the scuttle. When refitting the parts use strips of mastic 4, 503 sealing compound to make the joints waterproof. The attachment holes are slotted so that the scuttle can be aligned with the bonnet, but take care not to scratch the paintwork when carrying out adjustments.

After 1967 a cable-operated vent is fitted to the scuttle. Open the vent and remove the grille as shown in **FIG 13:25**. Peel out the sealing strip 2. Insert a screwdriver between the grille 1 and front scuttle frame 3 using a piece of rag 4 to protect the paint. Lever carefully to prevent distortion.

Disconnect the eye end 5 of the cable 2 from the spigot 3 on the vent flap 1, shown in **FIG 13:26** and then free

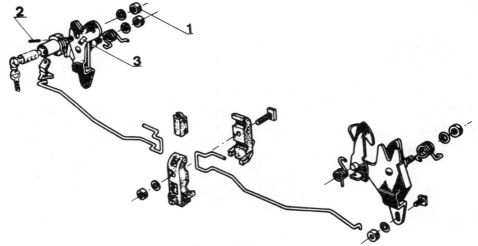

FIG 13:30   The bonnet lock components except R.1156

the clip 4 that holds the outer cable. The scuttle attachments are shown in **FIG 13:27** and once these have been freed the parts can be removed.

The parts on the later models are refitted in the reverse order of removal. Make sure that the rubber grommet around the vent cable is securely in place. When reconnecting the operating cable it will be found easier if the other end of the cable is freed from the control inside the car but take great care not to allow the cable to slide under the glove box. Secure the inner end of the cable with a piece of wire to prevent it from sliding under.

On the later models the vent operating cable does not always need to be disconnected, such as when obtaining access to parts fitted under the scuttle, and once the scuttle attachments have been freed the scuttle can be turned over and laid along the top of the front wing, using rags to protect the paintwork.

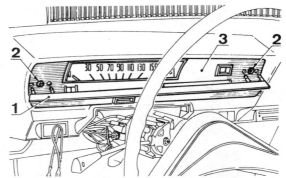

FIG 13:31   Removing the instrument panel on a R.1150 and early 1152, and 1153 models

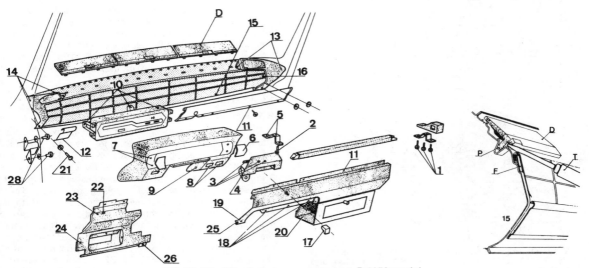

FIG 13:32   The dash components on a R.1150 model

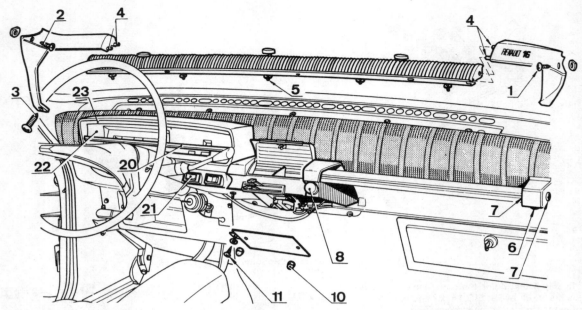

FIG 13:33 The dash components on later R.1152 and R.1153 models

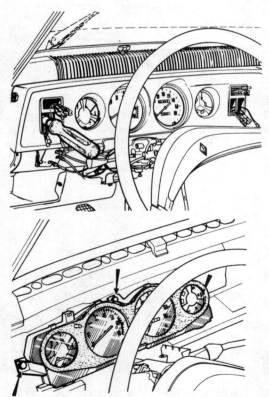

FIG 13:34 Removing the instrument panel on (top) early R.1151, and (bottom) later R.1151, R.1154 and R.1156 models

13:11 The bonnet (hood)

The bonnet attachments are shown in **FIG 13:28**. The bonnet can be removed after taking out the TACL screws 1. If the hinge arms are to be removed then the scuttle must first be removed and the clip washers 2 taken off.

The method of aligning the bonnet was changed in 1967 and if a new bonnet is to be fitted to an earlier model the new guide must be fitted as shown in **FIG 13:29**. The new holes 2 and 4 are drilled to 8 mm ($\frac{5}{16}$ inch), in the scuttle crossmember. Use the old holes 1 and 3 as the datum points.

The locking mechanism is shown in **FIG 13:30**. The nuts 1 hold the parts to the front panel and the rollpin 2 secures the lock barrel. The holes 3 are slotted to allow final adjustment when the parts are refitted.

The locking mechanism on the R.1156 has been simplified but can be dealt with in a similar manner.

13:12 The dash and instrument panel
R.1150 and early R.1152 and R.1153:

Disconnect the battery. Remove the cover from the lighting switch assembly on the steering column. Remove the beading 1, shown in **FIG 13:31**, and take out the two screws that secure the embellisher 3 in position. Take out the two switches and disconnect the wires from them, after labelling the leads. Take out the four screws that secure the cowl and then remove it. Unscrew the three bolts that hold the instrument panel in place and partially withdraw it. Disconnect the speedometer cable and electrical leads and then remove the instrument panel. The components of the earlier dash are shown in **FIG 13:32** and the components for models after 1967 are shown in **FIG 13:33**.

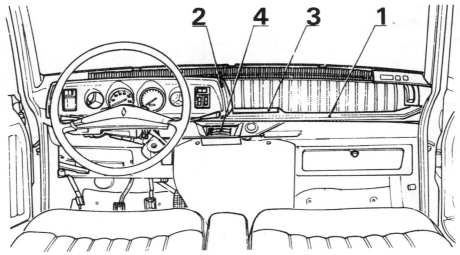

FIG 13:35   The dash on an early R.1151 model

R.1151 early:

The method of removing the instrument panel is shown in **FIG 13:34**. Remove the switches from the instrument panel, labelling the leads as they are disconnected and remove the lighting switch covers. Unscrew the two securing screws through the aperture for the switches. Partially withdraw the cowl and disconnect the leads for the panel lighting rheostat so that the cowl can be removed. Take out the three screws that secure the instrument panel and partially withdraw it so that the speedometer cable and two junction boxes can be disconnected.

To remove the retaining bar 1 attachments (shown in **FIG 13:35**) the cowl 2, ashtray 3 and heater control assembly 4 must be removed.

R.1152, R.1153 and R.1155:

The parts to be removed are shown in **FIG 13:36**. They are the two embellishers 1, the air distributor 2, the dashboard embellisher, and the steering wheel itself.

Remove the covers on the lighting switch and then free the attachments arrowed in **FIG 13:37** so that the instrument panel can be partially withdrawn and the leads and speedometer cable disconnected.

R.1151 later, R.1154 and R.1156:

Disconnect the battery and remove the facia board to give access to the instruments and their mounting panel.

Remove any switches and disconnect the associated wiring, being careful to clearly label the leads.

Remove the instrument panel bezel and unscrew the speedometer cable and the three mounting screws from the panel (see **FIG 13:34**).

Disconnect the two connector blocks and lift out the instrument panel assembly.

Refitting is carried out by reversing the above procedure.

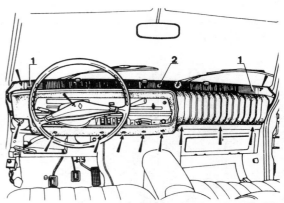

FIG 13:36   Removing the dash panel on a R.1152, R.1153 or R.1155 (USA/Canada) model

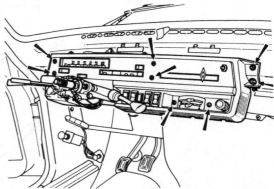

FIG 13:37   Removing the instrument panel on a R.1152, R.1153 or R.1155 (USA/Canada) model

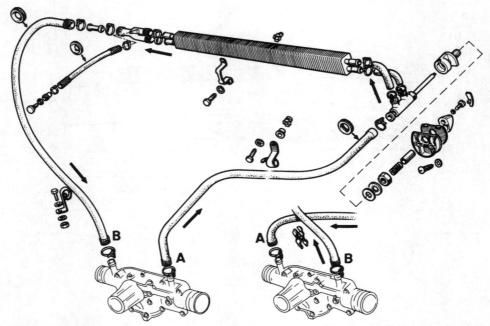

FIG 13:38 The heater components. The inset shows the hose run for righthand drive models

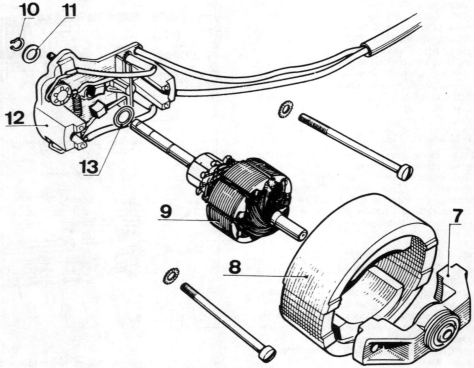

FIG 13:39 Typical heater motor components

Reassembly:

In all cases the parts are refitted in the reverse order of removal. Make sure that all the connections are correctly made before reconnecting the battery, **and note that the battery should always be disconnected when working on the instrument panel.**

It will be necessary to remove the instrument panel in order to change any instruments. To renew either the speedometer or rev counter (tachometer) it will be necessary to remove the glass.

13:13 The heater

The components are shown in **FIG 13:38**. The main figure shows the pipe run for lefthand drive models while the insert, with the hoses crossed, shows the run for righthand drive models.

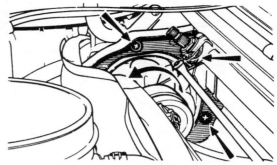

FIG 13:40   Heater motor and fan attachments

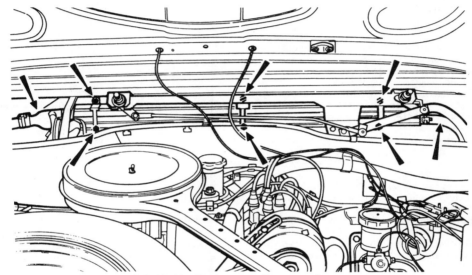

FIG 13:41   The heater radiator attachments

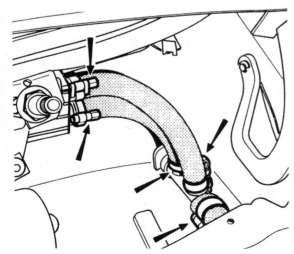

FIG 13:42   The control valve position

FIG 13:43   The attachment of the heater control head

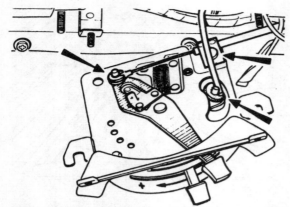

FIG 13:44 The attachments of the heater control cables

It should be noted that different types of motor are fitted to different models and special motors to 'Extreme cold' cars. This also applies to the heater radiator, so make sure that the correct replacement parts are obtained if any parts are found to be defective. Typical motor components are shown in **FIG 13:39** and instructions for servicing motors are given in **Chapter 12, Section 12:3**.

All the parts, except the control head, are fitted under the scuttle and it will be necessary to remove this (see **Section 13:10**) in order to gain access.

The attachments of the fan and motor assembly are shown in **FIG 13:40**. Take out the screws, disconnect the leads and remove the assembly. The arrow in the figure shows the direction in which the motor should turn when running.

Before removing either the radiator or the control valve the cooling system must be drained. **Once the parts have been refitted and the hoses reconnected the cooling system must be filled with coolant and correctly bled** (see **Chapter 4**).

Special hose clips are used for securing the hoses and only if the very greatest care is taken in undoing them can they be used again. The owner should therefore be prepared and have several standard worm-driven hose clips ready for reassembly.

The attachments of the radiator are shown in **FIG 13:41**. Disconnect the hoses and then free the clips that secure the radiator so that it can be lifted out.

The position of the control valve is shown in **FIG 13:42**. From inside the car remove the embellisher on the control handle with a small hook and then take out the screw exposed so that the handle can be removed. From under the scuttle, disconnect the hoses and then withdraw the valve so that its rod passes out through the dashboard.

The control attachments are shown in **FIG 13:43** and the attachments of the operating cables to the control head in **FIG 13:44**.

On 'extreme cold' cars metal ducts are fitted under the carpets to guide hot air to the rear compartment.

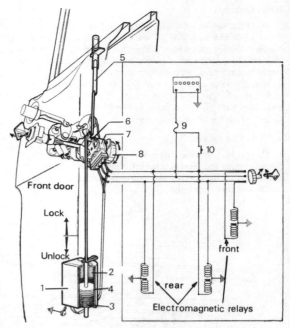

FIG 13:45 Electromagnetic system for locking all four doors

Key to Fig 13:45   1 Electromagnetic relay   2 Coil 1
3 Coil 2   4 Ferrite disc   5 Visual indicator   6 Locking lever
7 Switch   8 Interior control knob   9 Fuse   10 Inertia switch

13:14 Electric door locking system

FIG 13:45 is a diagram illustrating an optional system for the simultaneous locking of all four doors by turning the key in the lock of either of the two front doors. The operation is very simple: a quarter turn of the key—to the left for locking or to the right for unlocking—mechanically operates a switch which activates the electromagnetic relay, on each of the four doors. These relays are coupled directly to the locking levers.

Reference to the diagram shows how operation of the switch energizes one or other of the two coils in the four relays and causes the ferrite disc, and also the locking lever, to move in the appropriate direction: upwards to coil 1 for locking the door, downwards to coil 2 for unlocking.

The same operation can be performed from inside the car by rotating the control knob on the panel of each front door.

Each door is fitted with a red visual indicator to show when the door has been electrically secured.

A safety device is included whereby the doors are immediately unlocked in the event of a shock such as might be caused by an impact at about 10 miles per hour. At all times the conventional manual lock control overrides the electromagnetic system.

APPENDIX

Inches / Decimals / Millimetres Conversion

Inches	Decimals	Milli-metres	Inches to Millimetres (Inches)	Inches to Millimetres (mm)	Millimetres to Inches (mm)	Millimetres to Inches (Inches)
1/64	.015625	.3969	.001	.0254	.01	.00039
1/32	.03125	.7937	.002	.0508	.02	.00079
3/64	.046875	1.1906	.003	.0762	.03	.00118
1/16	.0625	1.5875	.004	.1016	.04	.00157
5/64	.078125	1.9844	.005	.1270	.05	.00197
3/32	.09375	2.3812	.006	.1524	.06	.00236
7/64	.109375	2.7781	.007	.1778	.07	.00276
1/8	.125	3.1750	.008	.2032	.08	.00315
9/64	.140625	3.5719	.009	.2286	.09	.00354
5/32	.15625	3.9687	.01	.254	.1	.00394
11/64	.171875	4.3656	.02	.508	.2	.00787
3/16	.1875	4.7625	.03	.762	.3	.01181
13/64	.203125	5.1594	.04	1.016	.4	.01575
7/32	.21875	5.5562	.05	1.270	.5	.01969
15/64	.234375	5.9531	.06	1.524	.6	.02362
1/4	.25	6.3500	.07	1.778	.7	.02756
17/64	.265625	6.7469	.08	2.032	.8	.03150
9/32	.28125	7.1437	.09	2.286	.9	.03543
19/64	.296875	7.5406	.1	2.54	1	.03937
5/16	.3125	7.9375	.2	5.08	2	.07874
21/64	.328125	8.3344	.3	7.62	3	.11811
11/32	.34375	8.7312	.4	10.16	4	.15748
23/64	.359375	9.1281	.5	12.70	5	.19685
3/8	.375	9.5250	.6	15.24	6	.23622
25/64	.390625	9.9219	.7	17.78	7	.27559
13/32	.40625	10.3187	.8	20.32	8	.31496
27/64	.421875	10.7156	.9	22.86	9	.35433
7/16	.4375	11.1125	1	25.4	10	.39370
29/64	.453125	11.5094	2	50.8	11	.43307
15/32	.46875	11.9062	3	76.2	12	.47244
31/64	.484375	12.3031	4	101.6	13	.51181
1/2	.5	12.7000	5	127.0	14	.55118
33/64	.515625	13.0969	6	152.4	15	.59055
17/32	.53125	13.4937	7	177.8	16	.62992
35/64	.546875	13.8906	8	203.2	17	.66929
9/16	.5625	14.2875	9	228.6	18	.70866
37/64	.578125	14.6844	10	254.0	19	.74803
19/32	.59375	15.0812	11	279.4	20	.78740
39/64	.609375	15.4781	12	304.8	21	.82677
5/8	.625	15.8750	13	330.2	22	.86614
41/64	.640625	16.2719	14	355.6	23	.90551
21/32	.65625	16.6687	15	381.0	24	.94488
43/64	.671875	17.0656	16	406.4	25	.98425
11/16	.6875	17.4625	17	431.8	26	1.02362
45/64	.703125	17.8594	18	457.2	27	1.06299
23/32	.71875	18.2562	19	482.6	28	1.10236
47/64	.734375	18.6531	20	508.0	29	1.14173
3/4	.75	19.0500	21	533.4	30	1.18110
49/64	.765625	19.4469	22	558.8	31	1.22047
25/32	.78125	19.8437	23	584.2	32	1.25984
51/64	.796875	20.2406	24	609.6	33	1.29921
13/16	.8125	20.6375	25	635.0	34	1.33858
53/64	.828125	21.0344	26	660.4	35	1.37795
27/32	.84375	21.4312	27	685.8	36	1.41732
55/64	.859375	21.8281	28	711.2	37	1.4567
7/8	.875	22.2250	29	736.6	38	1.4961
57/64	.890625	22.6219	30	762.0	39	1.5354
29/32	.90625	23.0187	31	787.4	40	1.5748
59/64	.921875	23.4156	32	812.8	41	1.6142
15/16	.9375	23.8125	33	838.2	42	1.6535
61/64	.953125	24.2094	34	863.6	43	1.6929
31/32	.96875	24.6062	35	889.0	44	1.7323
63/64	.984375	25.0031	36	914.4	45	1.7717

Volume, Distance and Pressure Conversions

UNITS	Pints to Litres	Gallons to Litres	Litres to Pints	Litres to Gallons	Miles to Kilometres	Kilometres to Miles	Lbs. per sq. In. to Kg. per sq. Cm.	Kg. per sq. Cm. to Lbs. per sq. In.
1	.57	4.55	1.76	.22	1.61	.62	.07	14.22
2	1.14	9.09	3.52	.44	3.22	1.24	.14	28.50
3	1.70	13.64	5.28	.66	4.83	1.86	.21	42.67
4	2.27	18.18	7.04	.88	6.44	2.49	.28	56.89
5	2.84	22.73	8.80	1.10	8.05	3.11	.35	71.12
6	3.41	27.28	10.56	1.32	9.66	3.73	.42	85.34
7	3.98	31.82	12.32	1.54	11.27	4.35	.49	99.56
8	4.55	36.37	14.08	1.76	12.88	4.97	.56	113.79
9		40.91	15.84	1.98	14.48	5.59	.63	128.00
10		45.46	17.60	2.20	16.09	6.21	.70	142.23
20				4.40	32.19	12.43	1.41	284.47
30				6.60	48.28	18.64	2.11	426.70
40				8.80	64.37	24.85		
50					80.47	31.07		
60					96.56	37.28		
70					112.65	43.50		
80					128.75	49.71		
90					144.84	55.92		
100					160.93	62.14		

Torque Conversions

UNITS	Lb ft to kgm	Kgm to lb ft	UNITS	Lb ft to kgm	Kgm to lb ft
1	.138	7.233	7	.967	50.631
2	.276	14.466	8	1.106	57.864
3	.414	21.699	9	1.244	65.097
4	.553	28.932	10	1.382	72.330
5	.691	36.165	20	2.765	144.660
6	.829	43.398	30	4.147	216.990

TECHNICAL DATA

Unless otherwise stated the dimension is given in millimetres and the dimension in the brackets is given in inches

ENGINE

General type	4 cylinder in-line
	Single camshaft in crankcase with OHV operated by pushrods and rockers
	Water-cooled and fitted with liners.
Castings	Extensive use made of light alloy

Specific engine models:

R 1150 (16)	697-01, 697-02
R 1151 (16 TS)	807-01 to 807-04
R 1152 (16 TL)	821-02, 821-03
R 1153 (16 TA)	821-01, 821-04
R 1154 (16TSA)	807-05, 807-06
R 1155 (USA)	841-04
R 1156 (16 TX)	843-01, 843-02

697, 821 and 841 are similar with single in-line bank of valves while 807 and 843 have two banks of valves

Compression ratio:

697-01, 807-01, 807-03 to 807-06 and all 821	8.6:1
697-02 and 807-02	7.6:1
841	7.5:1
843	9.25:1
821-02 (1976) low compression	8.0:1

Bore:

697	76 (2.992)
807 and 821	77 (3.032)
843	79 (3.110)

Stroke:

697	81 (3.189)
807 and 821	84 (3.307)

Cubic capacity:

697	1470 cc (90 cu inch)
807 and 821	1565 cc (95.5 cu inch)
841 and 843	1647 cc (100.4 cu inch)

Firing order	1–3–4–2

Crankshaft:

Number of main bearings	5
Bearing material:	
697	Whitemetal
All others	Aluminium/tin alloy
Hardening method	Roll hardened on all models except early R.1150
Journal diameter	54.8 mm (2.158)
Journal regrind diameter:	
Roll hardened	54.55 (2.148)
Non-roll hardened	54.30 (2.138)
Crankpin diameter	48 (1.890)
Crankpin regrind diameter:	
Roll hardened	47.75 (1.880)
Non-roll hardened	47.50 (1.870)
End float	.05 to .23 (.002 to .009)
Thrust washer thicknesses	2.80, 2.90, 2.95 (.110, .114, .116)

Camshaft:
Bearings   4
End float ..   ..   .05 to .12 (.002 to .0045)

Cylinder block:
Liner protrusion:
     697, 807 and 821   ., ...15 to .20 (.006 to .008)
     841 and 843 (less 'O' ring)   ..   ..   .10 to .17 (.004 to .0067)
     Bottom seal thickness, 697, 807 and 821:
         Blue spot ..   ..   .08 (.003)
         Red spot ..   ..   .10 (.004)
         Green spot ..   ..   .12 (.0047)
         'O' ring diameter, 841 and 843   ..   ..   1.15 to 1.35 (.045 to .053)

Cylinder head:

	Standard	Repair
Height:		
697 ..	80.65 (3.175)	80.15 (3.155)
807 and 843 ..	93.50 (3.681)	93 (3.661)
821 and 841 ..	81.45 (3.207)	80.95 (3.187)
Maximum bow ..	.05 (.002)	

Combustion chamber volume:
     697 ..   ..   40.70 cc (2.483 cu inch)
     807 and 843 ..   ..   43.45 cc (2.652 cu inch)
     821 and 841 ..   ..   43.72 cc (2.668 cu inch)
Valve seat width:
   Inlet:
     697, 821 and 841 ..   ..   ..   1.3 to 1.6 (.051 to .063)
     807 and 843   ..   ..   ..   1.5 to 1.8 (.059 to .071)
   Exhaust (all) ..   ..   1.7 to 2.0 (.067 to .079)
Valve seat angle ..   ..   90 deg. inclusive

Pistons and rings:
Gudgeon pin   ..   ..   Press fit in connecting rod, free fit in piston

Gudgeon pin length:
     697 ..   .. $67 (2\frac{5}{8})$
     807 and 821 ..   .. $68 (2\frac{11}{16})$
     841 and 843   69
Gudgeon pin diameter ..   ..   ..   20 (.787), 21 (.827)
Piston rings   ..   ..   Three per piston, supplied already gapped

Valve guides:
Internal diameter ..   ..   8 + .022, −.00 (.315 + .0008, −.00)
External diameter:
     Standard   ..   ..   13 (.512)
     1 groove   ..   ..   13.10 (.516)
     2 groove   ..   ..   13.25 (.522)

Valves:
Head diameter:
   Inlet:
     697, 821 and 841 ..   ..   ..   35 (1.378)
     807 and 843   ..   ..   ..   40 (1.575)
   Exhaust:
     697, 821 and 841 ..   ..   ..   31 (1.220)
     807 and 843   ..   ..   ..   35.35 (1.392)
Stem diameter   ..   ..   8 − 0.025, −.047 (.315 − 0.001, − 0.0019)

Included angle of bearing surface (all models)   ..   90 deg.

Valve springs:

Approximate free length:

697	.. 48.4 ($1\frac{29}{32}$)
821 and 841 outer	.. 48.4 ($1\frac{29}{32}$)
821 and 841 inner	.. 38.4 ($1\frac{1}{2}$)
807 and 843 outer	.. 54.3 ($2\frac{5}{32}$)
807 early inner	.. 44.7 ($1\frac{3}{4}$)
807 later 843, inner	.. 46.8 ($1\frac{27}{32}$)

Length under a load of:

9 kg (20 lb)—821 and 841, inner ..	.. 19 ($\frac{3}{4}$)
16 kg (35 lb)—807 later and 843, inner	.. 24.5 ($\frac{31}{32}$)
26 kg (57 lb)—807 early, inner ..	.. 26 ($1\frac{1}{32}$)
45 kg (99 lb)—697	.. 29 ($1\frac{9}{64}$)
807, 821 and 841, outer	.. 29 ($1\frac{9}{64}$)
52 kg (114 lb)—807 and 843, outer ..	.. 30.5 ($1\frac{13}{64}$)

Valve timing:

	697 and 841	807	821 (double valve springs)	821 (single valve springs)	843
Inlet opens BTDC	10°	21°	10°	18°	24°
Inlet closes ABDC	42°	59°	42°	54°	68°
Exhaust opens BBDC	46°	59°	46°	58°	68°
Exhaust closes ATDC	10°	21°	10°	18°	24°

Valve location.
697 and 821 .. E–I–I–E–E–I–I–E

Tappets (cam followers):

Diameter:

Standard	.. 12 − .010, − .024 (.472 − .0004, − .0010)
Repair size	.. 12.20 − .010, − .024 (.480 − .0004, − .0010)
Bore in block	.. 12 + .018, − .00 (.472 + .0007, − .00)

Pushrods:

Length:

697, 821 and 841	.. 88 ($3\frac{15}{32}$)
807 and 843 inlet	.. 78 ($3\frac{1}{8}$)
807 and 843 exhaust	.. 110 ($4\frac{11}{32}$)

Oil pressure at 80°C (176°F):

Minimum at 650 rev/min..	.. 2 to 2.5 kg/sq cm (30 to 35 lb/sq inch)
Minimum at 4000 rev/min	.. 4 to 5 kg/sq cm (60 to 70 lb/sq inch)

FUEL SYSTEM

Carburetter types:

R1150 (697 engine)	.. Solex 35 DISA, -2, -3 or -4
	Solex 35 DITA or -2
	Zenith 36 1F
R1151 (807 engine)	.. Weber 32 DIR-1, -16 or -28
	Weber 32 DAR-2, -4, -5 or -6
R1152 (821 engine)	.. Solex 26-32 DIDSA-3 or -8
	Weber 32 DIR-12, -19, -20, -35 or -36
R1153 (821 engine)	.. Solex 26-32 DIDSA-8
	Solex 32-32 SEIEA
	Weber 32 DIR-8, -10, -17, -18, -33 or -34

R1154 (807 engine)	..	..	..	..	Weber 32 DIR-13, -14, -22 or -27
R1155 (841 engine)	..	..	..	..	Solex 26-32 DIDSA-8
R1156 (843 engine)	..	..	..	..	Weber 32 DAR-7 or -8
R1152 (from 1976)	..	..	..	..	Solex MIMAT Mark 634
R1155 (from 1976)	..	..	..	..	Solex MIMAT Mark 633
R1157 (from 1976)	..	..	..	..	Solex MIMAT Mark 700

Idling speeds:
Engine type:

697, 807-01, 807-02, 807-03, 821-03	..	650 ± 25 rev/min
807-04, 821-02, 843-01	.. ..	700 ± 25 rev/min
807-05, 821-01, 843-02	.. ..	600 ± 25 rev/min
807-06, 821-04, 841-04	.. ..	625 ± 25 rev/min

Jet sizes:
35 DISA, mark 319, 319-1:

Choke tube	..	..	..	..	27
Main jet	..	..	..	..	140
Air compensator jet	..	..	..	..	135
Idling jet	..	..	..	..	50
Accelerator pump	..	..	..	..	50
Needle valve	..	..	..	..	1.5 mm
Float weight	..	..	..	..	7.3 g

35 DISA-2, mark 365, 365-1:
As 35 DISA except:

Main jet	..	..	..	..	142.5
Air compensator jet	..	..	..	..	160
Idling jet	..	..	..	..	42.5
Accelerator pump	..	..	..	..	40

35 DISA-2, mark 365-2, 370:
As 35 DISA-2, mark 365 except:

Air compensator jet	..	..	..	150
Needle valve	..	..	..	2 mm

35 DISA-3, mark 376, 376-1, 376-2
35 DISA-4, mark 445, 445-1, 454-HA:
As 35 DISA-2, mark 365-2 except:

Choke tube	..	..	..	26.5
Air compensator jet	..	..	..	155
Idling jet	..	..	..	50
Accelerator pump	..	..	..	50
Needle valve	..	..	..	1.7 mm

35 DISA-3, mark 366-HA:
As 35 DISA-3, mark 376 except:

Air compensator jet	..	..	145

35 DITA, mark 382, 382-1, 382-2, 387, 387-1
35 DITA-2, mark 405, 405-1:
As 35 DISA-3, mark 376 except:

Main jet	..	..	..	140

35 DITA, mark 388-HA
35 DITA-2, mark 406-HA:
As 35 DITA, mark 382 except:

Air compensator jet	..	..	145

36IF, mark V 10 003, V 10 005:

Choke tube	..	..	..	..	27
Main jet	..	..	..	..	135
Air compensator jet	..	..	..	..	100
Idling jet	..	..	..	..	40
Needle valve	..	..	..	..	1.5 mm
Enrichener	..	..	..	..	40

36IF, mark V 10 006:
  As 36IF, mark V 10 003 except:
    Main jet   145
36IF, mark V 10 007:
  As 36IF, mark V 10 006 except:
    Enrichener   95

32 DIR-1, mark 100
32 DAR-2, mark 101, 102, 103:

	Primary		Secondary
Choke tube	24		26
Main jet	140		150
Air compensator jet	190		140
Idling jet	50		80
Accelerator pump		60	
Needle valve		175	
Float		11 g	
Float level		5 mm	

32 DAR-4, mark 1100
32 DAR-5, mark 1800
32 DAR-6, mark 2400, 2401, 2402:
  As 32 DIR-1, mark 100 except:

	Primary		Secondary
Main jet	145		
Air compensator jet	180		
Accelerator pump		70	

32 DIR-16, mark 1600:
  As 32 DAR-4, mark 1100 except:

	Primary		Secondary
Main jet			160
Air compensator jet	170		170
Idling jet			45
Accelerator pump		60	
Float level		7 mm	

32 DIR-28, mark 3100, 3101, 3102:
  As 32 DIR-16, mark 1600 except:

	Primary		Secondary
Main jet	147		150
Air compensator jet	180		
Idling jet	60		

32 DIR-12, mark 1300
32 DIR-19, mark 2101, 2102
32 DIR-20, mark 2201, 2202:
  As 32 DIR-28, mark 3100 except:

	Primary		Secondary
Choke tube			24
Main jet			140
Air compensator jet	190		210
Idling jet	45		70
Accelerator pump		50	

32 DIR-19, mark 2100
32 DIR-20, mark 2200:
  As 32 DIR-12, mark 1300 except:

	Primary		Secondary
Accelerator pump		60	

32 DIR-35, mark 4000, 4001
32 DIR-36, mark 4100, 4101:
  As 32 DIR-12, mark 1300 except:

	Primary		Secondary
Main jet	150		132
Air compensator jet	165		185
Idling jet	55		45
Accelerator pump		45	

32 DIR-8, mark 600, 601

32 DIR-10, mark 700
32 DIR-17, mark 1900, 1901
32 DIR-18, mark 2000, 2001:

As 32 DIR-35, mark 4000 except:		
Main jet	140	140
Air compensator jet	190	165
Idling jet	45	70
Accelerator pump	40	

32 DIR-33, mark 3800, 3801
32 DIR-34, mark 3900, 3901:
As 32 DIR-8, mark 600 except:

Main jet	145	125
Air compensator jet	165	190
Idling jet	55	45
Accelerator pump	50	

32 DIR-13, mark 1400:

As 32 DIR-33, mark 3800 except:		
Choke tube		26
Main jet	145	160
Air compensator jet	180	140
Idling jet	50	80
Accelerator pump	40	

32 DIR-14, mark 1500
32 DIR-22, mark 2500, 2501, 2502:

As 32 DIR-13, mark 1400 except:		
Main jet	140	150
Air compensator jet	190	
Accelerator pump	50	
Float level	5 mm	

32 DIR-27, mark 3000, 3001, 3002, 3003:

As 32 DIR-14, mark 1500 except:		
Choke		24
Main jet	147	125
Air compensator jet	180	120
Idling jet	55	
Float level	7 mm	

32 DIR-42, mark 5000:

As 32 DIR-1, mark 100 except:		
Choke	24	24
Main jet	150	130
Air compensator jet	170	130
Idling jet	52	80
Float level	7	

32 DIR-43, mark 5100:

As 32 DIR-1, mark 100 except:		
Main jet	155	150
Air compensator jet	180	170 (1975 on, 150)
Idling jet	55	45
Float level	7	

32 DAR-7, mark 3700:

As 32 DIR-27, mark 3003 except:		
Choke		26
Main jet	135	135
Air compensator jet	170	145
Idling jet	52	45
Accelerator pump	60	

26-32 DIDSA-3, mark 439:

Choke tube	23.5	26
Main jet	120	140
Air compensator jet	125	130
Idling jet	65 with damper	95
Needle valve		1.7 mm
Float		7.3 g
Accelerator pump		40
Diffuser		3.2

26-32 DIDSA-8, mark 478, 478-1, 478-2:
As 26-32 DIDSA-3, mark 439 except:

• Main jet		155
Air compensator jet	120	100
Idling jet		90
Accelerator pump	35	

26-32 DIDSA-8, mark 502, 502-1:
As for 26-32 DIDSA-8, mark 478 except:

Air compensator jet		110
Idling jet	65	

26-32 DIDSA-8, mark 479, 479-1, 510, 510-1:
As for 26-32 DIDSA-8, mark 502 except:

Main jet		165
Air compensator jet	110	85
Idling jet		80

26-32 DIDSA-8, mark 479-2:
As 26-32 DIDSA-8, mark 479 except:

Needle valve	1.7 mm with built-in spring

26-32 DIDSA-8, mark 499:
As 26-32 DIDSA-8, mark 479 except:

Main jet	122.5	155
Air compensator jet	125	95
Idling jet	70	45
Needle valve	1.7 mm with built-in spring	

32-32 SEIEA, mark 549:

Choke tube	24	24
Main jet	130	145
Air compensator jet	140N3 *	200NH *
Idling jet	40 to 46	80
Needle valve	1.7 mm with built-in spring	
Accelerator pump	45	

Non-detachable

MIMAT, mark 634 and 700:

Choke tube	24	25
Main jet	127.5	140
Air compensator jet	140	165
Idling jet	38	45
Enrichment jet	50	
Pump jet	45	

MIMAT, mark 633:
As for mark 634 except:

Main jet	125	117.5
Air compensator jet	150	120
Idling jet	40	65
Enrichment jet	60	
Pump jet	40	

IGNITION SYSTEM

Firing order	1–3–4–2 (No. 1 in front)
Sparking plugs:	
Gap setting	.6 to .7 (.024 to .027)
Type:	
R1150	AC45 X L, Marchal 35HS
R1151, R1154	AC44 X L, Champion N3, Eyquem 750L, Marchal 35HSB NGK.-BP6ES
R1152, R1153	AC42 X LS, Champion N5, Eyquem 750L, NGK BP6ES
R1155	AC45 X L, Champion N5
R1156	AC 42 X LS, Champion N7Y, Eyquem 755L
Engines 821-01 to -04 from 1976 and 841-01	AC 42 XLS, Champion N9Y, Eyquem 600 LS
7.6 c.r.	AC45 X L
Ignition coil	Ducellier 2765.A
Static ignition timing:	
R.1150 pre-1969	0 ± 2 deg.
R.1150 1969 on	0 ± 1 deg.
R.1151 1968 model	2 BTDC ± 1 deg.
Later R.1151, R.1152 and R.1153 (USA) . .	0 ± 1 deg.
R.1153, R.1154 (early)	6 BTDC ± 1 deg. Later 10 BTDC
R.1156, manual	4 BTDC ± 1 deg.
R.1155	3 BTDC ± 1 deg.

COOLING SYSTEM

Normal operating temperature:	
R.1150 and R.1151:	
Hot climates	73°C (163°F)
Normal	84°C (183°F)
R.1152, R.1153, R.1154	84°C (183°F)
R.1156	82° to 92°C
Coolant:	
Ready mixed	6 litre drum, No. 806.834
	8 litre drum, No. 806.835
Antifreeze:	
Glaceol	1 litre tin, No. 805.332
	$2\frac{1}{2}$ litre tin, No. 806.142
Sexprot	Bulk only

CLUTCH

Type:	
R.1150 and early R.1151, and R.1152 . .	200D 325 with diaphragm spring and thrust ring
R.1151 and R.1152 later	200 DBR 325 diaphragm spring without thrust ring
R.1156	200 DBR 375 diaphragm spring without thrust ring
Disc thickness	7.7 (.304)
Operation	Cable from clutch pedal
Clearance	2 to 3 ($\frac{5}{64}$ to $\frac{1}{8}$) at end of withdrawal lever
Adjustment point	At cable on withdrawal lever

MANUAL TRANSMISSION

Type	336. Four forward speeds with all synchromesh engagement. Differential integral in transmission
Type (16TX)	385. Five forward speeds and reverse

Ratios:

	BV 336 early	BV 336 later
First	3.61 :1	3.46 :1
Second	2.25 :1	2.24 :1
Third	1.48 :1	1.48 :1
Fourth	1.03 :1	1.04 :1
Reverse	3.08 :1	3.08 :1
Differential	9 × 34 or 8 × 34	

Ratios:

	BV 385 early	BV 385 later
First	3.46 :1	3.82 :1
Second	2.24 :1	2.24 :1
Third	1.48 :1	1.48 :1
Fourth	1.04 :1	1.04 :1
Fifth	.91 :1	.86 :1
Reverse	3.08 :1	3.08 :1
Differential	8 × 31	

AUTOMATIC TRANSMISSION

Type	139.10 or 139.12
Weight	65 kg (143 lb)
Speeds	Three forward, one reverse

Ratios:

Torque converter	2.3 :1 maximum but normally 1 :1
Differential	9 × 34 (3.77:1)
Speedometer	1.41 :1

	First	Second	Third	Reverse
Gearbox	2.33 :1	1.44 :1	1 :1	2 :1
Overall	9.52 :1	5.606 :1	3.879 :1	7.759 :1

Type (16TX)	4139-12			
Ratios:	First	Second	Third	Reverse
Overall	8.74 :1	5.42 :1	3.75 :1	7.5 :1

Fluid	Elf Renault Matic or Mobil ATF.-200

SUSPENSION AND DRIVE SHAFTS

Drive shaft couplings:

Outboard	Bed or TE (cannot be serviced) or Spider GE86
Inboard	4-ball type or Spider G176

Torsion bars:

	Front	Rear
Length	1.035 metre ($40\frac{3}{4}$)	1.023 metre ($40\frac{9}{32}$)
Diameter:		
Standard	17.4 (.685)	21.6 (.850)
Poor roads	18.2 (.716)	22.5 (.886)
Number of splines:		
Suspension end	24	30
Anchor end	23	28

Dampers	Sealed telescopic double-acting

Anti-roll bar diameter:

Front	19 (.748)
Rear	14 (.551)

Suspension height settings:

Tolerance.. .. .. $+ 10$ ($\frac{3}{8}$) $- 15$ ($\frac{5}{8}$). Car must be on level ground, with tank full and tyres correctly inflated

Standard versions:

Vehicle type	Tyres	Front H1	Rear H2
R.1150	145 × 14 Radial	200 ($7\frac{7}{8}$ inch)	260 ($10\frac{1}{4}$ inch)
R.1152, R.1153	145 × 14 Radial	200 ($7\frac{7}{8}$ inch)	260 ($10\frac{1}{4}$ inch)
R.1150	155 × 14 Radial	210 ($8\frac{5}{16}$ inch)	270 ($10\frac{11}{16}$ inch)
R.1152, R.1153	155 × 14 Radial	210 ($8\frac{5}{16}$ inch)	270 ($10\frac{11}{16}$ inch)
R.1151, R.1154	155 × 14 Radial	195 ($7\frac{11}{16}$ inch)	255 ($10\frac{1}{16}$ inch)
R.1156	155 × 14 Radial	195 ($7\frac{11}{16}$ inch)	255 ($10\frac{1}{16}$ inch)

Kingpin inclination .. .. 13 to 15 deg.

Camber .. .. 15 min. to 1 deg.

Castor .. .. 1 deg. 40 min. to 3 deg. 40 min. empty

3 to 5 deg. with floor level

Track:

Early .. .. 0 to 3 mm toe-in

Later .. .. 0 to 3 mm toe-out

STEERING

Type .. .. Rack and pinion

Turns lock to lock 4

Reduction ratio 23:1

BRAKES

Type .. .. Hydraulically operated disc brakes on front wheels, drum brakes on rear brakes. Brake pressure limiter to rear wheels

Handbrake.. .. .. Cable operated on rear wheels only

Servo .. .. Master-Vac unit fitted to all models except R.1150

Adjustments .. .. At rear brakes and handbrake cables

Fluid:

Pre-1969 .. .. 70.R.1 or 70.R.3

1969 onwards 70.R.3

Limiter valve cut-off pressure .. .. 34 kg/sq cm + 0, −5 (415 to 485 lb/sq inch)

Hydraulic system:

Standard .. .. Single system

USA models .. .. Tandem system with pressure drop indicator

ELECTRICAL SYSTEM

Type .. .. 12-volt negative earth

Battery:

R.1150, R.1151 and R.1153 .. .. Fulmen AS.810, 40 amp/hr, 9 plate
Tudor 6RF.4, 40 amp/hr, 9 plate

R.1152 and 'extreme cold' .. .. Fulmen AS.910, 45 amp/hr, 11 plate
Tudor 2.HN, 45 amp/hr, 11 plate

Alternator:

Type	SEV-Motorola 26 607, 26 647 or 34 837
	Paris-Rhone A13 R 63 or A13 R 141

Output (warm):

SEV-Motorola	34 amp at 3000 rev/min
Paris-Rhone	30 amp at 3000 rev/min or 46 amp at 4000 rev/min

Alternator regulator:

Type	SEV 33 546 or Ducellier 8350, 8364 or 8371 or Paris-Rhone AYB 218
Checking speed	6000 rev/min
At 20°C and 30 amp	13.4 to 14.4 volts

Starter motor:

R.1150 (1966 to 1968)	Paris-Rhone D.8.E49 for normal use
	Paris-Rhone D.10.E43 for 'extreme cold'

All other models:

Lefthand drive	Ducellier 6183 or Paris-Rhone D8.E71
Righthand drive	Paris-Rhone D8.E84
'Extreme cold'	Paris-Rhone D10.E48

Locked torque and current:

Type Paris-Rhone	Locked pinion torque	Locked pinion current flow	Battery
D8.E49, D8.E71 and D8.E84	1.1 kgm (8 lb/ft)	355.A	12-volt, 40 amp/hr
D10.E43 and D10.E48 ..	1.8 kgm (13 lb/ft)	400.A	12-volt, 45 amp/hr
Ducellier 6183	1.25 kgm (9 lb/ft)	375.A	12-volt, 40 amp/hr

CAPACITIES

		Litres	Imperial	USA
Automatic transmission:				
Fluid		Elf Renault Matic or Mobil ATF.200		
Drain and refill		3	5 pints	$6\frac{1}{4}$ pints
From Empty		6	$10\frac{1}{2}$ pints	$12\frac{1}{2}$ pints
Cooling system:				
R.1150		5.8	10 pints	12 pints
R.1151, R.1154 and R.1156		6.8	12 pints	$14\frac{1}{2}$ pints
R.1152, R.1153 and R.1155		6.3	11 pints	$13\frac{1}{2}$ pints
Engine:				
Maximum		4	7 pints	$8\frac{1}{2}$ pints
Minimum		3	$5\frac{1}{2}$ pints	$6\frac{1}{2}$ pints
Fuel tank		50	11 galls	13 galls
Transmission:				
Oil		EP.80 or EP.80B		
Quantity		1.64	3 pints	$3\frac{1}{2}$ pints

TORQUE WRENCH SETTINGS

Settings are given kgm, figures in brackets are lb ft

Engine:

Cylinder head:

First stage	4 (30) cold
Second stage	7 to 7.75 (50 to 56), 697, 841 and 821
	7.5 to 8.25 (54 to 60), 807 and 843
Third stage*	8.25 to 8.75 (60 to 63), 697, 821 and 841
	8.5 to 9 (61 to 65), 807 and 843

* Engine must be run for 10 minutes and then allowed to cool for 50 minutes

Rocker shaft	2 to 2.75 (15 to 20)
Big-end bearings	4.5 (32)
Main bearings	6.5 (47)
Flywheel bolts	5 (36)

Oilway plugs:

Front face plug	8 (60)
Remainder	4.5 (32)

Oil pump bolts:

20 mm long	1.25 to 1.75 (9 to 12)
25 mm long	2.25 to 2.75 (16 to 20)
Crankshaft sprocket bolt	6 to 8 (44 to 58)

Manifolds:

697 and 821	1.5 to 2.5 (11 to 18)
807	2.5 to 3 (18 to 22) for inlet
	2 to 3 (15 to 22) for exhaust
Camshaft pulley bolt	10.3 (75)

Automatic transmission:

Drive plate attachments	4.5 to 5 (32 to 36)
Converter attachments	2.5 (18)
Lower cover	.6 (5)
Sump bolts	.45 (4)
Gearbox to engine	4 to 6 (29 to 44)

Steering:

Steering wheel nut	4.5 (32)
Rack to crossmember	2.5 (18)
Ball joint	3.5 ± .5 (25 ± 4)

Front suspension:

Hub nut	15 (110)
Lower damper attachment	4 (30)
Lower ball joint	5 (36)
Upper ball joint	3.5 (25)
Wishbone attachments	4.2 (31)

Rear suspension:

External bearing nuts	4.5 (32)
Internal bearing nuts	2.5 (18)
Anti-roll bar bearing	.8 (7)

Brakes:

Pipe unions	1.1 ± .2 (10)
Flexible hoses	2 ± .25 (15)
Bleed screws	.80 ± .2 (5 to 7)

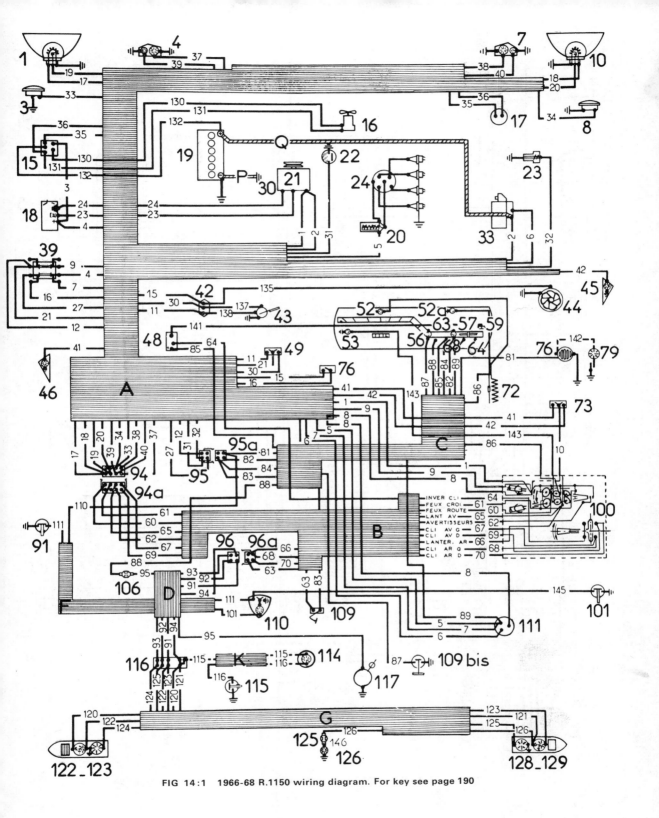

FIG 14:1   1966-68 R.1150 wiring diagram. For key see page 190

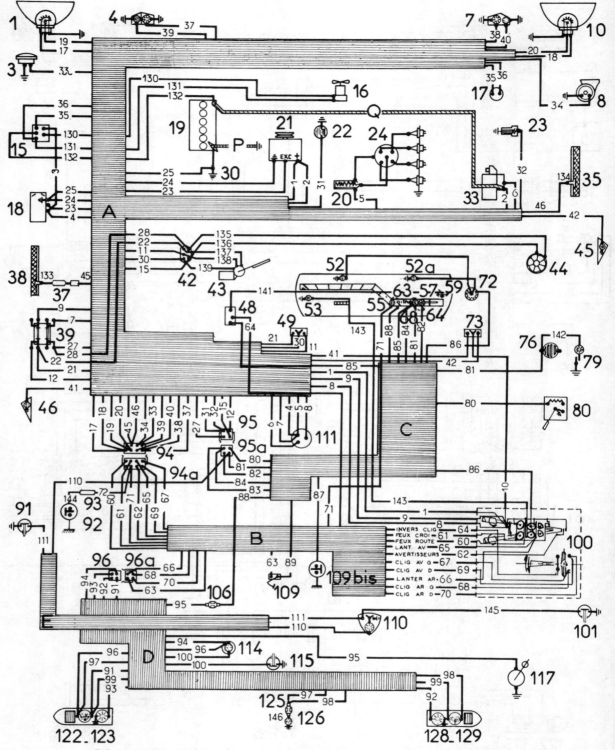

FIG 14:2   1969-72 R.1150, R.1152 and R.1153 wiring diagram. For key see page 190

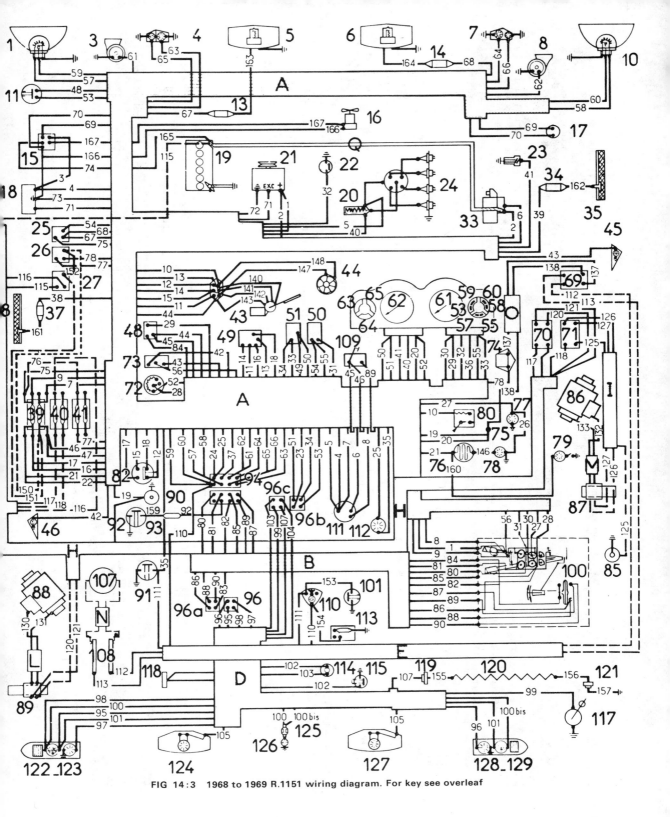

FIG 14:3   1968 to 1969 R.1151 wiring diagram. For key see overleaf

Key to Figs 14:1, 14:2 and 14:3

1 Lefthand headlight
2 Lefthand inner headlight (R.1151)
3 Lefthand horn
4 Lefthand sidelight and flasher
5 Lefthand Q.I. lamp (R.1151)
6 Righthand Q.I. lamp (R.1151)
7 Righthand sidelight and flasher
8 Righthand horn
9 Righthand inner headlight (R.1152)
10 Righthand headlight
11 Reverse light switch (R.1151, R.1152)
12 Lefthand headlight wires connection (R.1152)
12bis Righthand headlight wires connection (Mosta)
13 Lefthand Q.I. lamp junction (R.1151)
14 Righthand Q.I. lamp junction (R.1151)
15 Cooling fan motor relay
16 Cooling fan
17 Temperature switch (Mosta)
18 Regulator
19 Battery
20 Coil
21 Alternator
22 Oil pressure switch
23 Thermal resistance (R.1151) or thermal switch
24 Distributor
25 Q.I. lamps relay (R.1151)
26 Sun roof relay
27 Tachometer detector (R.1152)
28 Solenoid flap valve relay (R.1152)
29 Brake warning light switch (R.1152)
30 Battery earth (ground)
31 Idling speed damper
32 Idling speed damper
33 Starter
34 Righthand front brake pad
35 Righthand front brake pad junction
36 Solenoid flap valve (R.1152)
37 Lefthand front brake pad junction
38 Lefthand front brake pad
39 Main fuse box
40 Window winder fuse box
41 Sun roof fuse box
42 Cowl side junction box
43 Windscreen wiper
44 Heater/ventilator
45 Righthand parking light
46 Lefthand parking light switch (R.1151)
47 Foot-operated dipswitch (R.1152)
48 Flasher unit
49 Windscreen wiper switch
50 Q.I. lamp switch (R.1151)
51 Rear screen demister switch
52 Instrument panel lighting
52a Instrument panel lighting
53 Headlight main beam telltale
54 Brake warning light (R.1152)
55 Water temperature gauge (R.1151)
56 Choke warning light
57 Oil pressure and water temperature warning light
58 Q.I. lamp telltale (R.1151)
59 Flasher telltale
60 Rear screen demister telltale
61 Revolution counter
62 Speedometer
63 Fuel level indicator
64 Voltmeter
65 Handbrake and brake pad wear warning light
66 Instrument panel lefthand group connection (R.1151)
67 Instrument panel righthand group connection (R.1151)
68 Instrument panel + terminal
69 Sun roof switch
70 Lefthand window winder switch (R.1151)
71 Righthand window winder switch (R.1151)
72 Instrument panel rheostat
73 Parking light switch
74 Sun roof thermal cut-out
75 Instrument panel and sun roof earth (ground)
76 Cigar lighter
77 Ashtray illumination
78 Cigar lighter illumination
79 Glove compartment light
80 Heater rheostat
81 Brake pressure warning light switch (ground)
82 Windscreen washer pedal
83 Feed wire connection (R.1151)
84 Brake warning light connection
85 Righthand window winder earth (ground)
86 Righthand window winder junction (R.1151)
87 Righthand window winder junction (R.1151)
88 Lefthand window winder (R.1151)
89 Lefthand window winder junction (R.1151)
90 Lefthand door pillar switch
91 Lefthand window winder earth (ground)
92 Handbrake switch
93 Handbrake wires junction clip
94/94a/95 Group junction
95/95a/96 Group junction
96/96a Group junction
96b/96c Group junction
97/97a Group junction
98 Fuel level indicator junction clip (R.1152)
99 Brake pressure warning light switch earth (ground) (R.1152)
100 Combination lighting switch
101 Righthand door pillar junction (R.1152)
102 'Hazard' warning light fuse (R.1152)
103 'Hazard' warning light control unit (R.1152)
104 'Hazard' warning light switch (R.1152)
105 'Hazard' warning light junction clip (R.1152)
106 Fuel level indicator junction clip (R.1152)
107 Sun roof motor
108 Stop light switch
109 Sun roof track
109bis Choke switch
110 Interior light
111 Ignition (starter switch)
112 Neiman switch illumination (R.1151)
113 Map reading light
114 Luggage compartment light
115 Luggage compartment light switch
116 Rear harness junction box
117 Fuel level indicator
118 Reverse light junction
119 Rear screen demister + switch
120 Rear screen heating
121 Rear screen demister light
122 Lefthand rear and stop lights
123 Lefthand reverse light (R.1151, R.1152)
124 Lefthand rear flasher
125 Rear lights junction clip
126 Number plate light
127 Righthand rear harness
128 Righthand reverse light
129 Righthand rear and stop lights

List of wiring harnesses

A Front engine harness
B Combination lighting switch harness
C Instrument panel harness
D Chassis harness
E Interior light harness
F Rear harness (1966 R.1150)
G Sun roof harness
H Lefthand window winder harness (R.1151)
I Window winder harness
J 'Hazard' warning light harness (R.1152)
K Luggage compartment light harness
L Lefthand window winder motor harness
M Righthand window winder motor harness
N Sun roof motor harness
O Sun roof change-over switch harness
P Negative cable
Q Positive cable

Key to Fig 14:4

1 Side lamp and lefthand front flasher
2 Left headlamp
4 Horn
5 Spot lamp
6 Spot lamp
7 Horn
9 Right headlamp
10 Side lamp and righthand front flasher
14 Reverse light
15 Fan
16 Thermostatic switch for fan
18 Relay
19 Battery
20 Coil
22 Alternator
23 Oil pressure switch
26 Connector block
27 Regulator
28 Spot lamp relay
29 Sliding roof relay
30 Window winding relay
31 Parking lamp
32 Stop lamp switch
34 Distributor
35 Thermostatic switch
37 Starter
38 Parking lamp
40 Brake warning branch correction
41 Parking lamp
42 Earth
43 Brake pad
44 Clip
45 Connector block on bulkhead
46 Windscreen wiper
47 Heater
48 Clip for
49 Brake pad
50 Courtesy light switch
52 Flasher unit
53 Main beam warning light
57 Fuel gauge
58 Choke warning light
59 Oil and water warning light
60 Voltmeter
61 Flasher pilot light
62 Water temperature gauge
63 Spot lamp switch
64 Rear window heater switch
65 Wiper switch
66 Rear window warning lamp
67 Spot lamp warning light
68 Rev counter
69 Speedometer
70 Sliding roof switch
71 and 71a Window winder switches
72 Clock
72a Clock light
73 Panel light rheostat
74 Heater rheostat
75 Courtesy light
76 Parking lamp switch
84 Connector block
85 Connector block
86 Combination switch
88 Connector block
89 Flasher unit fuse
90 Connector block for ignition controlled circuits
91 Connector block (direct)
92 Facia wiring left
93 Facia wiring right
94 Window winder
95 Interior lighting
98 Handbrake switch
99 Thermal cut-out
100 Earthing point in cubby
101 Cubby light
102 Cigarette lighter
103 Ashtray light
104 Cigarette lighter light
105 Window winder earth
107 Boot light
108 Boot light switch
109 Windscreen wash pedal
110 Roof motor
111 Interior light
112 Fuel tank
115 Rear window switch
116 Heated rear window
117 Rear window switch
119 Reverse light branch connection
120 Flasher
121 Rear and stop lights
122 Connectors for rear lamps
123 Connectors for rear lamps
124 Number plate lamp
125 Reverse light
126 Rear and stoplights
127 Flasher

Each wire is identified by a number followed by letters to indicate the Colour of the wire and of the sleeve if applicable, then a number to show the wire diameter:

Colour of wires and sleeves:
Be Beige   Bc White   B Blue   C Clear   G Grey   J Yellow   M Maroon   N Black   S Pink   Ro Rose   R Red   V Green   Vi Violet

Wire diameters in mm: 1 9/10   2 12/10   3 16/10   4 20/10   5 25/10   6 30/10

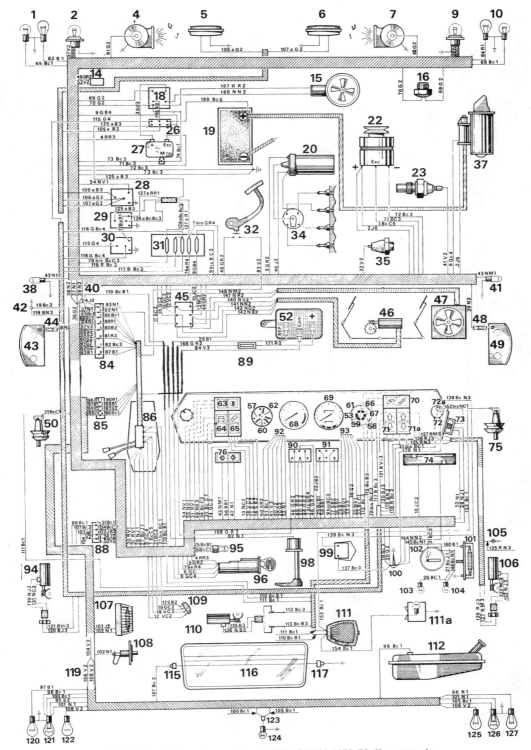

FIG 14:4   Wiring diagram for R.1151, R.1154 1970-73. Key opposite

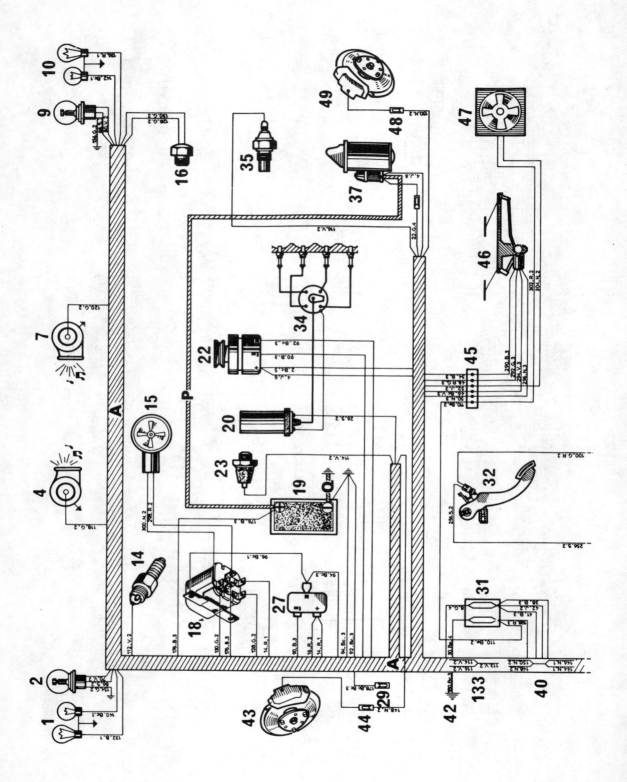

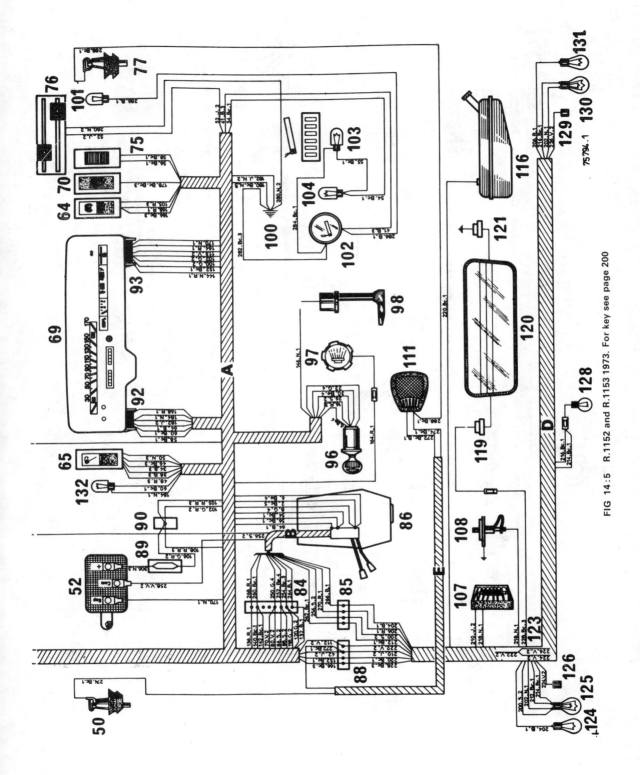

FIG 14:5 R.1152 and R.1153 1973. For key see page 200

75794.1

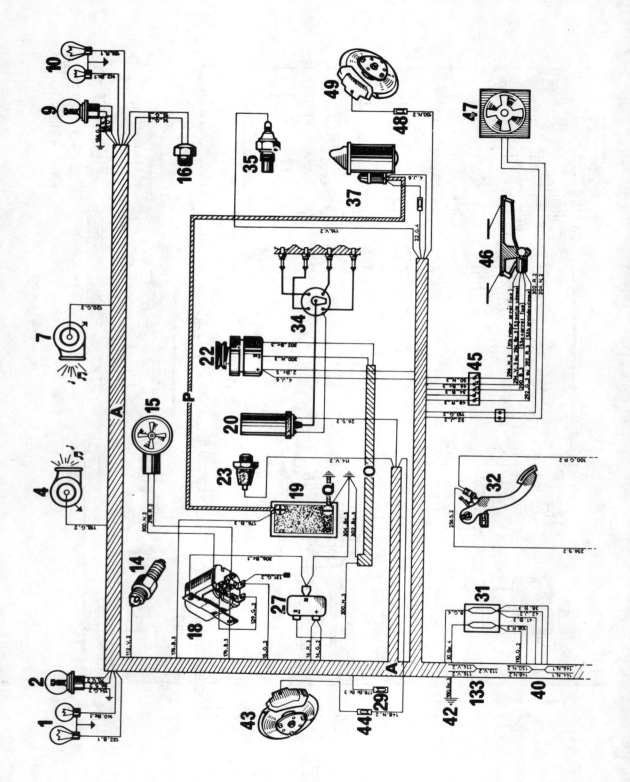

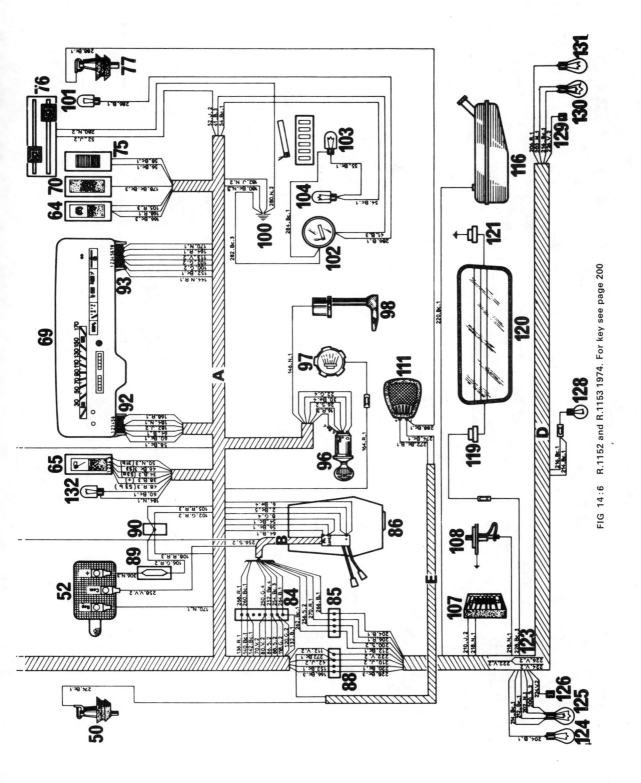

FIG 14:6   R.1152 and R.1153 1974. For key see page 200

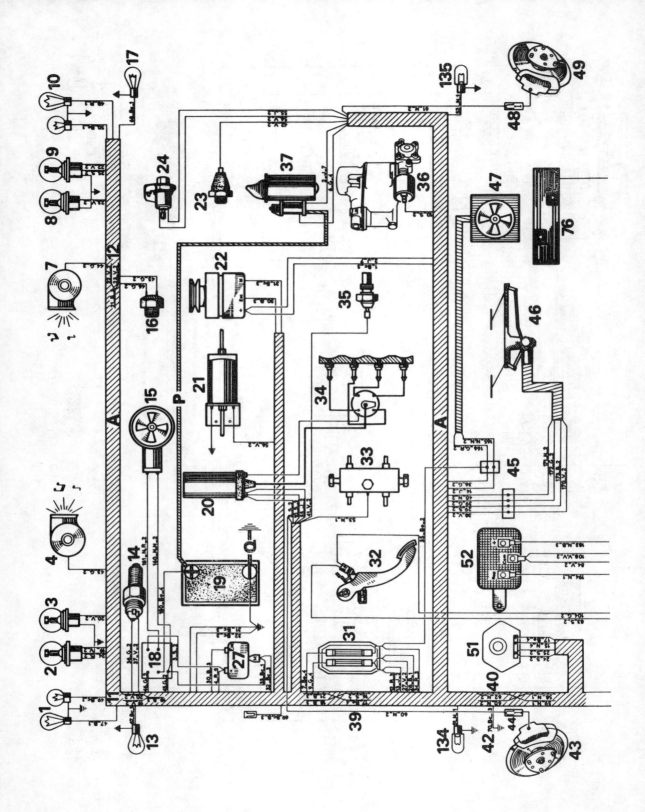

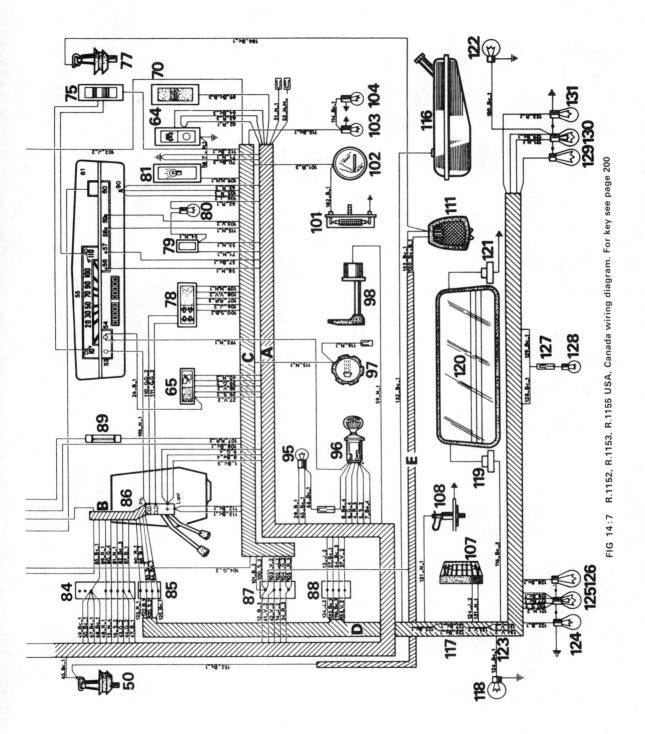

FIG 14:7 R.1152, R.1153, R.1155 USA, Canada wiring diagram. For key see page 200

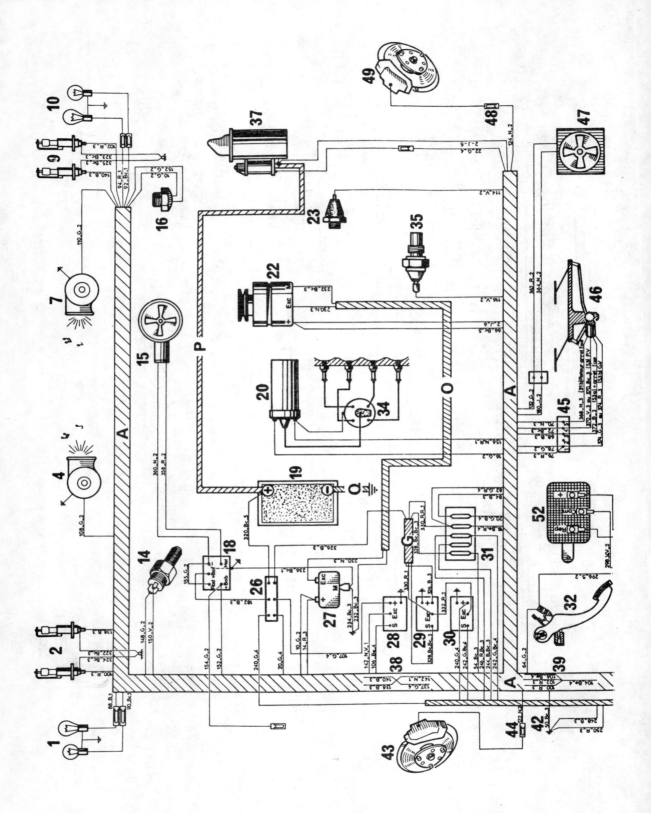

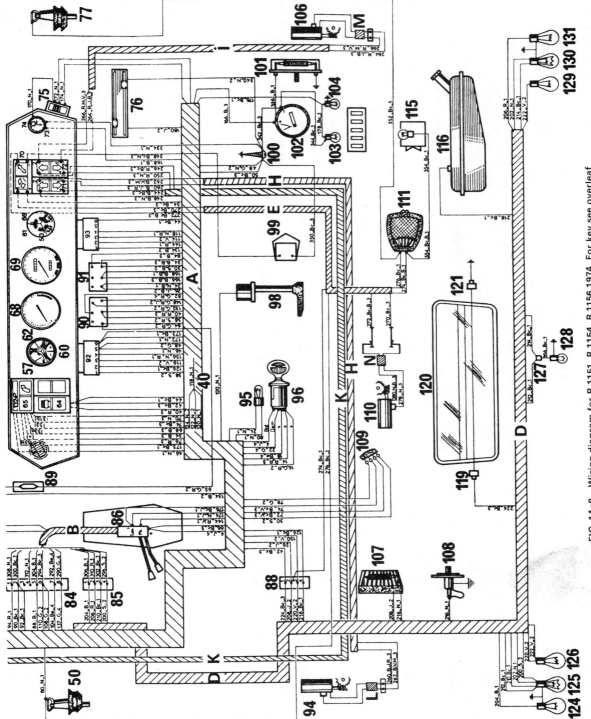

FIG 14:8   Wiring diagram for R.1151, R.1154, R.1156 1974. For key see overleaf

Key to Figs 14:5, 14:6, 14:7 and 14:8

1 Side and flasher lamps   2 Lefthand headlamps   4 and 7 Horns   9 Righthand headlamps   10 Side and flasher lamps
14 Reverse lamp switch   15 Electric fan   16 Thermo switch on radiator   18 Relay for engine fan   19 Battery   20 Coil   22 Alternator   23 Oil pressure switch
26 Connector   27 Regulator   28 Headlamp relay   29 Sliding roof relay   30 Window winder relay   31 Fuse box   32 Stop lamp switch   34 Distributor
35 Thermo switch or temperature transmitter   37 Starter   38 Splice in dip wires   39 Splice in main beam wires   40 Splice in brake warning wires   42 Earth for window winder
43 Fitting on lefthand front brake   44 Clips   45 Connector   46 Wiper motor   47 Heater   48 Clips   49 Fitting on righthand front brake   50 Door switch
52 Flasher unit   53 Main beam warning   55 Panel light   56 Warning for worn brake pads and handbrake   57 Fuel gauge   59 Oil and water warning lamp
60 Voltmeter   61 Flasher warning   62 Water temperature gauge   64 Heated rear window switch   65 Wiper switch   66 Heated rear window warning   68 Tachometer
69 Speedometer   70 Sliding roof switch   71 Switch for lefthand window   72 Switch for righthand window   73 Clock   74 Clock light   75 Rheostat for panel lighting
76 Heater rheostat   77 Door switch   84 and 85 Connectors for combination switch   86 Combination switch   88 Connector
90 Connector   91 Connector   92 Connector   93 Connector   94 Lefthand window motor   95 Ignition switch lamp   96 Ignition/starter switch   98 Handbrake switch
99 Sliding roof contact breaker   100 Panel earth   101 Glove box lights   102 Cigar lighter   103 Ashtray light   104 Cigar lighter light   106 Righthand window motor
107 Boot lamp   108 Boot lamp switch   109 Pedal for windscreen washer   110 Sliding roof motor   111 Interior light   115 Map reading light
116 Fuel tank   119 and 121 Heated window contacts   120 Heated window   124 Flasher   125 Rear and stop lamp   126 Reversing lamp   127 Clips   128 Number plate lamp
129 Reversing lamp   130 Rear and stop lamp   131 Flasher   132 Light for wiper switch

Each wire is identified by a number followed by letters to indicate the Colour of the wire and of the sleeve if applicable, then a number to show the wire diameter:

Colour of wires and sleeves: Be Beige   Bc White   B Blue   C Clear   G Grey   J Yellow   M Maroon   N Black   S Pink   Ro Rose   R Red   V Green
Vi Violet

Wire diameters in mm: 1 9/10   2 12/10   3 16/10   4 20/10   5 25/10   6 30/10

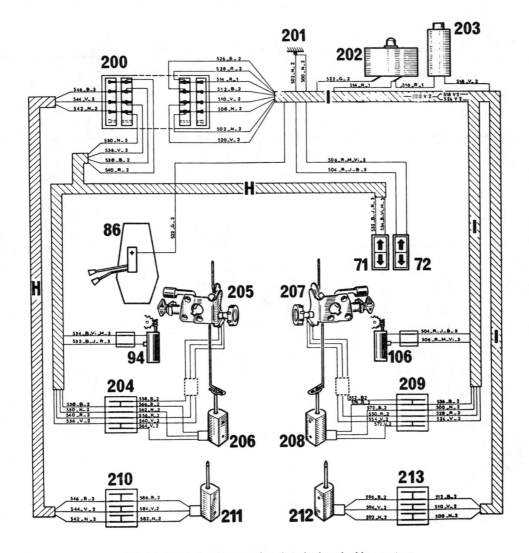

FIG 14:9   Wiring diagram for electric door locking system

Key to Fig 14:9   200 Connector   201 Earth   202 Thermal switch   203 Inertia switch   204 Lefthand front door connector   205 Lefthand front door lock   206 Lefthand front door relay   207 Righthand front door lock   208 Righthand front door relay   209 Righthand front door connector   210 Lefthand rear door connector   211 Lefthand rear door relay   212 Righthand rear door relay   213 Righthand rear door connector

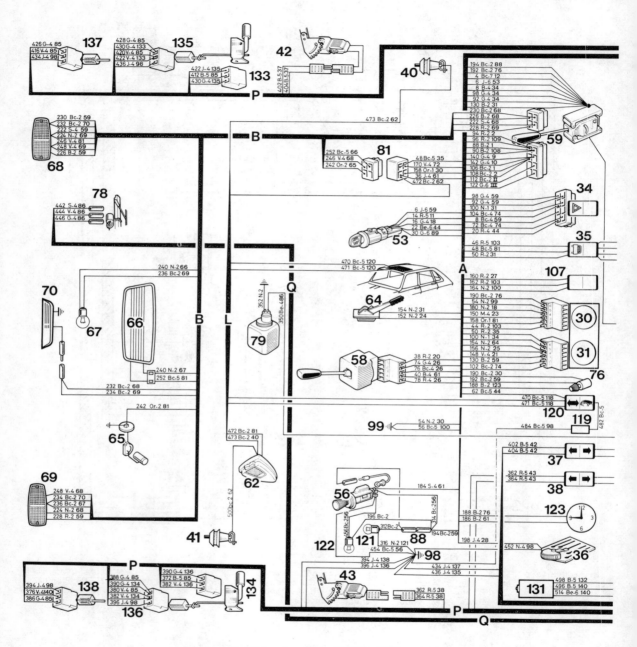

FIG 14:10   Wiring diagram for R.1156 – 1978 models

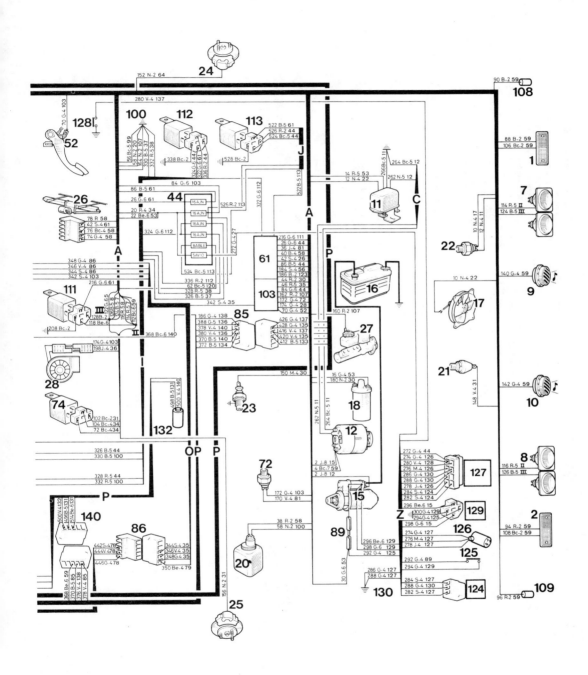

Key to Fig 14 : 10

1 Lefthand front sidelight and direction indicator
2 Righthand front sidelight and direction indicator
7 Lefthand headlight unit
8 Righthand headlight unit
9 Lefthand horn
10 Righthand horn
11 Regulator
12 Alternator
15 Starter
16 Battery
17 Engine cooling fan motor
18 Ignition coil
20 Windscreen washer pump
21 Oil pressure switch
22 Thermal switch on radiator
23 Thermal switch on cylinder head
24 Lefthand front brake
25 Righthand front brake
26 Windscreen wiper plate
27 Master cylinder
28 Heating/ventilating fan motor
30 Connector No. 1, instrument panel
31 Connector No. 2, instrument panel
34 'Hazard' warning lights switch
35 Rear screen demister switch
36 Heating/ventilating fan motor rheostat
37 Lefthand window winder switch
38 Righthand window winder switch
40 Lefthand door pillar switch
41 Righthand door pillar switch
42 Lefthand window winder
43 Righthand window winder
44 Accessories plate (fusebox)
52 Stoplights switch
53 Anti-theft switch
56 Cigar lighter
58 Windscreen wiper/washer switch
59 Lighting switch
61 Feed wire junction before switch
62 Interior light (lefthand)
64 Handbrake
65 Fuel gauge tank unit
66 Rear screen demister
67 Luggage compartment illumination
68 Lefthand rear light assembly
69 Righthand rear light assembly
70 Licence plate light

72 Reversing lights switch
74 Flasher unit
76 Instrument panel lighting rheostat
78 Rear screen wiper motor
79 Rear screen washer pump
81 Junction block, front and rear harnesses
85 Junction block, window winder harness
86 Junction block, chassis/tailgate harnesses
88 Wire junction, glove compartment illumination
89 Wire junction, starter wire
98 Glove compartment light earth
99 Dashboard earth
100 Lefthand inner wing panel gusset earth
103 Junction plate – + after switch
107 Brake circuit warning light bulb checking switch
108 Lefthand front width marker light
109 Righthand front width marker light
111 Headlight main beam relay
112 Window winder relay
113 Sunroof relay
118 Sunroof motor
119 Sunroof cutout
120 Sunroof changeover switch
121 Glove compartment illumination
122 Ashtray illumination
123 Clock
124 Automatic transmission
125 Automatic transmission starting authorisation switch
126 Sealed multiple plug on automatic transmission
128 Kick-down switch
129 Automatic transmission starting authorisation relay
130 Automatic transmission earth
131 Electro-magnetic locks cutout
132 Electro-magnetic locks inertia switch
133 Lefthand front door lock changeover switch
134 Righthand front door lock changeover switch
35 Lefthand front door electro-magnetic lock
136 Righthand front door electro-magnetic lock
137 Lefthand rear door electro-magnetic lock
138 Righthand rear door electro-magnetic lock
140 Junction block, electro-magnetic locks harness

Harness codes: A Engine front   B Rear   C Alternator   H Window winer relay   L Door switches   P Door locks   Q Tailgate

Each wire is identified by a number followed by letters indicating the colour code, then a number to show the wire diameter. The last number gives the unit of destination.

Wire colours: Vi Violet   Be Beige   Bc White   B Blue   C Clear   G Grey   J Yellow   M Maroon   N Black   Or Orange   R Red   S Pink   V Green

Wire number (diameter, mm): 1, 7/10   2, 9/10   3, 10/10   4, 12/10   5, 16/10   6, 20/10   7, 25/10   8, 30/10   9, 45/10

HINTS ON MAINTENANCE AND OVERHAUL

There are few things more rewarding than the restoration of a vehicle's original peak of efficiency and smooth performance.

The following notes are intended to help the owner to reach that state of perfection. Providing that he possesses the basic manual skills he should have no difficulty in performing most of the operations detailed in this manual. It must be stressed, however, that where recommended in the manual, highly-skilled operations ought to be entrusted to experts, who have the necessary equipment, to carry out the work satisfactorily.

Quality of workmanship :

The hazardous driving conditions on the roads to-day demand that vehicles should be as nearly perfect, mechanically, as possible. It is therefore most important that amateur work be carried out with care, bearing in mind the often inadequate working conditions, and also the inferior tools which may have to be used. It is easy to counsel perfection in all things, and we recognise that it may be setting an impossibly high standard. We do, however, suggest that every care should be taken to ensure that a vehicle is as safe to take on the road as it is humanly possible to make it.

Safe working conditions :

Even though a vehicle may be stationary, it is still potentially dangerous if certain sensible precautions are not taken when working on it while it is supported on jacks or blocks. It is indeed preferable not to use jacks alone, but to supplement them with carefully placed blocks, so that there will be plenty of support if the car rolls off the jacks during a strenuous manoeuvre. Axle stands are an excellent way of providing a rigid base which is not readily disturbed. Piles of bricks are a dangerous substitute. Be careful not to get under heavy loads on lifting tackle, the load could fall. It is preferable not to work alone when lifting an engine, or when working underneath a vehicle which is supported well off the ground. To be trapped, particularly under the vehicle, may have unpleasant results if help is not quickly forthcoming. Make some provision, how-ever humble, to deal with fires. Always disconnect a battery if there is a likelihood of electrical shorts. These may start a fire if there is leaking fuel about. This applies particularly to leads which can carry a heavy current, like those in the starter circuit. While on the subject of electricity, we must also stress the danger of using equipment which is run off the mains and which has no earth or has faulty wiring or connections. So many workshops have damp floors, and electrical shocks are of such a nature that it is sometimes impossible to let go of a live lead or piece of equipment due to the muscular spasms which take place.

Work demanding special care :

This involves the servicing of braking, steering and suspension systems. On the road, failure of the braking system may be disastrous. Make quite sure that there can be no possibility of failure through the bursting of rusty brake pipes or rotten hoses, nor to a sudden loss of pressure due to defective seals or valves.

Problems :

The chief problems which may face an operator are :
1 External dirt.
2 Difficulty in undoing tight fixings.
3 Dismantling unfamiliar mechanisms.
4 Deciding in what respect parts are defective.
5 Confusion about the correct order for reassembly.
6 Adjusting running clearance.
7 Road testing.
8 Final tuning.

Practical suggestions to solve the problems :

1 Preliminary cleaning of large parts – engines, trans-missions, steering, suspensions, etc, – should be carried out before removal from the car. Where road dirt and mud alone are present, wash clean with a high-pressure water jet, brush-ing to remove stubborn adhesions, and allow to drain and dry. Where oil or grease is also present, wash down with a proprietary compound (Gunk, Teepol etc,) applying with a stiff brush – an old paint brush is suitable – into all crevices. Cover the distributor and ignition coils with a polythene bag and then apply a strong water jet to clear the loosened deposits. Allow to drain and dry. The assemblies will then be sufficiently clean to remove and transfer to the bench for the next stage.

On the bench, further cleaning can be carried out, first wiping the parts as free as possible from grease with old newspaper. Avoid using rag or cotton waste which can leave clogging fibres behind. Any remaining grease can be removed with a brush dipped in paraffin. If necessary, traces of paraffin can be removed by carbon tetrachloride. Avoid using paraffin or petrol in large quantities for cleaning in enclosed areas, such as garages, on account of the high fire risk.

When all exteriors have been cleaned, and not before, dismantling can be commenced. This ensures that dirt will not enter into interiors and orifices revealed by dismantling. In the next phases, where components have to be cleaned, use carbon tetrachloride in preference to petrol and keep the containers covered except when in use. After the components have been cleaned, plug small holes with tapered hard wood plugs cut to size and blank off larger orifices with greaseproof paper and masking tape. Do not use soft wood plugs or matchsticks as they may break.

2 It is not advisable to hammer on the end of a screw thread, but if it must be done, first screw on a nut to protect the thread, and use a lead hammer. This applies particularly to the removal of tapered cotters. Nuts and bolts seem to 'grow' together, especially in exhaust systems. If penetrating oil does not work, try the judicious application of heat, but be careful of starting a fire. Asbestos sheet or cloth is useful to isolate heat.

Tight bushes or pieces of tail-pipe rusted into a silencer can be removed by splitting them with an open-ended hacksaw. Tight screws can sometimes be started by a tap from a hammer on the end of a suitable screwdriver. Many tight fittings will yield to the judicious use of a hammer, but it must be a soft-faced hammer, if damage is to be avoided, use a heavy block on the opposite side to absorb shock. Any parts of the steering system which have been damaged should be renewed, as attempts to repair them may lead to cracking and subsequent failure, and steering ball joints should be dis-connected using a recommended tool to prevent damage.

3 It often happens that an owner is baffled when trying to dismantle an unfamiliar piece of equipment. So many modern devices are pressed together or assembled by spinning-over flanges, that they must be sawn apart. The intention is that the whole assembly must be renewed. However, parts which appear to be in one piece to the naked eye may reveal close-fitting joint lines when inspected with a magnifying glass, and this may provide the necessary clue to dismantling. Left-handed screw threads are used where rotational forces would tend to unscrew a righthand screw thread.

Be very careful when dismantling mechanisms which may come apart suddenly. Work in an enclosed space where the parts will be contained, and drape a piece of cloth over the device if springs are likely to fly in all directions. Mark every-thing which might be reassembled in the wrong position, scratched symbols may be used on unstressed parts, or a sequence of tiny dots from a centre punch can be useful. Stressed parts should never be scratched or centre-popped as this may lead to cracking under working conditions. Store parts which look alike in the correct order for reassembly. Never rely upon memory to assist in the assembly of compli-cated mechanisms, especially when they will be dismantled for a long time, but make notes, and drawings to supplement the diagrams in the manual, and put labels on detached wires. Rust stains may indicate unlubricated wear. This can some-times be seen round the outside edge of a bearing cup in a universal joint. Look for bright rubbing marks on parts which normally should not make heavy contact. These might prove that something is bent or running out of truth. For example, there might be bright marks on one side of a piston, at the top near the ring grooves, and others at the bottom of the skirt on the other side. This could well be the clue to a bent connecting rod. Suspected cracks can be proved by heating the component in a light oil to approximately 100°C, removing, drying off, and dusting with french chalk. If a crack is present the oil retained in the crack will stain the french chalk.

4   In determining wear, and the degree, against the permis-sible limits set in the manual, accurate measurements can only be achieved by the use of a micrometer. In many cases, the wear is given to the fourth place of decimals; that is in ten-thousandths of an inch. This can be read by the vernier scale on the barrel of a good micrometer. Bore diameters are more difficult to determine. If, however, the matching shaft is accurately measured, the degree of play in the bore can be felt as a guide to its suitability. In other cases, the shank of a twist drill of known diameter is a handy check.

Many methods have been devised for determining the clearance between bearing surfaces. To-day the best and simplest is by the use of Plastigage, obtainable from most garages. A thin plastic thread is laid between the two surfaces and the bearing is tightened, flattening the thread. On removal, the width of the thread is compared with the scale supplied with the thread and the clearance is read off directly. Sometimes joint faces leak persistently, even after gasket renewal. The fault will then be traceable to distortion, dirt or burrs. Studs which are screwed into soft metal frequently raise burrs at the point of entry. A quick cure for this is to chamfer the edge of the hole in the part which fits over the stud.

5   **Always check a replacement part with the original one before it is fitted.**

If parts are not marked, and the order for reassembly is not known, a little detective work will help. Look for marks which are due to wear to see if they can be mated. Joint faces may not be identical due to manufacturing errors, and parts which overlap may be stained, giving a clue to the correct position. Most fixings leave identifying marks especially if they were painted over on assembly. It is then easier to decide whether a nut, for instance, has a plain, a spring, or a shakeproof washer under it. All running surfaces become 'bedded' together after long spells of work and tiny imperfections on one part will be found to have left corresponding marks on the other. This is particularly true of shafts and bearings and even a score on a cylinder wall will show on the piston.

6   Checking end float rocker clearances by feeler gauge may not always give accurate results because of wear. For instance, the rocker tip which bears on a valve stem may be deeply pitted, in which case the feeler will simply be bridging a depression. Thrust washers may also wear depressions in opposing faces to make accurate measurement difficult. End float is then easier to check by using a dial gauge. It is common practice to adjust end play in bearing assemblies, like front hubs with taper rollers, by doing up the axle nut until the hub becomes stiff to turn and then backing it off a little. Do not use this method with ballbearing hubs as the assembly is often preloaded by tightening the axle nut to its fullest extent. If the splitpin hole will not line up, file the base of the nut a little.

Steering assemblies often wear in the straightahead position. If any part is adjusted, make sure that it remains free when moved from lock to lock. Do not be surprised if an assembly like a steering gearbox, which is known to be care-fully adjusted outside the car, becomes stiff when it is bolted into place. This will be due to distortion of the case by the pull of the mounting bolts, particularly if the mounting points are not all touching together. This problem may be met in other equipment and is cured by careful attention to the alignment of mounting points.

When a spanner is stamped with a size and A/F it means that the dimension is the width between the jaws and has no connection with ANF, which is the designation for the American National Fine thread. Coarse threads like Whitworth are rarely used on cars to-day except for studs which screw into soft aluminium or cast iron. For this reason it might be found that the top end of a cylinder head stud has a fine thread and the lower end a coarse thread to screw into the cylinder block. If the car has mainly UNF threads then it is likely that any coarse threads will be UNC, which are not the same as Whitworth. Small sizes have the same number of threads in Whitworth and UNC, but in the $\frac{1}{2}$ in size for example, there are twelve threads to the inch in the former and thirteen in the latter.

7   After a major overhaul, particularly if a great deal of work has been done on the braking, steering and suspension systems, it is advisable to approach the problem of testing with care. If the braking system has been overhauled, apply heavy pressure to the brake pedal and get a second operator to check every possible source of leakage. The brakes may work extremely well, but a leak could cause complete failure after a few miles.

Do not fit the hub caps until every wheel nut has been checked for tightness, and make sure that the tyre pressures are correct. Check the levels of coolant, lubricants and hydraulic fluids. Being satisfied that all is well, take the car on the road and test the brakes at once. Check the steering and the action of the handbrake. Do all this at moderate speeds on quiet roads, and make sure there is no other vehicle behind you when you try a rapid stop.

Finally, remember that many parts settle down after a time, so check for tightness of all fixings after the car has been on the road a hundred miles or so.

8   It is useless to tune an engine which has not reached its normal running temperature. In the same way, the tune of an engine which is stiff after a rebore will be different when the engine is again running free. Remember too, that rocker clear-ances on pushrod operated valve gear will change when the cylinder head nuts are tightened after an initial period of running with a new head gasket.

Trouble may not always be due to what seems the obvious cause. Ignition, carburation and mechanical condition are interdependent and spitting back through the carburetter, which might be attributed to a weak mixture, can be caused by a sticking inlet valve.

For one final hint on tuning, never adjust more than one thing at a time or it will be impossible to tell which adjustment produced the desired result.

GLOSSARY OF TERMS

Allen key   Cranked wrench of hexagonal section for use with socket head screws.

Alternator   Electrical generator producing alternating or current. Rectified to direct current for battery charging.

Ambient temperature   Surrounding atmospheric temperature.

Annulus   Used in engineering to indicate the outer ring gear of an epicyclic gear train.

Armature   The shaft carrying the windings, which rotates in the magnetic field of a generator or starter motor. That part of a solenoid or relay which is activated by the magnetic field.

Axial   In line with, or pertaining to, an axis.

Backlash   Play in meshing gears.

Balance lever   A bar where force applied at the centre is equally divided between connections at the ends.

Banjo axle   Axle casing with large diameter housing for the crownwheel and differential.

Bendix pinion   A self-engaging and self-disengaging drive on a starter motor shaft.

Bevel pinion   A conical shaped gearwheel, designed to mesh with a similar gear with an axis usually at 90° to its own.

bhp   Brake horse power, measured on a dynamometer.

bmep   Brake mean effective pressure. Average pressure on a piston during the working stroke.

Brake cylinder   Cylinder with hydraulically operated piston(s) acting on brake shoes or pads.

Brake regulator   Control valve fitted in hydraulic braking system which limits brake pressure to rear brakes during heavy braking to prevent rear wheel locking.

Camber   Angle at which a wheel is tilted from the vertical.

Capacitor   Modern term for an electrical condenser. Part of distributor assembly, connected across contact breaker points, acts as an interference suppressor.

Castellated   Top face of a nut, slotted across the flats to take a locking splitpin.

Caster   Angle at which the kingpin or swivel pin is tilted when viewed from the side.

cc   Cubic centimetres. Engine capacity is arrived at by multiplying the area of the bore in sq cm by the stroke in cm by the number of cylinders.

Clevis   U-shaped forked connector used with a clevis pin, usually at handbrake connections.

Collet   A type of collar, usually split and located in a groove in a shaft, and held in place by a retainer. The arrangement used to retain the spring(s) on a valve stem in most cases.

Commutator   Rotating segmented current distributor between armature windings and brushes in generator or motor.

Compression ratio   The ratio, or quantitative relation, of the total volume (piston at bottom of stroke) to the unswept volume (piston at top of stroke) in an engine cylinder.

Condenser   See 'Capacitor'.

Core plug   Plug for blanking off a manufacturing hole in a casting.

Crownwheel   Large bevel gear in rear axle, driven by a bevel pinion attached to the propeller shaft. Sometimes called a 'ring gear'.

'C'-spanner   Like a 'C' with a handle. For use on screwed collars without flats, but with slots or holes.

Damper   Modern term for shock absorber, used in vehicle suspension systems to damp out spring oscillations.

Depression   The lowering of atmospheric pressure as in the inlet manifold and carburetter.

Dowel   Close tolerance pin, peg, tube or bolt, which accurately locates mating parts.

Drag link   Rod connecting steering box drop arm (pitman arm) to nearest front wheel steering arm in certain types of steering systems.

Dry liner   Thinwall tube pressed into cylinder bore.

Dry sump   Lubrication system where all oil is scavenged from the sump, and returned to a separate tank.

Dynamo   See 'Generator'.

Electrode   Terminal part of an electrical component, such as the points or 'Electrodes' of a sparking plug.

Electrolyte   In lead-acid car batteries a solution of sulphuric acid and distilled water.

End float   The axial movement between associated parts, end play.

EP   Extreme pressure. In lubricants, special grades for heavily loaded bearing surfaces, such as gear teeth in a gearbox, or crownwheel and pinion in a rear axle.

Fade   Of brakes. Reduced efficiency due to overheating.

Field coils   Windings on the polepieces of motors and generators.

Fillets   Narrow finishing strips usually applied to interior bodywork.

First motion shaft   Input shaft from clutch to gearbox.

Fullflow filter   Filters in which all the oil is pumped to the engine. If the element becomes clogged, a bypass valve operates to pass unfiltered oil to the engine.

FWD   Front wheel drive.

Gear pump   Two meshing gears in a close fitting casing. Oil is carried from the inlet round the outside of both gears in the spaces between the gear teeth and casing to the outlet, the meshing gear teeth prevent oil passing back to the inlet, and the oil is forced through the outlet port.

Generator   Modern term for 'Dynamo'. When rotated produces electrical current.

Grommet   A ring of protective or sealing material. Can be used to protect pipes or leads passing through bulkheads.

Grubscrew   Fully threaded headless screw with screwdriver slot. Used for locking or alignment purposes.

Gudgeon pin   Shaft which connects a piston to its connecting rod. Sometimes called 'wrist pin' or 'piston pin'.

Halfshaft   One of a pair transmitting drive from the differential.

Helical   In spiral form. The teeth of helical gears are cut at a spiral angle to the side faces of the gearwheel.

Hot spot   Hot area that assists vapourisation of fuel on its way to cylinders. Often provided by close contact between inlet and exhaust manifolds.

HT   High Tension. Applied to electrical current produced by the ignition coil for the sparking plugs.

Hydrometer   A device for checking specific gravity of liquids. Used to check specific gravity of electrolyte.

Hypoid bevel gears   A form of bevel gear used in the rear axle drive gears. The bevel pinion meshes below the centre line of the crownwheel, giving a lower propeller shaft line.

Idler   A device for passing on movement. A free running gear between driving and driven gears. A lever transmitting track rod movement to a side rod in steering gear.

Impeller   A centrifugal pumping element. Used in water pumps to stimulate flow.

Journals   Those parts of a shaft that are in contact with the bearings.

Kingpin   The main vertical pin which carries the front wheel spindle, and permits steering movement. May be called 'steering pin' or 'swivel pin'.

Layshaft   The shaft which carries the laygear in the gearbox. The laygear is driven by the first motion shaft and drives the third motion shaft according to the gear selected. Sometimes called the 'countershaft' or 'second motion shaft'.

lb ft   A measure of twist or torque. A pull of 10lb at a radius of 1ft is a torque of 10lb ft.

lb/sq in   Pounds per square inch.

Little-end   The small, or piston end of a connecting rod. Sometimes called the 'small-end'.

LT   Low Tension. The current output from the battery.

Mandrel   Accurately manufactured bar or rod used for test or centring purposes.

Manifold   A pipe, duct or chamber, with several branches.

Needle rollers   Bearing rollers with a length many times their diameter.

Oil bath   Reservoir which lubricates parts by immersion. In air filters, a separate oil supply for wetting a wire mesh element to hold the dust.

Oil wetted   In air filters, a wire mesh element lightly oiled to trap and hold airborne dust.

Overlap   Period during which inlet and exhaust valves are open together.

Panhard rod   Bar connected between fixed point on chassis and another on axle to control sideways movement.

Pawl   Pivoted catch which engages in the teeth of a ratchet to permit movement in one direction only.

Peg spanner   Tool with pegs, or pins, to engage in holes or slots in the part to be turned.

Pendant pedals   Pedals with levers that are pivoted at the top end.

Phillips screwdriver   A cross-point screwdriver for use with the cross-slotted heads of Phillips screws.

Pinion   A small gear, usually in relation to another gear.

Piston-type damper   Shock absorber in which damping is controlled by a piston working in a closed oil-filled cylinder.

Preloading   Preset static pressure on ball or roller bearings not due to working loads.

Radial   Radiating from a centre, like the spokes of a wheel.

Radius rod   Pivoted arm confining movement of a part to an arc of fixed radius.

Ratchet   Toothed wheel or rack which can move in one direction only, movement in the other being prevented by a pawl.

Ring gear   A gear tooth ring attached to outer periphery of flywheel. Starter pinion engages with it during starting.

Runout   Amount by which rotating part is out of true.

Semi-floating axle   Outer end of rear axle halfshaft is carried on bearing inside axle casing. Wheel hub is secured to end of shaft.

Servo   A hydraulic or pneumatic system for assisting, or, augmenting a physical effort. See 'Vacuum Servo'.

Setscrew   One which is threaded for the full length of the shank.

Shackle   A coupling link, used in the form of two parallel pins connected by side plates to secure the end of the master suspension spring and absorb the effects of deflection.

Shell bearing   Thinwalled steel shell lined with antifriction metal. Usually semi-circular and used in pairs for main and big-end bearings.

Shock absorber   See 'Damper'.

Silentbloc   Rubber bush bonded to inner and outer metal sleeves.

Socket-head screw   Screw with hexagonal socket for an Allen key.

Solenoid   A coil of wire creating a magnetic field when electric current passes through it. Used with a soft iron core to operate contacts or a mechanical device.

Spur gear   A gear with teeth cut axially across the periphery.

Stub axle   Short axle fixed at one end only.

Tachometer   An instrument for accurate measurement of rotating speed. Usually indicates in revolutions per minute.

TDC   Top Dead Centre. The highest point reached by a piston in a cylinder, with the crank and connecting rod in line.

Thermostat   Automatic device for regulating temperature. Used in vehicle coolant systems to open a valve which restricts circulation at low temperature.

Third motion shaft   Output shaft of gearbox.

Threequarter floating axle   Outer end of rear axle half-shaft flanged and bolted to wheel hub, which runs on bearing mounted on outside of axle casing. Vehicle weight is not carried by the axle shaft.

Thrust bearing or washer   Used to reduce friction in rotating parts subject to axial loads.

Torque   Turning or twisting effort. See 'lb ft'.

Track rod   The bar(s) across the vehicle which connect the steering arms and maintain the front wheels in their correct alignment.

UJ   Universal joint. A coupling between shafts which permits angular movement.

UNF   Unified National Fine screw thread.

Vacuum servo   Device used in brake system, using difference between atmospheric pressure and inlet manifold depression to operate a piston which acts to augment brake pressure as required. See 'Servo'.

Venturi   A restriction or 'choke' in a tube, as in a carburetter, used to increase velocity to obtain a reduction in pressure.

Vernier   A sliding scale for obtaining fractional readings of the graduations of an adjacent scale.

Welch plug   A domed thin metal disc which is partially flattened to lock in a recess. Used to plug core holes in castings.

Wet liner   Removable cylinder barrel, sealed against coolant leakage, where the coolant is in direct contact with the outer surface.

Wet sump   A reservoir attached to the crankcase to hold the lubricating oil.

INDEX